CODE WARS
- the Battle for Fans, Dollars and Survival

CODE WARS
– the Battle for Fans, Dollars and Survival

Dr Hunter Fujak

FAIRPLAY
PUBLISHING

First published in 2021 by Fair Play Publishing
PO Box 4101, Balgowlah Heights NSW 2093 Australia

www.fairplaypublishing.com.au
sales@fairplaypublishing.com.au

ISBN: 978-1-925914-15-3
ISBN: 978-1-925914-16-0 (ePUB)

© Dr Hunter Fujak 2021
The moral rights of the author have been asserted.

All rights reserved. Except as permitted under the *Australian Copyright Act 1968* (for example, a fair dealing for the purposes of study, research, criticism or review), no part of this book may be reproduced, stored in a retrieval system, communicated or transmitted in any form or by any means without prior written permission from the Publisher.

Cover design and page layout by Leslie Priestley.
Index produced by Mei Yen Chua.

All inquiries should be made to the Publisher via sales@fairplaypublishing.com.au

A catalogue record of this book is available from the National Library of Australia.

Contents

Prologue	vii
Part 1: Today	**1**
1.1 The Art of (Football) War	3
1.2 Australia's crowded, 'sport mad' market	6
1.3 The battlelines of Australia's code wars	14
1.4 Locating Australia's sport capital	23
1.5 The curious case of Sydney	30
1.6 The AFL's great northern incursion	40
1.7 The state of play	49
Part 2: Yesterday	**52**
2.1 In the beginning	54
2.2 Hybrid games	68
2.3 The 'sleeping giant'	83
2.4 Rugby union: Has professionalism been worthwhile?	95
2.5 Super League and the knee-capping of rugby league	110
Part 3: Tomorrow	**120**
3.1 Urbanisation and generational change in junior participation	129
3.2 Safetyism, CTE and the demise of contact football	134
3.3 Globalisation and the sleeping giant	141
3.4 Rugby league: a century of bad business	148
3.5 Rugby union: the game now mostly played in heaven	155
3.6 Culture war and the unassailable rise of Victorian rules football	160
Conclusion	169
Appendix	174
Glossary of Terms	178
Footnotes	180
Index	190

Prologue

Writing a book that covers all four Australian football codes is tricky, perhaps explaining why it is rarely attempted[1]. Writers, scholars and journalists typically tend to be experts within their football code of choice, and many excellent football books have been produced. *Code Wars* differs from such books, however, in that it explores the interrelationship between all four football codes and how they compete for our hearts, minds and wallets.

This book then, is about Australia's unique relationship to 'football' and explores the cut-throat cultural and commercial competition between the codes. To do this, it looks back at key historical moments that have shaped our football landscape, explores the modern sport landscape and finally, considers what the future may hold at a time of great uncertainty.

More interesting than debates around which football is 'best', this book explores the curiosities of Australia's sport landscape. Why are Melbourne and Sydney's sport cultures so different? How can a small town like Wagga Wagga simultaneously produce some of our best ever Australian Rules, rugby league, rugby union and cricket athletes? Will the Australian Football League (AFL) that runs the Australian Rules competition succeed in crushing its football competitors? Could concussion someday wipe out contact football entirely? This book is for those whose interest in football extends beyond the scoreboard, to that which occurs off the field. However, to probe questions such as the above two caveats are worth noting. First, this book makes a necessary sacrifice in individual focus upon any one code that comes from writing about the interrelationships between all four of them. Second, this book makes no attempt to sway the reader around which code is 'best' or 'worst' as sports. In my experience, debates around which football is 'the best' invariably result in stalemate and mutual frustration.

This book is underpinned by data from my PhD dissertation, further supported by interviews with experts as well as secondary academic, commercial and media research. The book attempts to translate what can often be dry scholarly research into something more accessible, as academia is often criticised for failing to reach the real world.

The book therefore has two guiding priorities. The first is to weave a narrative that is both interesting and intellectually informative, catering to both the casual reader interested in sport and the industry practitioner who may learn something new. The hardest challenge has been to try to distil information about four different football codes ranging from the highly opinionated to the highly statistical, while keeping the story flowing. Hopefully, I succeed in walking this tight-rope. The second priority is to be objective in the information provided, while offering my own perspective as a scholar and industry expert. This is important to acknowledge up front since, as you will see, I am critical of each code's management and/or behaviours at various points.

While I offer findings and insights that are impartial, one can never fully remove themselves from inherent biases.

I grew up in Sydney and support an eclectic mix of teams across all four football codes and sports generally. I became a member of the Sydney Cricket and Sports Ground Trust in 2015. I purchased this with about half my life-savings at the time, and it is not a perceptible reflection of any particular social class membership! From my time working in commercial research, I have directly or indirectly engaged with all four football codes in some capacity. I completed my PhD at the University of Technology Sydney in 2018 and am now a Lecturer in Sport Management at Deakin University in Melbourne.

In terms of personal football preferences, I consider all codes to have their advantages. I consider the way rugby union is played by New Zealanders the most aesthetically beautiful, while rugby league the code I'm personally most engaged by. As a sport management scholar, I consider the Australian Rules the 'best built' game, if I was designing a football code from scratch. Attending afternoon AFLW fixtures at suburban grounds, much like Shute Shield rugby in Sydney, brings me more enjoyment than big-stadium experiences. Soccer is the code I'd prefer my future children to play. As may already be apparent, this book henceforth avoids the use of the word 'football' except when referring to codes collectively. I do this in an attempt to avoid the obvious potential for reader confusion.

The book is a three part act, with each part almost independently readable. Part one critically discusses and evaluates the modern Australian sport landscape. Part two steps back in time to retrace vital moments in the historical development of the four codes. Here the objective is not to provide an exhaustive historical overview, but rather to single out key moments that have shaped the code war in some vital way. Part three focusses upon the future of the Australian sport landscape, made ever more timely by the onset of COVID-19 in 2020.

If the contents of this book prove particularly interesting to you, please consider becoming more involved in sport through further study, industry employment or community volunteering.

Part 1: Today
Australia's sport landscape

"Popular culture wars are extraordinarily passionate and strident affairs, especially when sport, and particularly 'football', is involved. Intense battles rage between groups with deeply held investments in their sports. Football fans in particular can be deeply attached to their teams and codes, which may even underpin their identities. The football wars as popular culture wars cannot simply be reduced to a preference for a particular football code, least of all in Australia. For the football wars in Australia offer a key site in which to examine questions of globalisation, and the sustainability of local and national culture within this process, and a debate as to which code can best unify and represent contemporary Australia" [2]

When Tom Wills crafted a set of rules for a new form of football for Victorians, he most likely didn't appreciate that some 150 years later, his creation would generate annual revenue of around $1.5 billion[3]. Rather, history tells us that he simply wanted to invent a game to keep cricketers fit over winter, in response to New South Wales having been so dominant in Sheffield Shield matches. The abridged story here of Tom Will's game is a microcosm for the transformation of sport generally.

The past 150 years has seen sport's role in society develop from a purely recreational past time centred on health and fitness, to becoming a consumer product of significant commercial value. It is a sad irony then, that despite the ever increasing availability of sport as a physical activity, Australian health is declining. The number of overweight or obese adult Australians reached 63% in 2015, while one in four children aged 5 to 17 are now overweight or obese. Although the exploits and prowess of Indigenous athletes are lauded across many sports, 43% of Indigenous adults are obese[4]. Sadly, a prolific volume of research has failed to find consistent evidence of a 'trickle-down effect' whereby elite sport inspires increased mass sport participation.

The acceleration in the financial growth of the sport industry can be traced to Kerry Packer's World Series Cricket of 1977, following the introduction of colour television in Australia in 1975. From this period, the sport industry has grown exponentially and it was no coincidence that in 1990, Deakin University in Melbourne was among the first universities in the world to offer sport management degrees within its business school. The modern sport industry is now more than just a peripheral component in the Australian economy. It employs around 100,000 people and accounts for 12% of total leisure and recreational spending[5], while approximately 2,000 students per annum study sport management in their undergraduate degrees. About 80% of the Australian population have an interest in sport, and about two-thirds of the population are interested in at least one football code.

For all the financial growth and professionalisation the sport industry has achieved, it is worth reinforcing why sport is so popular in the first place. Sport is able to form a deep part of many people's social identity, much like a religion or a political affiliation can. Arguably, with only 60% of people in the 2016 census identifying with a specific religious affiliation, it may be the case that sport teams are a more common source of social identity for Australians than religions. So too do our football grand final weeks, along with World Cup appearances, appear to capture public interest that exceeds our political elections. Correspondingly, sport has become entrenched as a large component of broader culture. That both news telecasts and newspapers devote their precious back-ends to sport coverage speaks volumes to its cultural prominence.

Australia is a particularly unique landscape, where sport is even more culturally prominent than in most nations. The most unique feature is, of course, the presence of four distinct football codes. Nowhere in the world is the word 'football' more contentious than here, creating unmatched cultural warfare. Ireland may perhaps come the closest with Gaelic football, soccer, rugby union and a very peripheral rugby league presence. America too has American football, soccer and a growing rugby union presence. New Zealand and England can point to interest in soccer, rugby league and rugby union. Yet common to most these comparison markets is the dominance of one particular 'football' over the rest. What makes Australia football so unique is not just having four codes, but that these co-exist in a hierarchy that sees each generate revenue in excess of $100 million annually and be considered broadly 'popular'.

Although the codes have been competing since their respective establishments, the commercialisation of sport has seen the stakes of such competition continue to rise and rise. As football rules were codified and football associations formed in the 1880s, a matter of only hundreds of men in each state decided which code to play.

Fast forward to 2019 and the AFL, NRL, FFA and Rugby Australia generated $1.56 billion in central league revenue between them. Accordingly what commenced as disagreements within our colonies about what game to play by, has evolved into a large-scale industry that is characterised by cut-throat cultural and commercial competition. While the football codes have long been at war, the stakes have therefore never been higher than today.

The Art of (Football) War

Although the Australian football landscape is constantly evolving, we are currently in the midst of the greatest period of industry change since perhaps the commercialisation of sport in the 1970s. Aside from the obvious impact of the COVID-19 pandemic, there have been broader shifts in the football landscape in the past decade to consider. The growth in women's football and short-form football, media fragmentation, globalisation and the growing awareness around concussion are mostly new or accelerating trends of the last decade. All these factors have only further contributed to the state of hyper-competition in which our football codes will increasingly find themselves.

Our football codes compete across many battlefronts, from attracting junior participants and then signing elite junior athletes, to attracting fans, sponsors, broadcasters and government support. The name 'football' itself is a highly contested battlefront, evidenced by the controversy summoned by Soccer Australia changing its name to Football Federation Australia from 1 January 2005.

As sociologist Buck Rosenberg notes: "This change of name is central to the 'football wars' and the struggle over the use of the name 'football' can be loosely understood as part of the 'culture wars'… Australian soccer, the new management team felt, was now 'mature' enough to claim its 'rightful' name of 'football'."[6] Indeed in my own teaching, I ban the word 'football' and 'footy' from the classroom lexicon due to the confusion it creates. For many of my undergraduate Victorian students in particular, it often appears like the first time they've contemplated that someone might misunderstand what is meant by their use of the term.

An interesting observation surrounding the modern code war is that we rarely see public acknowledgment across the leagues of the obvious and fierce competition that exists between them. This was best typified in a 2018 Melbourne radio interview with former NRL CEO Todd Greenberg: "Probably what's good commentary is the NRL and AFL are at war with these sort of things, but the reality is it couldn't be further from the truth… I feel as sports, we compete with a much wider variety of entertainment options. I think Netflix is a bigger competitor to rugby league than what any other sport is"[7].

Peter V'landys ascension to ARLC Chairmanship has perhaps reignited the code war in way that has disrupted a prolonged period of cordiality typified by Greenberg's quote. This is because V'landys is the quintessential wartime leader, and his many notable quotes leaves nobody unsure of where his loyalties are and who his enemy is:

"Melbourne has the smelly Yarra River, it's got the most dreary city on earth with the worst weather, yet NSW bows and scrapes to it all the time…We consume the Melbourne Cup, the AFL grand final, the Australian tennis open. In stark contrast, Sydney has the most beautiful city in the world and without any doubt the best harbour in the world and we do nothing to drive our own assets."[8]

Peter V'landys is in many ways, refreshingly transparent in an age where public relations has driven the code war into covert operations. Yet, this has not always been the case. Australian Rules for instance specifically dispersed 'propaganda' funding to northern markets from 1906. Specific use of language such as 'war', 'battle' or 'attack', particularly surrounding Australian Rules and rugby league, appeared more common between the 1950s to 1980s than today. The origin of the 'Barassi Line', a term developed to divide Australia between Australian Rules and rugby regions, is inherently associated with war. The expression is credited as being a play on the 'Brisbane Line': an alleged (but unsubstantiated) World War Two defence strategy to sacrifice all land north of the Queensland capital if Japanese forces were to have invaded. Consider the language in the following quote from a 1980 VFL corporate planning report, which reads as if it were written by an army general:

> "The Sydney sporting market will probably never be as ripe for an attack from Australian football as it is now. Rugby is in a state of organised chaos with a poor public image, and its participation and attendances are declining. The game and its stars are now well known and it is seen as a viable alternative to the violence of rugby"[9]

The shift from overt to covert rivalry between the codes perhaps reflects the growing commercial and strategic sophistication of sport management. Much of how the codes now compete has parallels to Sun Tzu's *Art of War*. Among the core principles of the text is that all warfare is based on deception: "Conceal your dispositions, and your condition will remain secret, which leads to victory; show your dispositions, and your condition will become patent, which leads to defeat". Other tenets also ring true. The AFL's progress has at least partially been propelled by a litany of historical calamities which have beset its competitors; "the opportunity of defeating the enemy is provided by the enemy himself". Detailing these litany of errors make up a large portion of part two of this book. Further consider the modern day practice of media releases, which often creatively manipulate statistics to trumpet the respective code's success: "When the outlook is bright, bring it before their eyes; but tell them nothing when the situation is gloomy".

Because highly prominent sport leagues exist in a kind of hybrid position between business and culture, it is easy to take for granted that they will always be around. This is a logic that is distinct from broader business, in which we accept the inevitable rise and fall of corporations. If we think of our football codes then, do they operate within a product life cycle in which one could end, or does their presence in the mainstream cultural sphere of society provide a higher barrier to failure? It is hard to imagine an Australian sport landscape without AFL, yet the comparatively strong growth of rugby union between 1995 and the 2003 World Cup and the 16 years of atrophy that have followed illustrates that the football landscape is not static.

Another certainty is our football codes are not inclined to help each other prosper. The FFA are perhaps the most acutely aware of this, given the lack of support provided by their counterparts in relation to ground availability during their failed bid to host the men's FIFA World Cup. Soccer more generally has faced over a century of oppression from its fellow codes, which have historically attempted to suppress the round ball game, particularly through a lack of infrastructure access[10]. Soccer also probably has the most right to feel aggrieved by a long running trend of negative media sentiment, particularly around fan behaviour, which we explore in part three of the book.

All codes, however, are guilty of harming each other, to the extent that they could, over the long span of history. Rugby union successfully contributed to eradicating Victorian rules from Sydney by 1893. They did so firstly by strategically declining invitations to play inter-colonial representative matches between the codes which would have provided Victorian rules much needed exposure. More nefariously, they did so by banning any individuals who played Victorian rules. Unintentionally, this may have been among Australian sports earliest 'square ups', after an influx of South Australians to Perth in 1885 contributed to the demise of rugby in Western Australia, supplanted by Victorian rules[11].

Banning people would in particular become a regular part of the rugby union play book during its amateur ethos. For instance, rugby league immortal Wally Lewis played both rugby league and union growing up, representing the Australian Schoolboys Union team on a 1977 tour of Great Britain. After returning, he would be told by the Queensland Rugby Union that he would not be selected in future representative teams if he continued to play rugby league. History shows he would choose league, contributing to a chain of events in which he became a prominent contributor to State of Origin's establishment, further cementing league's dominance in the state of Queensland.

Lewis choosing rugby league was consistent with the general flow of talent between these two codes from 1908 until the professionalism of union in 1995. Undoubtedly, rugby league was never terribly apologetic for this century of plundering players when they had the market advantage. For this reason the outcry within league circles at the turn of the millennium when the tide started to turn somewhat, with players like Tuqiri, Sailor, Rogers and Walker "defecting" to rugby union, appeared highly hypocritical. This was noted by nearly every union supporter at the time.

The poaching between rugby league and union now swings both ways. Rugby league, offering more opportunities to transition from elite junior to paid professional, almost needs rugby union as an athlete development pathway. Conversely, rugby league's cherry picking of Pacific Islander natives who have grown up with a love for union increasingly risks making the NRL a feeder pathway to French Rugby Union and the Wallabies.

The football codes are therefore much like competitors of any other typical industry:

each working towards their own goals, preferably at the expense of their competitors wherever possible. Yet, given Australia is apparently a 'sports mad' nation, can't all our sports prosper together?

Australia's crowded, 'sport mad' market

Australia is said to be the lucky country[12], and if you're a football fan, this is not least because there is a pool of 49 top-tier football teams to support. Factoring in the recent explosion in women's football leagues, there are now 80 discrete football teams to support from 2021. This is more than ever before. Yet once we reach a near one to one ratio of women's and men's teams within football clubs over the next decade, we'll be just shy of 100 discrete elite commercial football teams operating in Australia. Add cricket, netball and basketball across both genders, Australia has 121 teams across our seven mainstream team sports[13].

If a team for every 200,000 people was not enough sport content, consider that Australia hosts major sporting events that far exceed what our population and economic rank in the world hierarchy would predict.

Our hosting of the Australian Open tennis tournament provides an annual serving of the world's best tennis players, with the same true of hosting Formula 1 and MotoGP. So too has Australia exceeded at hosting mega sport events. Australia is one of only six countries to have hosted the Olympics twice, along with the UK, Greece, Germany, France and the USA. However if we exclude pre-World War 1 games, we are only one of four countries to have hosted the Olympics twice post-1914. Australia had hosted two games before all BRIC countries had (Brazil [2016], Russia [1980], India [nil], China [2008]). This means we had hosted more Olympics by 2000 than the combined total of countries which represent about 25% of the world's land mass and 40% of the global population. We have nearly hosted as many Commonwealth Games (five) as the United Kingdom has (six), which is more than Canada (four) or New Zealand (three). Australia has also hosted the second most Rugby World Cup fixtures (59 out of 374), behind only New Zealand (69). Australia too has among the most golf courses per capita in the world.

With all this in mind, it is understandable why Australia has long been considered such a sport obsessed, or "sports mad", nation.

As noted in the seminal book *Paradise of Sport*: "For better or worse, sport has become central to Australian life and the business of being Australian. Sporting culture is accessible and provides continuing satisfactions for many Australians. It is immensely popular and addresses some of the central issues of Australian life"[14]. This statement certainly appears supported by my empirical data. About two-thirds of the Australian population are interested in at least one football code, while only about 20% of the population are rejecters of sport broadly as a leisure category. Australia must certainly be a tough place to live for those individuals who dislike sport, particularly those who live in Melbourne.

However, what may often be taken for granted is whether Australia is a **uniquely** sport mad country by comparison to other nations. A Google search of 'sport obsessed nations' returns a potpourri of countries with loves for particular sports and events. A Google search of 'sport hating nations' does not provide any meaningful examples. The short answer here is that critical academic analysis has gradually moved from supporting, to qualifying and finally dismissing the idea that Australia is uniquely a sporting nation[15]. Such research has typically drawn on comparing our sport attendance rates, participation rates and international performance to other nations. In relation to the latter two in particular, such research has discovered only limited exceptionalism in the sporting domain at best (in recent times).

While a nation's gross domestic product (GDP) is the single best predictor of its Olympic performance[16], Australia has historically been able to outperform its GDP. This is because Australia has typically invested more than the average nation toward recreation, which in itself is a reflection of the cultural centrality of sport in Australia. As noted in one Olympic medal estimation study: "a measure of public spending in the broad area of recreation, explains the persistent tendency of countries such as Australia, New Zealand and The Netherlands, which are high spenders on recreation, to perform more strongly at the Olympic Games than the size of their economy suggests that they should"[17].

Yet our relative international performances have been sliding since 2000, corresponding to more prosperous nations investing more heavily in sport, concurrently to Australia reducing its own investment. In relation to Olympic performance, Australia finished 15th on a Weighted Medals per capita basis and 45th on a Weight Medals per GDP basis during the 2016 Rio Olympics[18]. In response, we have seen Sport Australia's previous 'Winning Edge' strategy, which was focussed entirely on elite performance and winning, replaced by the Sport 2030 national sport plan which sets more holistic, and less performance-ambitious targets:

"for the first time, Sport Australia has defined high performance Olympic and Paralympic success more broadly than just winning. Success at elite international level remains important to our nation and fundamental to the AIS, but the measurement of success must now also include the impact of athletes as role models, their engagement with the community, and delivering a respected system"[19]

The use of the Olympics and other international competition performance as a measure of our sporting prowess is also often mitigated by the claim that a large proportion of our best athletes gravitate towards Australian Rules, netball and rugby league. These sports, with either an absent or minor international presence, is said to dilute our athlete talent pool.

In some instances, we have a Ben Simmons' who reached NBA stardom and "always knew inside I wanted to play basketball and get to that next level and compete against the best"[20]. In many other cases we have Scott Pendlebury, Dean Brogan and Marcus Bontempelli among a litany of high level junior or senior basketballers who would become accomplished AFL players. Former rugby league player Tepai Moeroa was Australia's third ranked under 20s shot-putter when he signed with NRL club the Parramatta Eels[21]. Having hoped to still compete at the 2016 Rio games, he suffered a shoulder injury that scuppered his chances. For an aspiring shot-putter, the tackling involved in rugby league must be about as good for the shoulders as an aspiring pianist playing with hammers and chainsaws in their spare time.

In an attempt to try to quantify the impact of such non international sports, the Greatest Sporting Nation[22] attempts to quantify national elite performance utilising what appears to be a reasonable criteria on how to include performance in non-Olympic and non-fully international sports. According to their method, Australia finished 19th in 2018 on a per capita basis and 12th in aggregate as shown in Figure 1. Australia is never likely to finish atop either category because countries which dominate the aggregate list have particularly large populations and economies, while the top per capita countries are economically developed small countries. Australia straddles these two rankings methods due to a population that is middling, being approximately five times larger than the global median (5.5 million) but still less populous than 54 larger countries.

Rank	Per Capita	Aggregate
1	Norway	United States
2	Croatia	France
3	Switzerland	Russia
4	Sweden	Japan
5	Serbia	Germany
6	New Zealand	China
7	Slovenia	Great Britain
8	Netherlands	Italy
9	Belgium	Netherlands
10	Austria	Canada
11	Finland	Norway
12	Denmark	Australia
13	Latvia	Switzerland
14	Georgia	Spain
15	Belarus	Sweden
16	Czech Republic	South Korea
17	Hungary	Belgium
18	Slovakia	Croatia
19	Australia	Brazil
20	Ireland	Poland

Figure 1: Australian international performance in 2018.

While there appears to be some legitimate defence to our potentially diminished international sporting performance based on how widely we spread our athletes, this also perhaps speaks to a deeper truth about the Australian sport landscape. The comparison of Australia's 'sportiness' has appeared to focus on its output (how we perform), when what would appear to make Australia so sport-obsessed relates to input. It is the presence of so many sports within our mainstream culture, in particular four distinct football codes, that makes Australia a unique sport marketplace.

No other nation can claim, particularly relative to population size, to be home to as diverse a sport ecosystem as Australia. As noted by David Rowe, a professor of cultural research: "Britain, football mad, Italy is football mad, South America is football mad. But, not sport mad... What distinguishes Australia is a broader commitment to sport"[23]. This broader commitment to sport manifests not only in the variety of Australian sport opportunities that are available, but also that the remarkable balance between these sports in competing for the hearts, minds and wallets of sport fans. England for instance, despite being the source of most our historical sporting preferences, remains itself relatively narrowly enthusiastic with soccer.

The competitive tension within the Australian sport marketplace compared with other global contexts can be nicely visualised through the search data queries made through Google, analysed using open-access Google Trends data. Figure 2 illustrates the local search queries for the largest leagues across five countries. The annual search rate is averaged across each league's in-season period, to try account for the differing season lengths of each league[24]. Prophetic of Professor Rowe's critique, it is evident that in many nations, people are not so much obsessed with sport as they are obsessed with a particular sport.

This critical distinction is apparent in such varied contexts as the United Kingdom, Germany and India. In the United Kingdom, where there are also numerous football codes competing, the English Super League (rugby league) and Premiership Rugby (union) each receive only 2% of the search volume of the EPL (soccer). In Germany where there is a broader availability of professional sports, once more soccer is dominant with the Bundesliga generating nearly 30 times as much web traffic as Ice Hockey (5.3%), Basketball (2.6%) and Handball (2.5%). Over the four year period, German search traffic for the EPL was triple that of the country's domestic Handball and Basketball Bundesliga's competitions. India's reputation as being 'cricket mad' is validated by their search query behaviour, with the Indian Premier League generating 15 times the search volume of the Indian Soccer League and 20 times the volume of Pro Kabaddi League[25].

The most similar sport market to that of Australia is arguably the United States, where there are three sports which appear to genuinely compete at a tier one level (NFL, NBA and MLB) and several more on the fringe of mass popularity (NHL, MLS). These major leagues compete in the square of popular opinion to be considered America's most popular, each able to lean on a unique measure of popularity to do so.

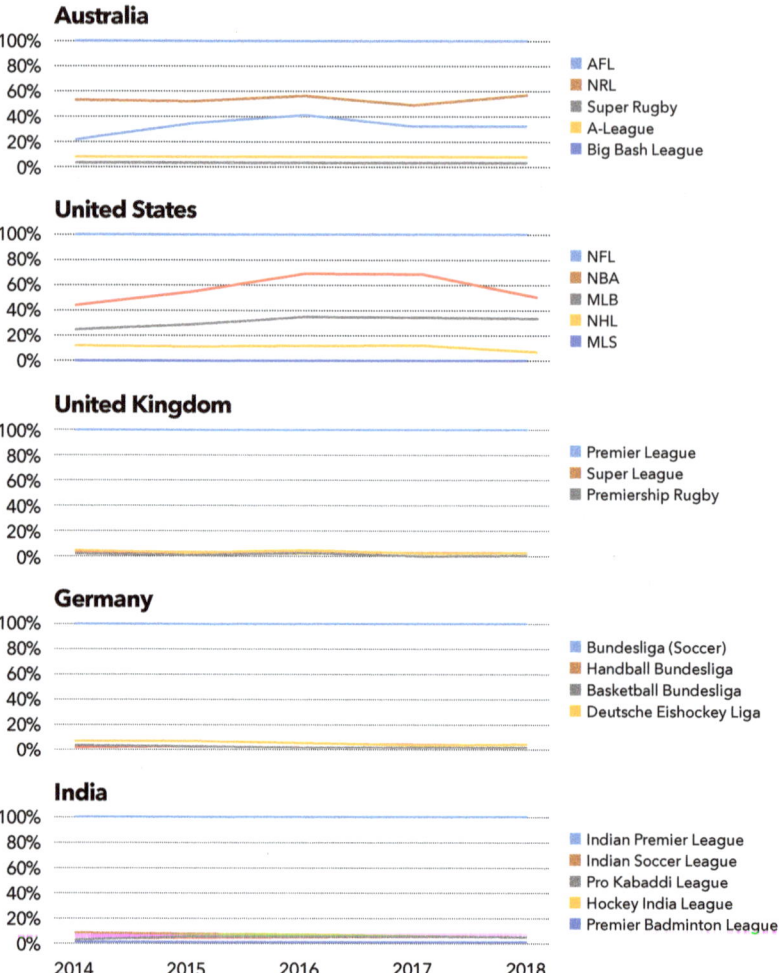

Figure 2: Google search trends by country and league

    Baseball has been considered 'America's pastime' for over 150 years and holds onto this mantle by claiming the greatest aggregate national attendance. However, the MLB's aggregate attendance largely reflects that each MLB team plays 162 regular season games. Basketball has a far higher participation rate than baseball and football and the NBA can therefore, in conjunction with strong media ratings, perhaps make the claim of being the most popular overall sport. The NFL points to its annual record of producing the largest national audiences for the Super Bowl, and television audiences generally, as a reflection of their supremacy. The NHL can at least rely on hockey mad Canada to underpin the league, much like Rugby Australia leans on New Zealand's rugby passion.

    The American example above, with each sport positioned according to their own particular unique measure of popularity, has parallels to the Australian sport market. The

FFA have long pointed to having the largest junior participation base as a source of their legitimacy in the Australian sport hierarchy. The AFL owns the largest media valuation and attendances in Australian sport. The NRL has the most top-rating television 'events' and has historically dominated the most watched programs on Foxtel. Even Rugby Australia, after the Wallabies won two World Cups in the 1990's and successfully hosted in 2003, had a national team arguably on par with men's cricket as Australia's premier national team around the turn of the millennium.

A further similarity to the American sport market has been an exponential growth in the volume of sport in the past several decades, as was illustrated at the start of this section. Around the turn of the millennium, academics began to observe that sport markets were beginning to appear crowded and hyper-competitive. It was estimated that by 2010, there were over 600 professional sport teams in the United States. This led some academics to predict that we had reached 'peak industry', which would result in a decline in revenue in the new millennium[26]. Although this was ultimately unfounded, such concerns spoke to the growing global concerns that commercial sport had reached a saturation point.

In Australia, fuelled by recent growth in women's team sport, the amount of commercial sport teams in operation has more than doubled from about 50 in 2005 to 121 by 2021[27]. Upon this basis, with our comparatively small population in mind, there is an argument to be made that Australia as a nation, and Sydney/Melbourne as individual cities, are among the most competitive sport markets in the world.

The task of empirically identifying which nation or city is in fact the 'most' sport saturated is difficult, given Europe and North America use distinct league structures that complicate comparisons. Europe's typical use of a promotion and relegation league system blurs the boundaries of defining which teams compete commercially, when considering the varying tiers of professionalism in which they operate. For instance, there are twelve soccer teams in London within the 'professional' leagues, although only six are in the Premier League, three in the second, two in third and one in the fourth division in season 2020/21. In Spain there is a 16 team league devoted to rink hockey, in which some teams are fully professional and others near amateur. Such variance unsurprisingly can lead to lopsided leagues, with the Barcelona rink hockey club winning 15 of 17 championships between 2002 and 2019 for instance.

By contrast, North America operates off a franchise model of league structure, to which Australia also subscribes. However, this is not without its complications when attempting to make comparisons to our local market. So called 'amateur' college teams in the NCAA are clearly professional in their structure and scale, when considering their income and expenditure. The athletics department of the NCAA's two highest grossing universities (Texas and Texas A&M) generated USD$437 million between them in 2018/2019[28]. Yet, they are not typical commercial enterprises like an NBA or NFL team because of their association and corresponding obligations within the collegiate system.

With such difficulties in comparisons acknowledged, we firstly consider how Australia compares with other nations. As of 2018, America and Canada had approximately 150 major league franchises (MLB, NHL, NFL, NBA, MLS) situated across 51 cities and a combined population of 365 million people. If we conservatively consider men's and women's teams as one unified club or 'franchise', Australia has approximately 74 franchises dispersed across 12 cities, with a population nearing 25 million people.

The concentration of our teams is therefore particularly evident on a per capita basis. Director of the prominent sport consultancy agency Gemba, Andrew Condon, made this observation in 2017 in comparing Australia with the state of California in the United States. According to his more liberal interpretation: Australia had a population of 24 million people and a GDP of $1.4 trillion, sustaining 90 professional men's and women's teams. California has a larger population and economy: 39 million people and a GDP of $US2.5 trillion, yet sustains only 20 teams[29].

Comparing Australia with countries of similar population and economic output further illustrates our sporting concentration. Taiwan is the country with among the next nearest population (23,773,876) to Australia, yet had only about 21 professional teams in 2019. A curiosity of Taiwan is that baseball represents a de facto national sport, yet their national league (Chinese Professional Baseball League) features only four teams. The competition will therefore grow a whopping 20% when the Wei Chuan Dragons re-join the major league in 2020/21. In addition to baseball, Taiwan's basketball league features five teams of both male and female orientation, under single franchises similar to the BBL/WBBL or AFL/AFLW model. Eight teams operate within the Taiwan Football Premier League, which commenced in only 2017.

Spain, with a similar GDP to Australia (1.43 trillion to Australia's 1.42 trillion per IMF, 2019) appears to have a similarly high concentration of sport teams, but has close to double Australia's population (46 million). Further, the standard of professionalism varies much more wildly than the Australian market. Spain's globally pre-eminent football competition La Liga features 20 teams, with the 22 teams in La Liga2 also of a professional standard. In addition, 18 teams feature at the top level in each of basketball (Liga ACB) and handball (Liga ASOBAL), the majority of which can be considered professional. However, levels of professionalism vary considerably across the 16 teams in Spain's rink hockey league (OK Liga) as mentioned, while the female rink hockey league (14 team) and women's soccer division (16 team), are still attempting to move beyond semi-professionalism.

An argument could also be made that Melbourne and Sydney are in fact the most competitive sport markets in the world, by virtue of their unique relationships to Australian Rules and rugby league. Across the seven commercial team sport leagues, Melbourne features 21 teams and Sydney 20. With respective populations of 4.94 million and 5.23 million, this leaves the two cities with 235,238 (Melbourne) and 261,500 (Sydney) people per top-tier commercial sport team. By contrast, Greater London (18 teams) and New York state (17 teams) each have a similar aggregate of elite sport teams[30], but considerably larger populous. With about 19.4 million people, these leaves New York state with a per capita ratio of 1,140,000 residents per team, while London's population of 8.91 million results in a ratio of 495,000 which is double that of Melbourne.

Undoubtedly, Australia retains a particularly unique sport landscape by world standards. In Sydney and Melbourne, Australia has two cities that have a particularly unique concentration of sport teams, despite populations that place them in the 50's bracket of global city population rankings. This sport concentration, in supply and demand terms, is fantastic for Australian sport fans. It means that Australians rarely run the risk of missing a sold-out fixture and can purchase a general admission football ticket in the vicinity of between $20 and $35. By contrast, the average ticket price to a Los Angeles Chargers NFL game was USD $165 in 2019. Meanwhile, it has been well documented that the financial growth of the English Premier League has been such that increasing ticket costs, necessitated by exploding player wage bills, have seen local fans increasingly frozen out of attending elite domestic soccer.

Further compare tennis' grand slam tournaments as a case study of how privileged Australian sport fans are by world standards. The Australian Open tennis can be attended with a general admission day pass that costs about $55 and usually remains available even to walk ups on the day in question. Compare this to how one can obtain a ticket to Wimbledon: 1) enter a public (or tennis club) ballot that is heavily over-subscribed, 2) win a ticket via the club lottery of national tennis club members, 3) join the queue at the venue, which in 2017 saw people start queuing 40 hours ahead of time to obtain a ticket or 4) invest in a debenture[31], which gives the holder a perpetual ticket for five years at the price of £50,000 each (for centre court).

While the Australian sport marketplace's relative supply to demand is fantastic for consumers, it forces sport organisations into a state of cut-throat competition of the highest order.

Although a slight simplification, the changing of the seasons between summer and winter could be historically marked as a handover from cricket to Australian Rules and rugby, with a month or so intermission between each season for consumers to rebuild their sporting appetite. Increasingly, this is no longer the case. The advent of the Big Bash Leagues and the shift of the WBBL to precede the BBL, the development of the ANZ Championship and then Super Netball, summer A-League and W-League, and the AFLW have blurred and stretched the seasonal sporting calendar. In any one moment of the year, there will now likely be at least three major leagues in-season, all competing for Australia's hearts, minds, eyes and wallets.

Further stoking competition is that these Australian hearts, minds and eyes have also never been more valuable. The 'big five' of the AFL, NRL, RA, FFA and CA saw their collective central revenue nearly double in seven years, growing from $1.1 billion in 2012 to break the $2 billion mark in 2019. With the Australian sport market never having been so valuable, yet never so crowded, can the football codes co-exist in peace? Or will cut-throat competition eventually see the code war conclude with clear victors and casualties?

The battlelines of Australia's code war

What differentiates Australia from more typical sport settings is not only that we have multiple football codes, but that their origins are so heavily geographic-centric. We explore the history of this in far greater detail in part two, instead focusing here upon the implications of this in the modern environment. Despite each football code having over a century of local history, there remain big geographic divisions in our football preferences. This socio-geographic division is colloquially referred to as the Barassi Line, coined by history professor Ian Turner during his annual lectures between 1965 and 1978. The line is named after AFL player/coach Ron Barassi, who exhibited particular enthusiasm towards propagating Australian Rules north of the code's traditional heartlands during a period where such enthusiasm was yet to be fully embraced. Turner described this dividing line between Australian Rules and rugby as curving in an arc from Eden in coastal New South Wales, through Canberra, Broken Hill, Birdsville in south-west Queensland and into Arnhem Land in the north east of the Northern Territory.

Although the expression is now 50 years old, and technology is globalising our media consumption, where you live and were raised in Australia in fact still has a remarkably strong bearing on your likely football preferences. While this may seem like an obvious statement to any observant football fan, it is the degree of such differences that are particularly noteworthy. To illustrate this, I draw on television ratings, survey data and Google Trends data below.

In a study I published in 2013 which analysed television ratings data for the period 2007 to 2011, 93% of NRL audiences came from the northern states (NSW and Queensland) and 81% of AFL viewership came from southern states (VIC/SA/WA/TAS).

Looking more recently at season 2019, this has not changed much. NRL matches held an average rating in Sydney of 198,000 for games involving Sydney teams and 186,000 for games without, compared with AFL figures of 51,000 for Sydney Swans matches and 21,000 for matches involving neither Sydney team. The NRL's 2019 audience in Brisbane was 173,000 for Broncos games and 107,000 for games not involving Queensland teams, compared with AFL figures of 43,000 for Brisbane Lions matches and 28,000 for fixtures not involving Queensland teams. By comparison, the AFL's 2019 average audience in Melbourne was 261,000, 92,000 in Adelaide and 95,000 in Perth, whereas a rating for 10,000 to 20,000 would be typical for the NRL in these markets. As judged by television ratings then, the NRL remains hardly national, nor the AFL particularly Australia-wide – despite both of those concepts being implicit in their titles.

THE BATTLE FOR FANS, DOLLARS AND SURVIVAL

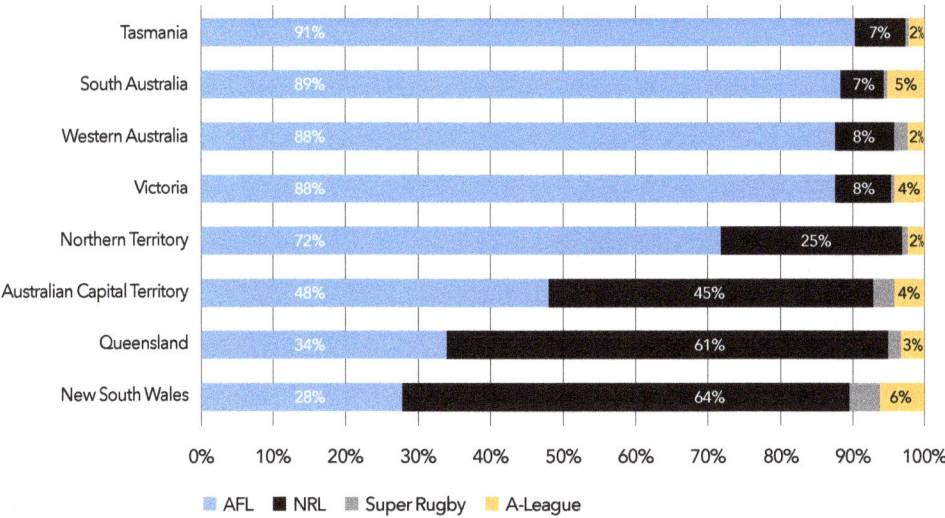

Figure 3: Comparative Google search volume of AFL/NRLS/Super Rubgy/A-League in Australia by state (2014-2018)

This is further evident in Google search data, displayed above. Figure 3 illustrates the share of search volume associated with each code's respective domestic league, by state/territory, for the period 2014 to 2018. This is perhaps among the fairest ways to perform a like-for-like comparison of the codes' respective popularity, given Google is available to all, overcoming the limitations of trying to compare television ratings that are limited by differing accessibility across codes. This data once more illustrates a clear divide between north-east and south-west Australia. In the southern states, AFL retains an average 89% share of annual search volume across the four leagues, which declines to 31% across New South Wales and Queensland. The NRL's 63% share of northern search volume declines to just 7% in southern states.

The Google search data reveals several notable points about the geographical divides of Australia. First, it is clear that AFL is becoming embedded north of the Barassi Line at a far quicker rate than rugby league to the south. Second, Turner's original mapping of the Barassi Line appears to remain reasonably consistent with modern data. He included Canberra along the line, which is the most evenly contested territory within the data. Turner also included Arnhem Land, which is in the north-east corner of the Northern Territory. Although the specific choice of Arnhem Land was most likely geometric, to allow for a neat dividing line, the Northern Territory also remains more evenly contested between AFL and NRL than any of the surrounding states. Finally, Figure 3 also reveals the significant gap in search volume between AFL and NRL versus Super Rugby and A-League. New South Wales in fact has the most shared search volume, with 8% of searches relating to Super Rugby and the A-League, while in Tasmania the two leagues account for only 2% of search volume. Tasmania has stayed impeccably loyal to AFL for a state that does not feature in the top-flight competition. It should also be noted that soccer and rugby union benefit from international team interest not captured in the comparison, and hence the focus on domestic league search volume undoubtedly under-reports the total search volume somewhat.

What is interesting about the Google data is how strong the preferences for the big two codes remain, despite the freedom the internet provides to explore anything of interest. For this reason, the 'information superhighway' was originally predicted to improve the dispersion of interest among sports (much like all culture generally).

The logic was, if sports operate as cultural oligarchies that result in newspapers focussing their attention only on the most popular sports, the internet would provide the accessibility to break down these content barriers. This has proven not to be the case as was illustrated starkly in early 2020. AFL journalist Mark Robinson of the *Herald Sun* was asked on Twitter why coverage of the AFL Women's was positioned four pages deep behind comparatively meaningless AFL Men's practice matches and general commentary. His response: "It's not positioned in the first four pages because our data shows us not many people are reading AFLW articles". Rather than expand our opportunities to explore broadly as was predicted, digital analytics are in fact driving the opposite outcome and refining our consumption behaviours.

This is not limited to sport. The same is true of much of our digital behaviours around media, which has embraced algorithmic patterns to try maximise the consumer experience. However, it has been well-publicised that such predictive algorithms increasingly risk shrinking our exposure to the new, unknown, disliked and contrary, in favour of that with which we are comfortable. For instance, a music industry report found that despite the increased accessibility of music through digital platforms, the top 10% of albums accounted for 95% of total sales and 99.2% of total digital streams in 2018[32]. Despite platforms like Spotify making all music more accessible than ever before, perversely, our behaviours are narrowing.

The Australian experience is best contrasted to the American setting identified earlier where there are also several top tier, 'mainstream' sports. What is particularly interesting is that there is comparatively small variance between regions in their interest toward these four major leagues as seen in Figure 4. This manifests in two respects.

First, the NFL is the most popular American sports league across every state. Only in Oklahoma (3% gap), Utah (5%) and Oregon (6%) is the NFL/NBA search volume differential close, and these regions are home to NBA teams without a corresponding NFL team (but have strong college football programs). New York (4%) and California (5%) have the closest NFL/NBA search volume differential among regions that feature teams of all major leagues.

Second, the variance in interest between states is relatively small compared with the Australian market. The NFL's comparative share of interest is highest in Wyoming (63%)

THE BATTLE FOR FANS, DOLLARS AND SURVIVAL

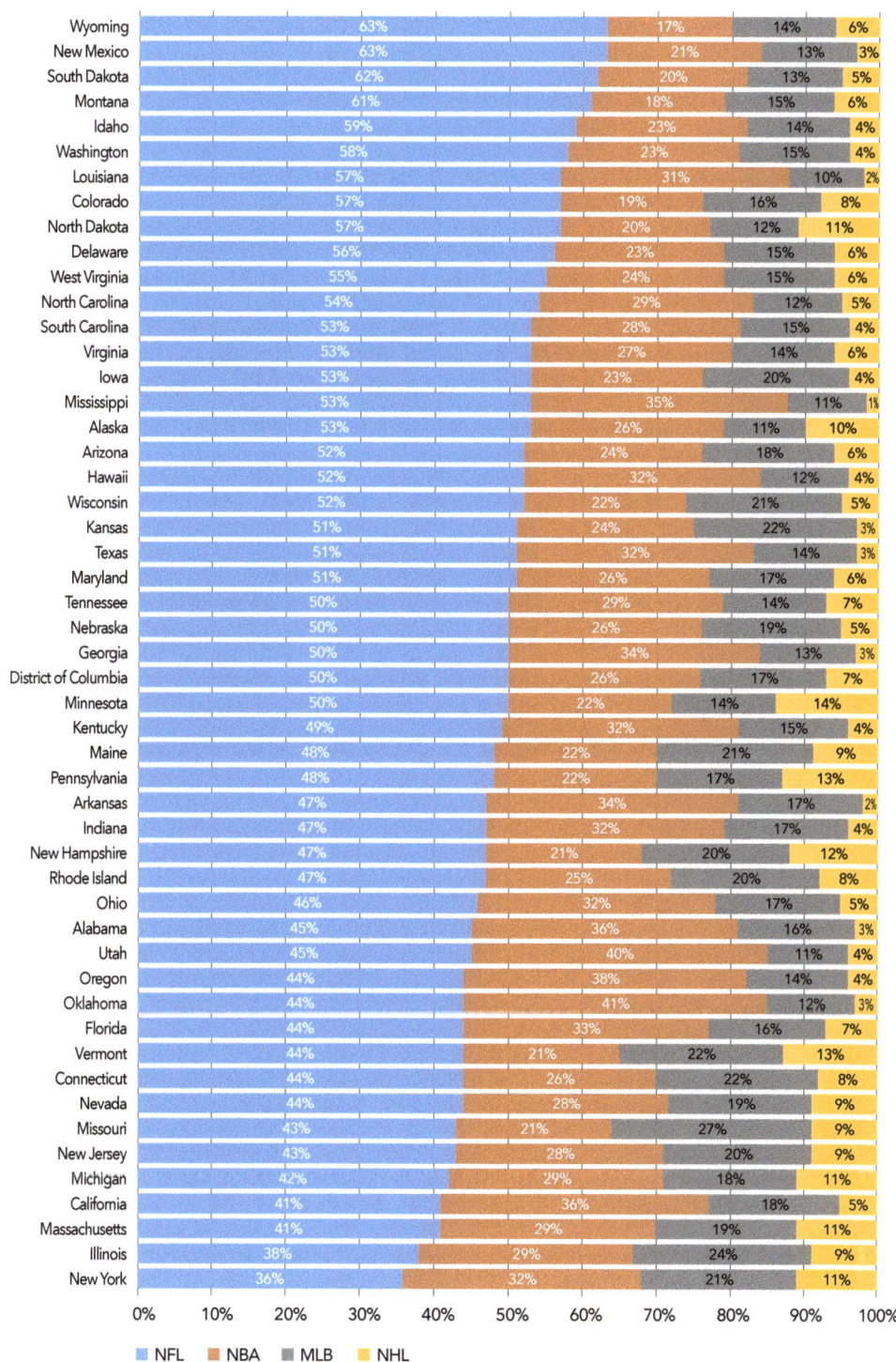

Figure 4: Comparative search volume of US Major Leagues by State (2014-2018).

and smallest in New York (36%) across 51 regions. By contrast, the AFL hold a 91% share of search volume in Tasmania, but only a 28% share in New South Wales, a range of 63% across only eight regions. The Australian market therefore displays much more variance among far fewer regions. That there isn't more variation in America is also surprising, given the country experiences diverse seasonality across regions. American regions vary from extreme cold and to extreme hot; vital considering the nature of ice hockey or baseball. By contrast, weather conditions across Australian cities are relatively consistent.

If you boarded a mystery flight to a random American state and then went directly to the nearest sports bar, it would be similarly probable that you would be surrounded by approximately half a venue of NFL leaning fans, a third of NBA leaning, and a remaining corner of MLB and NHL leaning fans. In contrast, if you boarded a mystery flight to a random Australian state, there is every chance that the NRL would either be on the main screen or barely televised. Therefore, the key to understanding Australia's crowded sport and football market is to consider how each state and capital city contributes to Australia as a whole.

To hammer home the geographical differences in Australian football preferences, I share below research findings derived from a commercial research panel's national database from 2017. The database includes over 27,000 respondents, their identified interest level in sport and which sports, among a list of 34 alternatives, they were interested in. After applying statistical processes to make the data output representative and valid, it is able to illustrate the vast differences in football and overall sporting interest across regions. I'll refer back to this data throughout the book.

Although the regions of Australia seem to hold similar levels of interest in sport overall, it is in fact the type of sports they enjoy where we see the most variance. Figure 5 tallies the interest in the football codes across the five mainland capital cities, the state of Tasmania and nationally.

While the rugby league versus Australian Rules difference between north and south is obvious, it is the differing cultural strength of the two codes that is far more interesting and insightful. The single largest difference between regions which emerges is in relation to the number of people who support only one football code. In both Sydney and Brisbane, rugby league is the most supported football code, with 14% of the population solely interested in rugby league to the exclusion of all other codes. By contrast, in Melbourne, Adelaide, Perth and Tasmania, Australian Rules is the most popular code, with 35% of the population solely interested to the exclusion of all other football codes.

Reframing this distinction reinforces the difference between Australian rules and rugby league support across Australia. Among people who are interested in only one code south of the Barassi Line, 76% of people nominate Australian Rules as their sole football code of interest. By contrast, among people who are interested in only one code north of the Barassi Line, less than half (45%) choose rugby league. From the AFL's perspective, it is impressive

THE BATTLE FOR FANS, DOLLARS AND SURVIVAL

	Sydney	Brisbane	Melb.	Adelaide	Perth	Tasmania	National
No codes	37%	38%	32%	32%	36%	34%	35%
AFL only	4%	6%	34%	35%	28%	35%	19%
League only	14%	14%	1%	1%	1%	2%	9%
Union only	2%	3%	1%	1%	2%	2%	2%
Soccer only	11%	7%	8%	8%	9%	5%	7%
Main code	14%	14%	34%	35%	28%	35%	
Other codes	17%	16%	10%	10%	12%	9%	
AFL & Union	1%	1%	1%	1%	3%	1%	1%
AFL & Soccer	2%	2%	10%	12%	7%	5%	5%
AFL & League	3%	5%	3%	2%	2%	4%	4%
League & Union	4%	6%	1%	1%	1%	2%	3%
League & Soccer	6%	3%	-%	1%	1%	-%	2%
Union & Soccer	1%	1%	-%	-%	1%	1%	1%
Two codes	18%	18%	16%	17%	16%	13%	16%
AFL & Union & Soccer	1%	-%	1%	1%	2%	1%	1%
AFL & League & Union	3%	5%	2%	2%	3%	4%	3%
AFL & League & Soccer	3%	1%	2%	1%	1%	1%	2%
League & Union & Soccer	3%	3%	-%	1%	1%	-%	1%
Three codes	8%	9%	5%	4%	5%	6%	7%
All four codes	5%	4%	3%	2%	3%	3%	4%

Figure 5: Football repertoires across our capital cities.

to consider the following three statistical observations. If one were to walk down the streets of Melbourne, Adelaide or Tasmania:

1. Every third person you walked by on the street would be interested in AFL and no other football code.
2. If you were in a pub filled with people interested in football, 82% of those people would be interested in AFL.
3. More than half of the pub above would be solely interested in AFL and no other football code.

As a matter of contrast, if you were hoping to open a sports bar tailored exclusively to those interested in rugby union, you'd be best served opening in Brisbane. This would be quite a niche bar, given you'd only be catering to 23% of the local population who are interested in the code. In particular, only 3% of the Brisbane population are solely interested in the code and no others.

Although geography is undoubtedly the most prominent defining feature of the Australian football landscape, the shifting sands of demography are also a key influence. Like any consumer product, sport teams and leagues are susceptible to changes in population tastes and preferences.

During the first decade of television in America, wrestling, roller derby and boxing were in fact among America's most popular sports. This was because they were the dominant TV sports of the time, needing only a single camera to be broadcast. Thus improvements in broadcast technology would erode this advantage quite quickly. By the 1950s and 1960s, NFL broadcasting exploded, relegating these sports from the screens and also largely bringing the radio sport broadcasting era to an end.

A key historical leaning from the American context is that sports cannot take as a given that their popularity will perpetuate. Gallup polling has tracked America's favourite spectator sports for nearly a century, illustrating how what might appear like gradual shifts in preferences can eventually change entire landscapes. In 1937, 34% of Americans identified baseball as their favourite spectator sport, making it Americans' favourite sport by a considerable margin. By 2017, this had declined to only 9% of Americans, placing it a distant third. Its place has been taken by American football and fragmentation. American football has grown from 23% to 37% during this period, while 8% less people indicated American football, baseball or basketball to be their favourite sport[33].

Population demographics have also contributed to shaping changing Australian sport preferences, and here I illustrate the particular implications of age upon the football landscape.

In a survey I conducted of Sydney and Melbourne based residents and the sport teams they support, perhaps the most striking feature is the evident youthfulness in the fan base of NBA and EPL teams, compared with local teams. The average age of supporters among Manchester United, Liverpool and Arsenal fans in these two cities was found to be 43.4, while the group average age of Los Angeles Lakers, Chicago Bulls or Golden State Warriors (NBA) supporters was 36.6. People aged 18 to 39 account for 39% of the general population, yet this group represent 68% of the fan base for the three NBA teams surveyed.

By contrast, the South Sydney Rabbitohs has the oldest fan base of all football clubs (48.3), followed by St George Illawarra (47.9) and Wests Tigers (47.6). The Geelong Cats (46.2) and St Kilda Saints (46.1) retain the oldest fan bases amongst Melbourne football teams.

In academic terms, support of overseas teams has been dubbed 'satellite fandom' or 'satellite support', and its growth recognised as increasingly important to understand as part of a globalising economy[34]. Unsurprisingly, growth in satellite fandom has been fuelled by digital technology, which has made overseas leagues increasingly available to domestic consumers around the world. Given new technologies are typically diffused at greater rates by younger individuals, satellite fandom appears a particularly young person phenomena. This is a trend I have observed first-hand in teaching undergraduate sport management students for a decade now. Between 2010 and 2019 I have seen students, during their introductions, increasingly identify as fans of Manchester rather than Melbourne, Arsenal rather than Adelaide, or the Bulls rather than Bullets.

In the best case, the support of global leagues by younger sport fans does not necessarily replace interest for local teams and leagues. However, it forces local teams to share fans with a growing array of local and domestic competitors. In a piece of scholarly research around Liverpool's global fan base, it was suggested that the globalising nature of sport leagues would result in football consumers supporting both a local side, and one of the world's big six as a cultural norm[35]. We explore this hypothesis further in part three in considering what the future holds for football in Australia.

The changing preferences of younger sport fandom however are becoming evident when juxtaposing the average age of NBA fans (36.6), with AFL (49.1), rugby league (49.5) and rugby union (51.3) fans as illustrated later in Figure 6[36].

Empirically, the impact of younger fandom is becoming apparent in commercial sport trends. Roy Morgan research for instance illustrated that in the case of the NRL, the proportion of Australians aged under 25 who had watched NRL on conventional television had declined by 32% between 2016 and 2020 (from 29% to 20%). By contrast, this decline was only 14% amongst those aged 65+ (37% to 32%)[37].

Furthermore, although it may be hard to believe given our relative population size, Australia is the number one country outside of the United States and China in terms of both total revenue and total subscribers for the NBA League Pass streaming platform. Australia, with the world's 55th largest population, provides the NBA more subscribers to its streaming platform than countries like Brazil (209 million people), Japan (126 million), Germany (84 million) or France (65 million).

Consider also that while the A-League's final season on Fox Sports is valued at $32 million, the EPL derives $50 to $60 million in annual revenue from Australia via their agreement with Optus Sport.

Focussing upon sports more broadly by using a nationally representative sample, Figure 6 further illustrates that sports have varying age profiles. The contrast between Boxing and MMA makes for a particularly interesting observation. MMA exhibits a similar national popularity (9.7%) as Boxing (9.0%), yet, the data suggests one sport's future is far more promising than the other. The average age of Boxing fans was 49 in comparison to MMA's 39. Although a difference of a decade in the average age of fans is already quite consequential, the data in fact hides a larger gap because these two sports share their fan bases. Approximately 40% of the fans for each of MMA and Boxing also enjoy the other code, thereby bringing the average age of the two sports closer together. Looking at unique fans, that is fans of MMA who are not Boxing fans and Boxing fans who are not MMA fans, reveals the true age gap in the fan bases of these combat sports. The average age of MMA exclusive fans is 38.1, with 61% of such fans aged 18-39. The average age of Boxing exclusive fans is 53.3, with a 41% aged over 60 and only 26% aged 18-39. MMA is a young and growing sport, undoubtedly contributing to the pre-eminent fighting league UFC being valued at USD $4 billion when purchased by private equity in 2016.

Sport	Average	18-39	40-59	60+
Golf	58.15 ↑	16.3% ↓	32.3% ↓	51.4% ↑
Cricket	52.19 ↑	27.7% ↓	35.4	36.9% ↑
Rugby Union	51.34 ↑	29.3% ↓	35.1	35.6% ↑
Rugby League	49.51 ↑	32.8% ↓	36.2% ↑	31.0% ↑
AFL	49.10 ↑	33.5% ↓	36.4% ↑	30.2% ↑
Tennis	48.98 ↑	36.4% ↓	32.3% ↓	31.3% ↑
Boxing	48.53 ↑	36.1% ↓	33.6%	30.3% ↑
Netball	47.22	38.5%	34.5%	27.0%
Average	46.93	39.0%	35.0%	26.0%
Soccer	46.52	41.7% ↑	31.6% ↓	26.7%
Basketball	42.03 ↓	51.8% ↑	30.9% ↓	17.4% ↓
MMA/UFC	39.46 ↓	56.5% ↑	32.0% ↓	11.6% ↓

Figure 6: Age of sport fan bases.

Locating Australia's sport capital

Given the previous section has illustrated how much variance exists in our football preferences across regions, an understanding of today's Australian football market is incomplete without considering in further detail the individual markets in which they operate. This section therefore takes a brief detour to explore the development of our major cities, as the homes of our major sports codes.

Melbourne has long been uncontested in its positioning as Australia's 'sport capital', but how valid is this claim? The 'sportiness' of Australia's cities has typically focussed on sport attendance as the basis of comparison, in which Melbourne certainly performs exceptionally. However, to a degree, this could be considered a biased measure, as a local population can only attend sport to the degree that sport is physically available to them. Sydney and Melbourne benefit from considerably more sport availability then Australia's remaining cities.

Two particularly noteworthy historical periods have largely shaped Melbourne's modern sport status. Firstly, the early availability of recreational space, along with the early establishment of corresponding sporting institutions and infrastructure, provided Melbourne a strong foundation upon which a sport culture could develop. The city of Melbourne was officially founded in 1835 and it would only take three years for the Melbourne Cricket Club to form. Vitally, the Melbourne Cricket Ground was opened in 1853.

Sydney cricket officials by contrast, struggled for several more decades to find an appropriate ground for major cricket events. One reason proposed for this difference is that Melbourne had a greater amount of centralised flat land than Sydney, which is comparatively hillier. The flatter terrain of Melbourne would also parlay into the development of a superior transport network, again contributing to perceived advantages in drawing crowds. As noted by Australia's most venerable sport historian, Richard Cashman, in distinguishing the cultural differences between Sydney and Melbourne sport landscapes: "It is far more difficult to travel from one suburb to another because Sydney's immediate hinterland is intersected by rivers, coves and bays"[38].

Melbourne also established a racecourse much quicker than Sydney. The first race at Melbourne's Flemington Racecourse occurred on March 3rd 1840, while Sydney settled for Randwick as the home of racing in 1860. Again, this occurred because the city of Melbourne was much less densely developed at this time, providing freedoms to locate such a facility. By contrast inner-city land in Sydney was, from inception, at a premium due to its proximity to both water supply and the harbour. In a testament to their divergent development, by 1890, the population of the two cities was roughly equal but Melbourne covered twice the area of Sydney.

The early establishment of infrastructure was not only an advantage in itself, but most definitely had a compounding benefit over time. This is perhaps best exemplified by comparing the rival city's establishment of cricket grounds. The enclosed nature of the MCG meant that the first inter-colonial cricket game played in the MCG in 1856 was immediately able to collect gate revenue. By contrast, cricket was not played in permanently enclosed grounds in Sydney until 1871, and not at what would become the Sydney Cricket Ground (SCG) until 1878. In an attempt to collect gate revenue during the 1850s, Sydney officials would pay to erect a temporary grand stand and fencing for inter-colonial matches at the Domain, which were largely avoidable anyway. Accordingly: "The great majority of the large crowds which attended the first Sydney intercolonial in 1857 - an estimated 9-10,000 on the first day and 15,000 on the second - did not pay"[39]. Not only did fans have better infrastructure to watch sport, but the Melbourne Cricket Club got a 15 year head start in collecting gate receipts.

As an aside, the comparative scarcity of centralised flat space in Sydney as compared to Melbourne also helps to explain why ovals in Melbourne are typically larger than in Sydney, as best contrasted by the cavernous MCG and boutique SCG.

With strong foundations built and a century of exemplary sport patronage to follow, it was then the 1980s when Melbourne's positioning as Australia's sporting capital begun to take its modern form as part of the economic plan of Premier John Cain for the city. Although the 1956 Melbourne Olympics were demonstrative of the city's historical enthusiasm towards sport, the 1980s saw Melbourne turn to sport and culture as a form of 'economic salvation' in which the urban economy was diversified away from manufacturing employment towards tourism, leisure and spectacle. This was a response to a significant period of government deregulation throughout the 1960s and 1970s, in which Sydney became the preferred economic location while Melbourne languished comparatively[40].

Up until Melbourne was placed into Australia's toughest ever lockdown restrictions due to the coronavirus pandemic in mid-2020, it is hard to imagine a time where Melbourne was not Australia's most vibrant city. Yet during the 1970s, the city faced quite a stark reality. Manufacturing jobs in inner Melbourne declined by one-third during the 1970s from 120,000 to fewer than 90,000. A further third of inner Melbourne manufacturing jobs were lost again after the recession of 1982. The 1970s also saw a one-quarter decline in inner city retail jobs in this period. Meanwhile, Sydney became the preferred destination of economic investment and accordingly continued to grow quicker than Melbourne in both population and economic terms. The state of play at this time is neatly summarised by scholar Seamus O'Hanlon[41]:

"As manufacturing declined in importance, newer industries such as financial services, the media, and high technology appeared to be locating in Sydney, then fast becoming Australia's gateway city. There was also emerging evidence of population drift to sunny Queensland, which was going through a resources and tourism boom and to a lesser extent Western Australia, which was experiencing massive investment in resource-based projects. A strong sense emerged that, like many other Western cities with a manufacturing-focused economy, Melbourne was entering a period of decline."

In response to a desire to transform Melbourne's economy towards events, the 1980s saw a period of significant infrastructure investment. This included additions to the grandstand capacity at Flemington Racecourse, the installation of lights at the Melbourne Cricket Ground, the AFL grand final designated as a 'major sporting event' in legislation and perhaps most importantly, the establishment of the Flinders Park sport precinct which would result in the permanent domiciling of the Australian Open tennis tournament in Melbourne.

Among these initiatives, perhaps the most significant was securing the Australian Open tennis tournament in 1988. Although most would now only know of the Australian Open tennis tournament as an iconic Melbourne event, it is notable that from 1905 to 1972, the tournament was rotated around Australasia. Prior to being staged in Kooyong (an inner Melbourne suburb) more permanently from 1972, the tournament had in fact been staged in Sydney (17 times), Adelaide (14), Brisbane (7), Perth (3) and even New Zealand (2). Once the event had outgrown Kooyong and the club did not wish to pursue necessary capital works to retain the event, the decision was made to develop a new precinct for the event as we now know it.

Notably, Sydney had indicated an interest in hosting the Australian Open if Tennis Australia decided to move the event from Kooyong, yet the event appeared destined to remain in Victoria[42]. Despite the sportiness of the city, the establishment of a permanent facility within inner Melbourne was not without controversy. To obtain the land required, the government passed legislation to favourably rezone the required land, to the criticism of some stakeholders. However, the move was a success, resulting in an increased attendance from 140,000 to 266,436 in its first year in the new home, helping to cement Melbourne's positioning as the sport capital of Australia[43].

Since this seminal period, Melbourne has maintained its status as a sport event destination. It acquired the Formula 1 rights from Adelaide in 1993 as part of Premier Jeff Kennett's continued growth agenda for the state, which once more, was not without public controversy, given this was done without public consultation[44]. The city also competed fiercely and won against Sydney to become Australia's unsuccessful bid city for the 1996 Olympics. Melbourne would then successfully host the 2006 Commonwealth games. From an infrastructure perspective, a rectangular stadium was purpose built to coincide with acquiring a top level rugby union franchise in 2011, while the MCG has regularly received capital improvements. Most recently, a further redevelopment of Melbourne Park has been completed to secure the future of the Australia Open tennis tournament.

Scholars have argued that Melbourne's exceptional rates of spectatorship, distinguishing the city from other Australian and international contexts, is driven by a unique sport culture[45]. This culture is said to have developed because sport spectating as a consumer ethic became ingrained among the working class due to highly affordable ticket pricing. The culture was further ingrained because women were a significant part of the spectating crowd, with accounts of female spectatorship ranging from 25% to 50% of Australian Rules patronage. A counter-theory, albeit somewhat facetious in nature, is that Melbourne's exceptional sport patronage stems from its comparative dullness as a city. By contrast, Sydney is; "the sort of town where passions are diffused… You don't have your whole sense of self invested in your team winning the game. He or she in Sydney has more to fall back on"[46]. While PhDs[47], books[48] and much popular press have evaluated Melbourne's sport pedigree, there has been perhaps as much fan-faring as there has been genuine critique.

An under-acknowledged factor in Melbourne's impressive sport spectatorship is that structurally, the city retains an accessibility to sport unmatched elsewhere in Australia. This superior accessibility manifests in two forms. First, the city of Melbourne established sport infrastructure early and soundly, resulting in a compounding social benefit in terms of access. The 1980s and 1990s then saw Victoria's government place sport infrastructure and events as a state priority, once more leading to advantages in Melbourne's sport landscape which remain today. The second element of accessibility is in relation to content. Melbourne has the most professional sport clubs (21) in the country and has also secured the lion's share of major recurring sport events. On this basis, Sydney and Melbourne represent the most comparable cluster of cities, and Melbourne appears undoubtedly sportier in its culture than Sydney. But comparing Melbourne to Adelaide, Brisbane, Perth or Hobart is inherently more problematic given considerable differences in access to commercial sport and population size.

Australia's sportiness, however, could be measured in less overt ways than infrastructure, attendances and events, which are all interrelated measures that reinforce Melbourne's status as capital.

For instance, sport participation data released by Sport Australia for the period of October 2015 to June 2019 does not reveal a compelling Victorian dominance. Victoria's adult participation rate (people aged 15+) is indeed the highest at 89.8%, but closely followed by New South Wales (89.3%), South Australia (89.3%) and Western Australia (88.8%). Similarly among adolescent (0-14 year olds) participation, Victoria (76.5%) only marginally exceeds South Australia (74.3%) and New South Wales (74.1%).

Perhaps more interesting in considering what makes a 'sport capital' is the relative contribution of regions in producing elite Australian athletes. A 2017 PhD thesis by Kristy O'Neill from the University of Sydney evaluated the profiles of 2,160 Australian athletes who competed at the summer Olympic Games between 1984 and 2012. By evaluating biographical and archival data, O'Neill traced each athlete to the corresponding local government area where they were born or raised. The goal was to find potential sporting "hot spots": an environment or community in which a particular type of talent or expertise has been consistently produced and maintained at a high level of achievement. Her findings appear quite conclusive surrounding which state features the most hotspots that produce elite Olympians: Western Australia.

Western Australian hot spots feature nine times in the top twenty Local Government Areas on the basis of per capita production of Olympians. They also hold three of the top four hotspots: Narrogin, Claremont and Nedlands, while Perth city is the only Urban Capital City to feature. New South Wales features on the list five times, while Victoria and South Australia LGAs each appear three times. Given Claremont, Nedlands, Cambridge and Perth city are neighbouring LGAs that surround the University of Western Australia which is itself a sports hub, O'Neill therefore identifies Perth to be Australia's elite sporting hot spot, benefitting from a more Mediterranean climate. As the author noted:

"Perth is big enough to have world-class sporting facilities but is not as large as Sydney or Melbourne, meaning that promising athletes were more likely to be noticed early on by coaches or talent spotters"[49]

O'Neill's above explanation surrounding a population sweet spot conceptually aligns to our broad, but still developing, understanding of the relationship between population size and elite athlete development. For instance, a similar conclusion that small cities trumped larger ones was reached in Israel, where the optimal city size for prospective draftees into elite football was found to be between 50,000 and 200,000 residents[50]. Locally, the 'Wagga Effect' has been coined to describe Wagga Wagga's unusually high production of elite athletes, as first described by an Australian Institute of Sport analysis from 2005[51].

The 'Wagga Effect' is distinct from O'Neil's analysis because Olympic performance fails to capture athlete production in nearly all our primary sports; i.e. our football codes, cricket and netball. It is postulated that Wagga produces a disproportionate amount of athletes not only because it is a small town (population 46,735), but also because it is a place where children typically play many different sports, often entering in senior or adult competition just prior to specialisation[52]. This latter point is particularly important because scientific consensus in the context of athlete development is moving away from early specialisation (focussing on one sport with all one's attention) and towards generalist skills as the best path to sporting success[53]. Sitting along the Barassi Line, where kids are more inclined to participate in a greater variety of sports, creates a sport 'multiculturalism' that may therefore explain why Wagga is a production line of champions.

A review of the list of famous Wagga athletes is both compelling and amazingly diverse across codes. Alumnus include Wayne Carey and Paul Kelly (AFL), the Mortimer brothers and Peter Sterling (rugby league), Nathan Sharpe and Alicia Quirk (rugby union), Sally Shipard (soccer) as well as Michael Slater and Mark Taylor (cricket). Unfortunately for

Taylor, being from the same town as Slater didn't seem to help their batting rapport, with Slater shaving five runs off Taylor's final batting average through calamitous run outs[54]. Much of New South Wales's AFL State of Origin team, when such games were still played, were disproportionally derived from such towns as Wagga rather than Sydney.

Reinforcing the tenuous nature of Melbourne's claim to being Australia's sports capital is that the state of Victoria is an under-performer in contributing to our national teams. This was already evidenced in O'Neill's study of Australian Olympians, but also true in other contexts. It has long been said in cricket circles that when a player receives their blue cap (playing for NSW), they also receive their baggy green. This jest reflects that NSW has been a historical powerhouse in contributing to our national cricket team, perhaps most visibly evident by virtue of a New South Welshman having been captain of the men's national team for roughly 26 of the past 40 years. As was noted by Cricket Victoria's CEO in 2014 prior to the Boxing Day test: "It does hurt us as well. We want more Victorians out here on Boxing Day.... We're not getting players, and batsmen specifically, playing long-form cricket for Australia and that is something we want to rectify".

Victoria has also underperformed in contributing to our national teams in soccer, which represents the one football code in which we can expect the various states to have contributed toward with reasonable equality. For a definitive answer, Greg Werner, who has co-authored the Encyclopedia of Matildas[55], was able to provide revealing insights. Of the 205 women capped in 'A' internationals to the end of June 2020, Victoria has only supplied 14 of them. This equates to a contribution of 6.8% of players from a state that accounts for 26% of the population[56]. The bulk of Matildas have come from NSW and Queensland; there hasn't been a Victorian capped since 2012 when Brianna Davey, Ash Brown and Steph Catley made the grade. The figures don't get much better for Victoria in respect to the Socceroos. There were 107 players capped before a Victorian born player represented Australia. This would take until 1948, when Angus Drennan from Sunshine United became the 108th Socceroo. Of the 606 Socceroos to have been capped through to December 2020, only 71 have been home grown in Victoria. This equates to a 12% contribution of players from a State that accounts for 26% of the population.

To further explore alternate ways of examining Australia's sportiness, sport preferences are once again considered here. A national sample of respondents asked respondents to self-assess their interest toward sport, on a scale from 1 to 10. The interesting observation that comes from the results in Figure 7 is that there is very little difference in the level of sport passion across the Australia's capital cities. As a result, the average sport interest score across Australian regions is remarkably similar, with a national mean of 5.06 (out of 10), a low of 4.84 in Perth and a high of 5.26 in Melbourne among capital cities. The mean scores of Perth (4.94) and Brisbane (4.91) are below the national mean by a large enough proportion to be 'statistically significant' in their difference, as are Sydney (5.15) and Melbourne (5.23) above the national average.

	Score				Fan Groups	
Region	All	Men	Women	Total Sports Supported (All)	% of Non-sport fans**	% of Avid Sport fans***
Melbourne	5.26*	6.14	4.36*	4.72	32.31*	27.05*
Sydney	5.15	6.19	4.18	4.79	33.14*	24.86
Adelaide	5.13	6.1	4.09	4.72	34.14	25.86
Reg. Victoria	5.09	6.04	4.12	4.93	34.76	25.69
Reg. South Australia	5.07	6.07	3.97	4.85	35.37	26.17
AVERAGE	5.06	6.01	4.13	4.81	35.17	24.96
Reg. Queensland	5.02	5.94	4.14	4.92	35.8	24.98
Hobart	4.99	5.87	4.25	4.73	37.41	24.36
Perth	4.94	5.87	3.96	4.55	36.77	23.26
Darwin	4.93	6.03	3.92	4.67	40.06	25.72
Reg. Western Australia	4.92	5.73	3.96	5.49	33.79	21.1
Brisbane	4.91*	5.8	4.02	4.76	37.96*	23.36
Reg. NSW	4.91*	5.85	4.06	4.99	38.00*	24.62
Reg. Tasmania	4.84	5.81	3.93	4.87	39.23	24.76
Canberra	4.81	5.95	3.74	4.42	38.05	20.07

Figure 7: Australian sporting preferences by region. [57]

However, statistical significance should not be translated to a practical real world significance (which is measured statistically in other ways such as 'effect sizes'). In evaluating practical significance through effect sizes, this difference equates to approximately 54% of Melbournians exhibiting a sport avidity higher than the average (50%) across the remainder of Australia. Notably, underpinning Melbourne's overall slightly superior attitudinal sport avidity are women, who exhibit a significantly higher score than any other cohort of women across the nation. This finding seems consistent with previous scholarship that has suggested that the core to the development of Melbourne's sport culture has been the comparatively stronger involvement of women.

The absence of larger differences in self-appraised sport avidity between regions seems strange when you consider Melbourne's evident superior attendance behaviour. How can Melbournians, who regularly attract over 100,000 to a grand final parade, be as attitudinally passionate sport fans as Sydneysiders, where 20,000 is considered a strong NRL or

Super Rugby crowd? Several potential explanations can be offered for this. The first is methodological. Measuring attitudinal sport passion by nature, requires respondents to self-assess, and human nature dictates that respondents are likely to assess themselves against familiar baseline comparisons. A Melbourne respondent assessing their sport avidity may therefore self-assess against a higher standard of fandom given they live in Australia's 'sports capital'.

A further explanation can be found in the crucial role of accessibility to infrastructure, which impacts behaviours more than attitudes. This explanation is akin to saying that Australians are similarly positive in their attitudes towards beach-going, irrespective of where one lives. However, rates of actual beach attendance are higher in Sydney or the Gold Coast than in Melbourne or Hobart due to differences in accessibility, given the latter have fewer beaches of note.

The implication of this hypothesis is that, if Australians are broadly similar in attitudinal passion toward sport, then every major city has the potential to develop a sport spectatorship culture similar to Melbourne, given appropriate investment in infrastructure and accessibility.

The conclusion is that while broad consensus has Melbourne as Australia's sporting capital, the way in which this has been historically assessed (sport attendance) is self-fulfilling once you consider accessibility. Arguably, Wagga Wagga or Perth can stake a claim for being Australia's sports capital upon alternate criteria of sport performance. More broadly, Australians across the entire country are in fact surprisingly invariant in their passion for sport, illustrating that we are perhaps in fact a widely 'sport mad' nation. That Australian cities are similarly passionate towards sport as Melbourne suggests there is hope for a city like Sydney to build a sport attendance culture through shrewd investment in infrastructure and events.

The curious case of Sydney

Sydney's relationship with football is different from every other major city in the country. What makes the city different is that where you specifically live in Sydney has a huge influence upon which football code you're likely to prefer and the degree to which you like football generally. The sub-regions of Sydney display erratic football preferences. Despite being neighbours, North Sydney is very different from the Northern Beaches. The Northern Beaches is very different from Liverpool, which is again different from Bondi. This is quite distinct from Melbourne, Brisbane, Adelaide and Perth. I'll firstly explain why this is, and then illustrate the effect it has.

Although we have discussed the formation and cementing of Melbourne's status as Australia's 'sports capital', Sydney retains an unmatched distinction in the annals of Australian sport history. Sydney is the birthplace to three of Australia's four football codes, and New South Wales arguably the fourth. Rugby union was the first code established in Sydney, with the Sydney University Club founded in 1863. For comparison, Melbourne played its first game of what would become 'Australian Rules' only marginally earlier in 1858, with the Melbourne Football Club also formed that year. It may come as some surprise, given current conditions, that rugby union in fact enjoyed early popularity. In 1907, Australia played New Zealand at the Sydney Cricket Ground in front of approximately 50,000 attendees, a then record crowd[58]. New South Wales too could be considered the birthplace of Victorian rules football, given the game's founder Tom Wills was born in what was New South Wales at the time[59].

While there are some reports of earlier games taking place (notably in Tasmania and Queensland), the first recorded game of soccer under modern laws is widely believed to have occurred in Sydney in 1880, with the New South Wales English Football Association the first governing body of soccer within Australia in 1882[60]. The name arose because the New South Wales Football Association had been taken in 1880 by those who supported Victorian rules football. Soccer would establish its national body in 1911.

Finally in 1907, rugby league was formed in Sydney as a breakaway code from rugby union due to the well-known desire by players to be financially compensated should they be unable to work as a consequence of being injured playing sport. The formation of rugby league is likely well understood by most readers, but it is important to emphasise two particular points here. Firstly, the concept of amateurism was so important to rugby union that the sport did not officially go professional until global market forces compelled it to do so in 1995. That a popular sport, with a global governing body and several successful World Cup renditions, nearly reached the turn of the millennium as an amateur sport is astounding in its own right. Second, the practicalities of the split over money were a deeper reflection of philosophical and societal differences. As noted by sociologist Peter Horton: "The rift further assumed a class basis, with the rugby league fixtures being heavily supported by the working class. This polarisation established the ground rules for the future relationship between the two codes"[61]. This provides us with another clue as to the differences in Sydney sport fandom from other Australian cities.

The inaugural 1908 New South Wales Rugby League season would follow, featuring eight Sydney based clubs and a ninth northern New South Wales team. The eight Sydney teams played out of three locations: Birchgrove Oval, Wentworth Park and Moore Park. Observing the modern day map of Sydney, these once dispersed locations in the 1908 colony are today nearby inner city venues. Unsurprisingly, the location of the eight Sydney clubs reflected the concentration of the colonial population within the inner regions of the settlement at the time. In this respect, the movements of the inaugural Western Suburbs club are a harbinger for the broader geographical sprawl of Sydney that has occurred over the century which has followed. The club was founded at Ashfield Town Hall in 1908, located just ten kilometres west of central Sydney. In 1967 the club moved games to Lidcombe oval, 20 kilometres west of central Sydney. By 1987, the Western Suburbs had relocated again to play out of Campbelltown stadium, 55 kilometres south-west of central Sydney.

The sprawl of rugby league clubs in Sydney and the development of the city over the century that has followed would not seem all that unique when considering Melbourne has experienced largely similar conditions in respect to AFL clubs. However, two particularly significant events distinguish the two cities and their respective association to NRL and AFL teams[62].

The first is that Melbourne AFL teams have successfully migrated to centralised inner-city stadiums between 1970 and 2000, whereas Sydney rugby league teams still largely play in local suburban venues.

Among Melbourne AFL teams, centralisation can be attributed to the opening of Waverley Park in 1970, then finalised by Docklands stadium at the turn of the millennium[63]. By contrast, over half of Sydney's NRL teams still play in suburban venues to this day[64]. Accordingly, while Melbourne retains a comparable concentration of AFL teams to that of NRL teams in Sydney, there is less reason for Melbourne AFL teams to rely on tightly defined geographic boundaries to attract fans. As a crude example, the suburb of Collingwood had a population of 8,513 in the 2016 census, while the Collingwood Football Club had 74,643 members the same year. Playing in centralised stadiums is conceptually supported by marketing theory, which contends that the ease of product availability contributes strongly to its overall popularity. By playing in suburban venues, Sydney NRL clubs essentially position themselves as region-centric niche brands.

The second significant difference between the Sydney and Melbourne football clubs is the turbulence experienced through relocation and rationalisation. In particular, the key difference between Australia's two dominant football codes was the Super League war of the late 1990s. It is important to note that while the Super League war directly influenced the distribution of rugby league clubs in Sydney and Australia more broadly, Australian Rules also faced grave fears about its concentration of clubs in Melbourne at the same time. By the mid 1990s and advanced upon a national expansion path, the AFL had identified that the Melbourne market was over represented by teams. This resulted in discussions around potential mergers and even financial incentives to do so. By mid-1996, $8 million was on the table for Melbourne AFL teams to merge, with Melbourne, Hawthorn, St Kilda, Western Bulldogs, Fitzroy, North Melbourne and even Richmond considered vulnerable at the time.

As we now know, the AFL's territorial presence in Melbourne remained relatively stable in the end, with only Fitzroy relocating to Brisbane in 1996. Aside from this, the composition of Melbourne teams remained unchanged since South Melbourne relocated to Sydney in 1982, after a rumored plan by Fitzroy in 1978 to move to Sydney was squashed by its members. The closest merger proposal during the period was that of Melbourne and Hawthorn to form the Melbourne Hawks. The Melbourne Demons in fact voted in favour of merging (scraping home by 52.5% vote margin), while Hawthorn blocked the merger with a pronounced but not unequivocal no vote of 65%[65].

North Melbourne have also teetered on the edge of relocation since this period, most notably to the Gold Coast in the mid 2000s, but have remained stubbornly resistant. Melbourne AFL teams are therefore considerably more embedded in Melbourne than their corresponding Sydney rugby league counterparts, as many more of the foundational VFA/VFL clubs remain. If we look at the two leagues overall, the AFL's 18 clubs have an accumulated 1,881 years of existence between 1858 to 2020, compared with 794 years among the NRL's 16 clubs between 1908 and 2020.

By contrast to the AFL's period of introspection, rugby league's rationalisation of Sydney teams was much more traumatic. The Cronulla Sharks and Penrith Panthers were the last Sydney teams to be added to the competition in 1967, while Newtown's exit in 1983 was the only departure from the top flight competition between 1938 and 1998. Therefore, the turbulence of club rationalisation during Super League was in stark contrast to the four decades of relative stability that preceded this period. The formation of the NRL was contingent on the goal of rationalising the competition from the pool of 22 existing clubs to 14, with an emphasis upon reducing the number of teams in Sydney. As history now shows us, this period saw four clubs, Wests, Balmain, St George and Illawarra, embrace mergers to form two new merged entities. Rationalisation would also see South Sydney given a two year sabbatical and the North Sydney Bears lost to top flight rugby league.

This section then, illustrates how the final dispersion of NRL clubs in Sydney has appeared to influence rugby league interest in Sydney today, and how this differs from how Brisbane supports rugby league, and Adelaide, Perth and Melbourne support Australian Rules. Figure 8 looks at the 15 sub-regions of Sydney. The horizontal axis plots the population

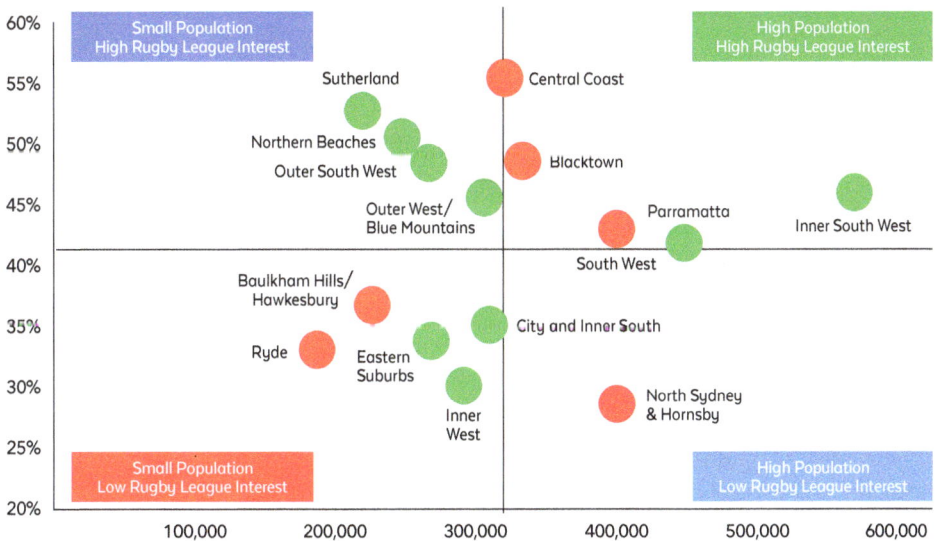

Figure 8: Relationship between Population Size and rugby league Interest across Sydney Regions.

of that region and the vertical axis the interest that region exhibits towards rugby league. This illustrates which regions of Sydney underpin the sport's popularity, and which regions are comparatively less interested. Where a region is represented by a local NRL team, I have overlayed a green bubble upon the respective region and a red bubble upon unrepresented regions. This, it should be noted, is an inexact science given a team's fan base can come from any region and conversely, a region will be home to fans of different teams. However, it provides some face value evidence of which teams are likely and less likely to benefit from large fan bases for the purposes of our discussion.

The data reveals that 42% of the general Sydney population is interested in rugby league, but of more importance, such interest is varied across the city. Sydney's interest in rugby league statistically demarcates along a north-east versus south-west divide. Of the six regions which record below average rugby league interest in Sydney, five are located on the north-east side of the city. This is probably of no surprise to rugby league fans, and it is well known that Sydney's west is considered rugby league heartland.

Across broader Sydney, rugby union exhibits an inverse popularity positioning to rugby league. Rugby union is 33% more popular in the north-east regions (24.2%) of Sydney compared with the south-west (18.0%). Of concern for rugby union is that it is the least popular of the four codes in southern and western Sydney, which accounts for 63% of the city's population.

Figure 8 provides an opportunity to compare the underpinning support not only for rugby league in Sydney, but to consider the market position of specific NRL clubs. The divergent rugby league interest observed in Sutherland compared with the Eastern Suburbs is instructive of Sydney's varying rugby league interest. The Eastern Suburbs population is 23% larger (267,031) than Sutherland, yet interest in rugby league is considerably lower (34%) than in Sutherland (52.5%). Accordingly, the available 'pool' of local rugby league fans from which the Cronulla Sharks team (Sutherland) can draw from is higher (114,385) despite a smaller local population than the Roosters in the Eastern Suburbs.

Professor Sean Brawley, whose unintentionally ironic research interests have included both the 'white peril' of Asian immigration and the Cronulla Sharks, makes him an expert on such localised football clubs. Brawley observes that the Sharks' admission to the competition was underpinned by a strong junior nursery and local support, and this helped them survive the Super League period stronger than counterparts[66].

The fandom concentration that has previously helped them, however, also limits the team's commercial growth potential. Reflecting upon the growth of Sydney, the implications of introducing the Cronulla Sharks and Penrith Panthers in 1967 have been antithetical from a population growth perspective. The Sutherland Local Government Area (LGA) accounted for 5.4% of Sydney's population in 1966. In the 50 years that have followed, the Sutherland LGA has grown by only 65%, resulting in the region shrinking to accounting for 4.5% of Sydney's population by 2016. In this corresponding period, the Penrith LGA grew from 1.5% (35,979) of Sydney's population to 4.1% by 2016 (196,066). Professor Brawley observed that it took the Sharks ten years to be embraced by the local community, given their entry coincided with the final period of neighbouring St George's 11 year run of premierships between 1956 and 1966. Ironically then, the merger of St George and Illawarra geographically enclosed the club to within the Sutherland shire, which was not growing in population relative to the rest of Sydney.

With only 89,138 rugby league fans living in the Eastern Suburbs, the Sydney Roosters have the smallest direct geographical catchment to attract fans. This helps to explain why the club has in recent years attempted to develop a greater presence on the Central Coast, which retains a high level of rugby league interest with no team to represent them. Notably, Sydney's Eastern Suburbs has the strongest access to sport, with the Sydney Football Stadium and Sydney Cricket Ground residing within their boundary, making Moore Park somewhat of a physical epicentre between the Waratahs (rugby), Roosters (rugby league), Sydney FC (soccer) and the Sydney Swans (Australian Rules).

Ironically then, despite the region having the privilege of the highest absolute access to football, the Eastern Suburbs has the highest rate of people not at all interested in football (45%). The Eastern Suburbs in fact has the highest rate of non-interest in football across the country, but Sydney in general is well represented on this list. Across the six state capitals, Sydney regions account for 11 of 20 most football disinterested regions of Australia. Across all of the 107 sub-regions that make up the Australian Bureau of Statistics (ABS) map, Sydney accounts for 8 of 20 of Australia's least interested footy regions.

The territorial implications of team rationalisation from the turn of the millennium are also evident in Figure 8. The Wests Tigers merged entity is associated with regions that exhibit distinct compositions. The Inner West (293,303) has a larger population than the Outer South West (262,065) but the regions' local residents retain the second lowest interest in rugby league in Sydney (29.5%). Accordingly, the Outer South West has considerably more rugby league fans (127,720) than the Inner West (86,647) despite a smaller population. However, this doesn't translate into fan attendance patterns. Notably, the Wests Tigers have recorded higher average attendance at Leichhardt (13,243) in the Inner West than at Campbelltown (12,225) in the Outer South West, despite more rugby league supporters residing in the latter. This reflects the West Tigers' tendency (conscious or otherwise) to position themselves more as a Balmain than a Campbelltown club, despite the latter being a far stronger strategic positioning looking forward.

The growth of Sydney's population, particularly in the south-west, hasn't really appeared to benefit the West Tigers as strongly as you would expect. The merged entity has recorded higher average attendances at the two venues than the unmerged Balmain (8,608) and Wests (7,897) did previously from 1957 to 1999, but this should not be considered a particularly impressive achievement. This is because the Tigers' attendance growth is in line with the overall average NRL attendance growth of 50%, when comparing 2019 to 1957.

While NRL average attendances have grown by 50%, Sydney's population has also more than doubled in the same timeframe.

With the entrance of a south-west Sydney A-League team playing from Campbelltown in season 2020/21, the West Tigers should be nervous. A brand's popularity is closely tied to their accessibility to consumers. The NRL's West Tigers will be defending their home market by playing approximately three fixtures at Campbelltown. Macarthur FC are scheduled to play thirteen regular season A-League fixtures at Campbelltown. This region is also younger and with greater cultural diversity, playing directly into the strengths of the soccer fan base as previously described.

The NRL should most certainly be paying attention to defending its 'heartland'. A problem here however is that the NRL has historically allowed clubs incredible autonomy in their respective operations. Rather, the NRL would do well to become more interventionalist in coordinating all-of-game strategy on behalf of clubs. For instance, there is a strategic argument to be made that the Canterbury Bulldogs should play at least a portion of their fixtures from Campbelltown, to increase the supply of desirable NRL fixtures and defend the region for the code.

What is perhaps most interesting within Figure 8 is spotting the rugby league wastelands that can be found within northern Sydney. Rugby league interest is lowest in North Sydney and Hornsby (28.4%) and highest on the Central Coast (55.4%)[67]. Adjacent to North Sydney and Hornsby, Ryde records the third lowest rugby league interest in Sydney (32.6%) while the outer northern region of Baulkham Hills and Hawkesbury also recorded below average rugby league interest (36.7%). Northern Sydney therefore appears to be itself divided into two distinct zones. The most north-eastern zone (Central Coast and Northern Beaches) exhibit among the strongest interest (52.9%), while the south-western zone (North Sydney & Hornsby, Ryde, Baulkham Hills) exhibit among the weakest interest in rugby league (32.2%), despite being geographically adjacent regions.

Such statistics tie together the impact of the Super League war with the current-day commercial impact some 20 years later. The primary victim of the Super League upheaval were the now relegated North Sydney Bears. Despite being a foundation member of the league, they were relegated from top-flight competition in 2002 after their ill-fated merger with local rival Manly. This unsuccessful merger illustrated one particular difference between good management principles in general business versus in sport. Although the merger was logical from a territorial/geographic perspective - being neighbouring clubs within northern Sydney - the rivalry between the teams that stemmed from their direct proximity ultimately made the merger unpalatable.

The loss of the Bears from top flight rugby league[68] has never really been analysed comprehensively from a quantitative perspective, at least in the public domain, but it undoubtedly cost the game many fans. According to Andrew Moore, the most prominent historian/expert of the club: 'Rugby league "churned" many fans. Many supporters of the

North Sydney Bears have never watched another game of rugby league since the demise of their club at the first grade level in 1999'[69].

Although it's easy to write off Moore's words as hyperbole, a booked named The Convert by Peter Lewis speaks to this point. An early giveaway to this is the title of the first chapter, 'Death of League'. Lewis's book details his conversion from growing up in North Sydney as an ardent Bears fan to stumbling into becoming a Sydney Swans supporter in 1996. Before the Super League war, he recounts: "I was a fan for life, uninterested in other diversions; I was a Bear man and that was my sole pervasion". By the time the Super League war had broken out: "League is dead... I needed a new sport with no emotional baggage"[70]. By chance, Lewis was in Moore Park and reflecting upon the circumstances of Super League when he walked into the Swans office and bought a members ticket. An AFL fan was gained thereafter.

In one of the last moments of normalcy 2020 provided, I caught up with Peter Lewis, approaching 25 years since he wrote his highly emotive chronicle of converting to Australian Rules in 1996. I was curious to see if Moore's broad claim that Bears fans 'have never watched another game of rugby league since the demise of their club' had held true or was an overreaction typical of highly charged moments in history. Lewis seemed like a good case study for this assertion, given the tone of his book aligned to Moore's claim. So, was Lewis's dalliance with Australian Rules in 1996 temporary or embedding?

Since falling in love with Australian Rules and the Sydney Swans in 1996, Lewis has been a member for most of the proceeding 24 seasons, typically attending between five and six Swans games a year. By comparison, he has attended "two or three" NRL games in all of the 24 years that have followed. In describing these few NRL games, he did so with almost an almost apologetic tone. He explained that he had received free tickets and lives near Leichhardt Oval. This is how Lewis, who once described his passion for rugby league as 'a fan for life... a Bear man', describes the two sports today; "one is junk food [NRL] and the other fine dining [AFL]".

Perhaps more interesting than Lewis's personal journey is how his preferences have been passed onto his Sydney-raised children, illustrating a generational challenge faced by the NRL in Sydney caused by Super League. Lewis's two sons would grow up playing Australian Rules as their childhood sport of choice in the Inner West of Sydney. His daughter has made junior representative teams in Sydney's AFL competition. His children have little connection to NRL or other competing football codes. This generational shift may not be an isolated case. Lewis estimates that among his high school friends, who attended school all of 200 metres from North Sydney Oval, half adopted the Swans and shifted away from rugby league while half migrated to another rugby league team.

The timing of the Super League and in particular the Bears' demise coincided with an acceleration in the competitive tension between football codes in Sydney. The Super League war has a shared back story with the creation of Super Rugby in 1995, and no doubt the latter induced a portion of rugby league's sparse white collar supporters back to union. Then the Sydney Swans would finally arise from relative obscurity in 1996, after Tony Lockett's iconic post-siren kick to win the preliminary final. By the time the NRL had normalised in the early 2000s, other football codes were once again making further in-roads. The 2003 Rugby World Cup coincided within rugby union's golden period, the 'A-League' would launch only a few years later in 2005/06, after the former NSL had failed to live up to expectations after 27 years, and the Sydney Swans finally converted performance into a premiership in 2005.

Today, the geographic catchments formally represented by the North Sydney Bears exhibit the lowest interested towards rugby league in all of Sydney. Meanwhile, the adjacent Northern Beaches region that is directly represented by local team the Manly Sea Eagles recorded the second highest interest toward rugby league in Sydney (49.7%). Is this a coincidence?

It is possible that North Sydney retained lower rugby league interest than other parts of Sydney prior to the Bear's expulsion, particularly as it has been commented that the clubs fans were not particularly parochial compared with others. But the attendances of the Norths and Manly clubs before the merger are instructive. In the decade prior to rationalisation (1990-99), Manly maintained an average crowd of 13,641 to North Sydney's 11,655. Therefore, while the Northern Beaches club held a 17% larger average attendance during the 1990s, by 2018 the Northern Beaches population was 79% more interested in rugby league than their North Sydney neighbours.

When looking at a map of Sydney and overlaying the geographic territories of its NRL teams, it becomes clear that there is a significant misalignment between people and clubs. North Sydney and Hornsby represent the equal third most populous region in Sydney (405,354), yet record the lowest interest in rugby league. When combined with the adjacent region of Ryde (182,120) and Baulkham Hills/Hawkesbury (227,741), approximately 815,000 people reside in the broader territorial catchment of the lost Bears club. Given the combined Parramatta/Blacktown population is 788,000 and the combined South-West/Outer South-West population is 668,000, the club with perhaps the largest geographic catchment in Sydney is the one no longer in the competition. Consider further that it had also been identified as early as the 1980s that Campbelltown was a growing regional hub which required greater access to rugby league, yet by 2019 the region hosted just three NRL fixtures.

This is an incredible strategic weakness in the NRL club footprint. Despite the NRL essentially committing more than half its competition licences to Sydney, the league does not even have all of Sydney adequately represented by clubs.

The FFA have been first to latch onto this weakness with the introduction of a south-west A-League team. With soccer angling toward future promotion and relegation to and from the A-League, it is not inconceivable that a fourth strong A-League team could sprout from the northern region of Sydney, perhaps even a rekindling of Northern Spirit, to further weaken rugby league's grip upon the Sydney market. So too would an expansion in Rugby Australia's domestic footprint in the future undoubtedly result in the admission of at least another Sydney team to increase competitive intensity.

The regional variance found in Sydney is made more curious by the fact that no other capital city exhibits a similar pattern in respect to their preferred football code. Figure 9 illustrates this, although some explanation is needed of what is being presented. Figure 9 illustrates the variation in football interest across the sub-regions of each mainland capital city. Each region is plotted on the graph according to whether their football interest (either AFL or NRL, depending on the city) exceeds or falls below the city average, which is set at 100%. As an example, the city-wide interest in AFL in Melbourne is 56.4%, with the North-East recording the highest interest at 63.0%, therefore 12% larger than the city-wide average.

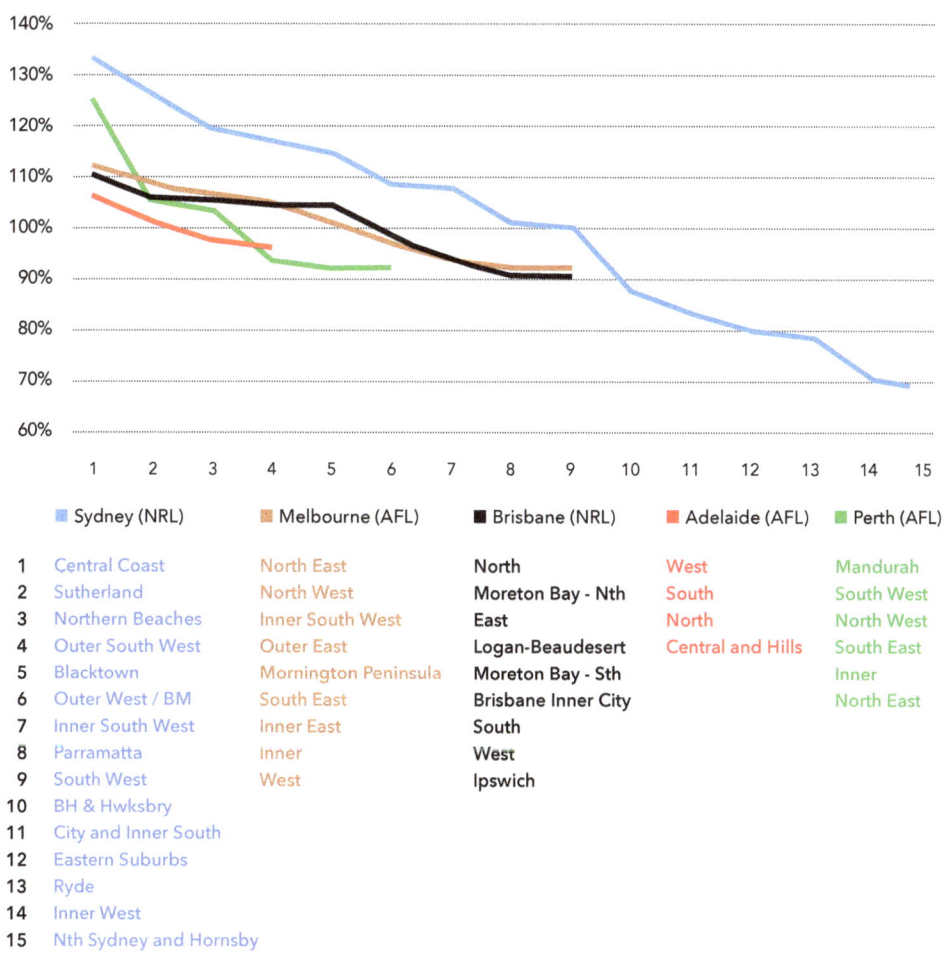

Figure 9: Standardised Football Interest by City Sub-Region across Australia.

Melbourne West records the weakest average (50.8%), nearing 10% below the city average.

In the case of Melbourne, Brisbane, Adelaide and Perth, football interest within individual city sub-regions falls between 90% and 110% of the city-wide average. The exception appears to be Mandurah in Perth, which is particularly enthusiastic towards AFL. Mandurah, however, is somewhat of an outlier as it is statistically grouped with Perth on account of freeway and railway connections built in the late 2000s, but is 72km south of Perth. Adelaide is remarkably even across the city in terms of being AFL-mad. In the Central and Hills district, you would expect to see 54 people at the pub watching AFL compared with 59 people in an equivalent pub in West Adelaide. So too in Brisbane, you'd expect to see 40 people watching NRL in the Ipswich pub compared with 47 people in north Brisbane[71].

Sydney is shockingly different. In Sydney, you would see a comparatively paltry 29 people at the North Sydney pub, compared with a near double amount of 55 people on the Central Coast. Having frequented the North Sydney Hotel, situated opposite North Sydney Oval, I can confirm from personal experience the general malaise towards NRL found here. A kilometre from North Sydney Oval, the Crows Nest Hotel in fact reserves a large portion of their viewing screens exclusively for AFL telecasts.

The differences in Sydney, however, are not just a tale of North Sydney. The broader point here is that, across Melbourne, Brisbane, Adelaide and Perth, you could walk into any sports pub and likely encounter a similar looking set of people. Sydney is comprised of 15 regions each doing their own thing, and often that is not NRL - nor any type of football at all.

The AFL's great northern incursion

Depending on which football code you support, you're likely to take a different view on how successful the various codes have been in expanding their national presence. What is incontestable, however, is that the AFL have been the most successful organisation in terms of overall growth from their establishment to 2021. The AFL's success can be at least partially attributed to two areas of management in which they appear to have displayed far more competence than their counterparts. First, has been the regular development of strategic visions and plans for their sport, rather than simply relying on organic development. Second has been a stronger propensity to execute strategic plans in the face of both risk and resourcing requirements. Both these features are evident in the AFL's highly organised attempts to develop the sport in the northern states, which are briefly revisited below for context as informed thorough the sociological research of Healey and Sharp[72].

Australian Rules football has had northern expansion on its mind for over 100 years. This was evident as early as 1877 upon the formation of the VFA, whereby a national game was firmly on the agenda. In 1877, the secretary of the VFA proposed to New South Wales'

South Rugby Football Union (SRFU) to organise an inter-colonial football match, or matches, between the colonies.

The VFA believed that by exposing their game to Sydneysiders through such contests, their sports' perceived superior aesthetics would win over northerners. The SRFU refused to sanction a representative inter-colonial match, but gave permission to a NSW club to play a Victorian club under the outlined proposal. So it was in June 1877 that the first reported game of Victorian rules football occurred in Sydney, between Sydney's Waratah club and Melbourne's Carlton club over two matches, one under Victorian rules and one under rugby rules. Although this didn't catalyse into entrenched support for the code, it is notable because it coerced rugby out of its malaise to successfully defend its territory by developing the rules of their game.

The establishment of the VFL and the Australian Football Council in 1906 ensured that expansion into Sydney remained high on the agenda. Between 1903 and 1910, the VFL would spend over £10,000 promoting football in Sydney. It was literally called 'propaganda' funding, which saw northern investment in the form of footballs, jumpers, and coaches for schools. This period saw the VFL bring games to Sydney, both VFL matches and exhibition matches against NSW representative teams. In 1903, a reported 20,000 spectators witnessed Fitzroy and Collingwood square off at the SCG. VFL games were able to generate typical crowds of 5,000+, while matches featuring NSW representative teams ranged between 1,000 and 4,000. Yet by 1905, Sydney's interest in Victorian Rules once again began to fade and the birth of rugby league in 1908 ensured the code was a non-presence for decades to follow.

The VFL would continue to make concerted attempts to propagate the game in the century that followed. Notably, in 1952, a series of VFL competition matches were played in Sydney and country NSW as part of a 'National Day' experiment, which represents the first attempt of Australian football to position the code on an Australian-wide front. Games were played in Hobart, Yallourn, Brisbane, Euroa and Albury. In 1967, the VFL made the historic agreement to telecast a replay of VFL games, upon a one week delay, in Sydney. The agreement was a wild success, with an estimated 70,000 viewers watching such replays on a one week delay. By 1971 VFL telecasts on Channel Nine were live, with an estimated audience of 100,000 viewers, which is more than the average audience of AFL telecasts in 2020[73].

In 1979 and 1980 further games were played in what became known as the 'Sydney Experiment', with 31,395 watching Hawthorn play North Melbourne at the SCG. Following the establishment of an independent commission in 1984, the VFL produced a strategic plan titled 'Establishing the Basis for Future Success' in which 'a programme of national expansion' was one of four key pillars. This agenda was also reflected in the marketing campaigns of the AFL, which as early as 1993 were geared towards New South Wales and Queensland audiences through the promotion of a 'national game'[74].

The AFL's historical focus on becoming entrenched in Sydney reflects the commercial centrality of Sydney and Melbourne to Australia. Today, the two cities account for 44% of national GDP and 40% of the national population. Although Melbourne in periods had the larger population, Sydney has been Australia's largest city for most of the time since the 19th century. Melbourne was predicted to eclipse Sydney again by the end of the 2020s before the onset of COVID-19.

Inconveniently for the AFL, Sydney and the northern advertising markets have generally been more valuable than southern markets. This is in part able to explain why NRL broadcast rights are particularly valuable despite appearing so much less national than the AFL. For instance, total advertising expenditure on FTA commercial networks in the first half of 2015 was $1.05 billion for New South Wales and Queensland, compared with $0.77 billion for the remaining south-western states. Gross advertising revenue in Sydney was $525 million, compared with $382 million in Melbourne for this period.

For this reason, Sydney in particular has been a holy grail of Australian Rules administrators. This was particularly apparent in the late 1980s and early 1990s with the Sydney Swans in the midst of a calamitous period which culminated in 1992 with a request for special assistance. Here, the Swans released a statement that without AFL assistance, the owners of the club would not renew their licences. Support for Sydney among Melbourne clubs was wavering as such clubs were battling their own survival fights, while the AFL Commission began developing alternative options. Yet, the inclusion of a Sydney team in the AFL competition was considered to be worth a quarter of the $40 million deal signed with Channel Seven for the period 1990-1995 and it was feared that a lack of a Sydney team could allow the network to review its agreement.

The Sydney Swans were too important to fail. This was already apparent in 1986 when the club breached the inaugural salary cap and went largely unpunished. The Swans were estimated to have spent $2.5 million in 1986, over double the salary cap in their first year of operation. For comparative context, the Melbourne Storm salary cap scandal of 2006-2010, dubbed by *The Age* as "*The biggest scandal in Australian sports history*" at the time, resulted in overpayments that equated to 19% of the salary cap over the five year period.

The Sydney Swans were fined $20,000 for breaching the salary cap breach by over 100%. The sentiment surrounding the Sydney Swans was noted by journalist and author Gary Linnell:

"Sydney was too important a market and too crucial in the television rights equation to drag it back to the same level on which other clubs were operating"[75].

As a historical curiosity, the Canberra Raiders similarly breached the $1.5 million salary cap in its first year of operation in 1990, when the club won the Premiership[76]. Hence, in both Australian Rules and rugby league, the era of salary caps commenced with teams cheating the cap. How prevalent cheating has been since is an uncomfortable question, given most breaches since have been identified due to whistleblowers rather than policing. Only a small cabal of individuals are likely to know the answer to this question in each code.

While the focus on Sydney when discussing the AFL's northern expansion is understandable due to the commercial aspects described above, Sydney is but one piece of the expansion strategy. The use of the terminology 'northern states' and 'southern states' in fact represents an oversimplification of the geographic divide between Australian Rules and rugby league. This is apparent when considering the Barassi Line as originally defined by Turner does not run along state boundaries, but rather through Canberra, Broken Hill, Birdsville and Maningrida and curves in an arc from Eden in coastal NSW all the way up to Arnhem Land in the Northern Territory.

This was evident as far back as 1893, when there remained an insufficient number of clubs to continue the Sydney competition. The closure of the Sydney competition did not mean the end of Australian Rules in New South Wales, rather, the code remained prosperous in Albury, the Riverina and Wagga. The reason for this, as described by historian Peter Sharp, is that these areas were economically and culturally bound to Melbourne, rather than Sydney. Evidence of this is scattered throughout history. For instance, the 1952 VFL season 'National Day' round that featured a game between North and South Melbourne in Albury, which drew a crowd of 15,000. Many AFL champions in fact originate from these regions, not least Wayne Carey, Paul Kelly, Cameron Mooney and Neale Daniher from Wagga Wagga as previously discussed. Perhaps for this reason, esteemed former rugby league player and Wagga native Steve Mortimer wrote when prognosticating about rugby league's future expansion targets in 1987:

> "The game of Rugby League should now head into the war zone. Take on Aussie Rules head to head and establish the Winfield cup 16th team at Albury. I've rarely felt more strongly about anything in the game than that the next and critical step should be to create a club taking in the Albury-Wodonga-Wagga area. That would be taking it right to the Aussie Rules mob"[77]

New South Wales is not a pure 'rugby' state like Victoria largely is in relation to Australian Rules. What is of particular interest then, is where the Barassi Line lies in 2021 compared with how it was originally set by Ian Turner some 50 years ago.

Although my own research in 2013 stated that the line had not moved much, television ratings are not a particularly nuanced tool when exploring individual regions. To better understand the state of the Barassi Line in 2021, we deep dive into this northern battlefront to see how AFL and rugby league interest compare. To do this, we analyse the football preferences of 27,000 people across the 107 statistical regions that comprise Australia.

The results of this data come in the form of a data visualisation known as a 'heat map', displayed in Figure 10 below. The greener a region, the more it prefers Australian Rules while the redder the region, the more it prefers rugby league. Regions with light colouring are more neutral, indicating a smaller difference in preference between Australian Rules and rugby league.

That the Australian map is comprised of many shades, rather than directly contrasting red and green, illustrates the falsehood of there being 'pure' Australian Rules and rugby league states. Notably, that Western Australia is a lighter shade of green (AFL) than South Australia and Victoria perhaps belies ARLC Chairman Peter V'Landys' dismissiveness that Perth is a 'rusted on AFL state' in which millions of dollars would be 'wasted' by introducing an NRL team[78]. Similarly, that a New South Wales region is green (i.e. an AFL region) illustrates clearly the AFL's successful march across the Barassi Line and into regional New South Wales.

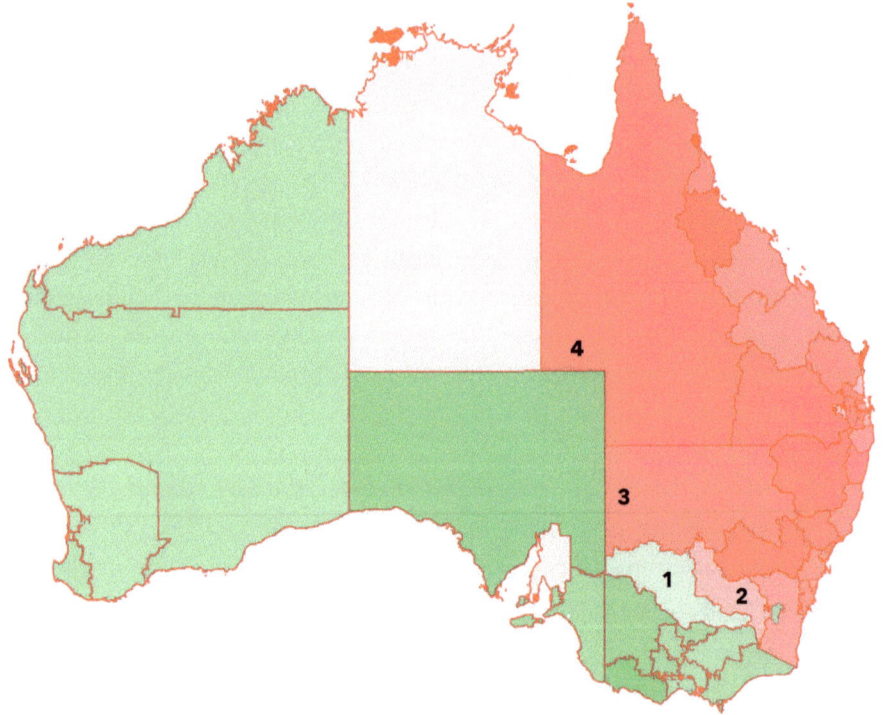

Figure 10: AFL (green) versus combined Rugby (red) interest across Australia by region.

The Murray region ('1')

The most striking region in Figure 10 is the Murray region, identified with a '1' in the diagram. The Murray region of New South Wales, which straddles the majority of the Victorian border, is undoubtedly an AFL region. A total of 55% of local residents indicate an interest in AFL, individually higher than rugby league (33%), rugby union (16%) and soccer (15%). As a matter of comparison, the rate of Australian Rules interest in Sydney (21.5%) is less than half that of the Murray. Unsurprisingly then, the Murray records the highest level of AFL interest north of the Barassi Line. The interest in AFL compared with alternatives is stark. More people in the Murray are interested in AFL (55%) than the combined total of all rugby league, union and soccer fans (45%)[79].

The Murray region is home to approximately 116,000 residents, and is comprised of three sub-regions: Albury, Upper Murray and Lower Murray. These are positioned in right to left order within '1' of Figure 10. While Australian Rules interest is broadly strong across the whole region, it is noticeable that rugby league interest shrivels the closer one approaches Albury. Rugby league interest starts at 46% in the Lower Murray, before declining to 36% in the Upper Murray to then further erode to 29% in Albury. Notably, Albury and Wodonga really are sister-cities when it comes to football preferences. On the other side of the Victorian border is Albury's sister city Wodonga, within Wodonga-Alpine. Wodonga, on the Victorian side of the border, records the highest interest towards rugby league in Victoria, at 30%, essentially equal to Albury in NSW. AFL also is similarly popular in Albury (52%) as in Wodonga (58%).

Within the Upper Murray is the town of Corowa, which straddles the interstate border and has a Victorian sister city in Wahgunyah. In 2014 the town erected a plaque to commemorate the Barassi Line, thus claiming some intersectionality to the divide. A ceremony was even held with Ron Barassi in attendance to unveil the plaque. When I spoke

The Barassi Line: A plaque has even been erected in the town of Corowa-Wahgunyah.

to the editor of the *Corowa Free Press* for his perspective on the paper's local readership, he stated: "I think you'll find this is an Aussie Rules area around here".

The Riverina ('2')

The Riverina is undoubtedly a contested region when it comes to football allegiances, although sport diversity in this region has appeared to benefit all codes as previously mentioned.

Perhaps the most public skirmish upon this battlefront occurred in 2012, when the Wagga Wagga City council agreed to enter a $300,000 funding deal with the Greater Western Sydney Giants to play annual pre-season games and promotions in the city for three years. The public back and forth between the city's Mayor, NRL and AFL advocates are instructive of how ill-equipped rugby league has been at defending its heartland.

Reflecting the importance of this football border town, then NRL CEO David Gallop flew down to Wagga Wagga the following day to meet Wagga's mayor. The day prior, he made the following statement: "I'll be going down there arm in arm with the CRL to try to get some answers as to why the council is making an investment of this type with the AFL with no similar support for our code".

In response, Wagga mayor noted: "We met with a representative from the NRL about five years ago, when Wagga Leagues Club folded and the main ground, Eric Weissel Oval, and the junior fields closed…But we haven't seen them since. I'm glad this has come to the surface".

GWS Giants CEO Dave Matthews responded to the controversy by saying: "The reality is we are investing significantly… It is disappointing that Wagga City Council have tried to do a meaningful partnership on behalf of its community, and develop ongoing benefits, and get questioned for it"[80].

As Fairfax reporter Andrew Webster noted in covering this story at the time, the Wagga case was a bellwether for the general state of affairs that sees Australian Rules consistently playing offence, and rugby league defence across all major battlefronts. Whereas in 2012, a rugby league trial match between Canberra and Canterbury generated $40,000 to fund improvements to Wagga's McDonald Park, the AFL had accumulated $8.5 million in investment within the Riverina region in the decade prior to 2012, as well as $250,000 in capital funding to Robertson Oval. Rugby league advocates and officials therefore regularly experience outrage from the financial clout the AFL exerts, but have rarely counter-punched with any strategic nous. As Webster noted in the Wagga case: "The AFL is too powerful, too cunning, too quick. Australian sport's version of Predator".

Today, the Riverina region of NSW is home to roughly 156,000 residents. The region includes Wagga Wagga, but also Tumut and Griffith. Notably it has been commonly said that rugby league 'has lost the Riverina', and incidents such as the above do not bode well for the code. Yet the data does not paint as stark a picture. Rugby league remains the most popular sport in the region (50.1%), although local interest in Australian Rules (38.3%) trails by a comparatively small margin. The Riverina's expressed interest in AFL is the second strongest amongst north Barassi regions, made more impressive by the perhaps surprisingly weak support for rugby union (13.1%) and soccer (11.5%) in the region.

Broken Hill and the Far West ('3')

Broken Hill is perhaps most famous as the birthplace of BHP and remains Australia's longest running mining town. However, Broken Hill is also notable for its geographic positioning, being New South Wales' most western outpost and straddling the South Australian border.

For anyone who has lived entirely within a capital city, the quirks of Broken Hill will be hard to imagine. This is because despite being located in New South Wales, the city for all intents and purposes is a South Australian outpost. First, Broken Hill observes Australian Central Standard Time (SA) rather than Eastern Standard Time (NSW). This peculiarity is attributed to the fact that when the dominions adopted standard time, Broken Hill's only direct rail line was to Adelaide and not Sydney. It also reflects the city's relative proximity, being a six hour drive from Adelaide and thirteen hours from Sydney. Broken Hill's media also reflects its South Australian leaning. While the major metropolitan newspapers from both Adelaide and Sydney are available locally, the local programming schedules of Channel Nine, Ten and Seven correspond to Adelaide, not Sydney. So, does Broken Hill have the footy preferences of a South Australian or New South Wales city?

Broken Hill is part of the 'Far West and Orana' region. As you can see in Figure 10 ('3'), this region accounts for about a third of the physical space of NSW, but only 1.5% of NSW's population. Across the region in totality, rugby league remains the premier football code. A total of 44% of people in the Far West indicate an interest in rugby league, followed by a clustered pack of Australian Rules (19%), rugby union (19%) and soccer (18%). However, whether this holds true in Broken Hill on the most western tip of New South Wales is questionable. Among my small sample, 50% of people from Broken Hill indicated an interest in AFL, followed by 31% for each of rugby league, union and soccer.

Birdsville and Outback Queensland ('4')

Next up the chain in the plotting of the original Barassi Line is the town of Birdsville, located on the south-western edge of Queensland, straddling the Northern Territory. Birdsville has a local population of 160 people according to the 2016 census, and thus is too small to have any organised football leagues. The town, however, enters a team in the annual Bedourie Rugby League Nines. After contemplating whether to try call 160 Birdsville residents and ask them directly, I instead called up the local (and iconic) pub, the Birdsville Hotel as a good authority of the town's football interest. I spoke with the manager in early 2020 to understand which footy prevails in the small town: "It's a rugby league town among the locals. Tourists are 50-50"[81]. Despite geographic similarities to Broken Hill, Birdsville still firmly cheers for Queensland during State of Origin.

Brisbane & Queensland

Perhaps the most overt aggression in the modern code war occurred on September 2nd 2020, when the AFL CEO Gill McLachlan announced that the 2020 AFL Grand Final would be played at Brisbane's 'Gabba stadium. This was followed about a month later by a cheeky crack by ARLC Chairman Peter V'landys in response: "They can huff, they can puff, but they won't blow our house down, it's solid brick".

Reflecting the AFL's strategic ability to capitalise upon unexpected circumstances, 2020 would become historic for becoming the first season in which AFL Grand Final was held outside of Victoria. The difference between the AFL and NRL here is telling. While the NRL are willing to play marquee fixtures like State of Origin or NRL Nines in Adelaide or Perth, the code does little to capitalise on such events with further strategic follow-up. By comparison, the AFL will most certainly leverage the Queensland Grand Final to try expand the code's northern fan base. This was foreshadowed in the AFL's initial press release, with Queensland to host "a festival of football from Far North Queensland to the Gold Coast, which will include a Premiership Cup tour across the state"[82].

The timing of the Queensland Grand Final could arguably have not been better for the AFL and worse for the NRL. None of the NRL's three Queensland teams qualified for the 2020 finals series, while flagship club the Brisbane Broncos experienced perhaps the worst season ever achieved by an NRL team, if measured by scrutiny, criticism and under performance. Although Queensland's State of Origin would save some face, the damage to the rugby league's grip on the State may have already been done. Concurrently to the NRL, the AFL's Brisbane Lions finished atop the competition table and the Gold Coast Suns surpassed their membership record in 2020 (16,236) despite COVID-19 which had been set in their inaugural season (14,311).

Perhaps the most notable proof is in the respective grand final television ratings. In 2019, a year in which both codes recorded similarly poor grand final television audiences by historical standards, the Brisbane audience was 68% larger for the NRL final (534,000) than for the AFL (317,000). In 2020, the Brisbane audience was only 28% larger for the NRL (492,000), as compared to the AFL (383,000). Evident in these numbers is a simultaneous weakening of NRL figures (down 8%) and significant improvement in AFL figures (up 21%).

In relation to the AFL, shifting the game to an evening timeslot, playing at the Gabba and Queensland hosting hubs for much of the 2020 Covid-affected season provided perhaps an unsurprising local ratings boost. It is the declining NRL rating that is more concerning, because it is a trend rather than an anomaly. Brisbane had never recorded an NRL grand final audience below 500,000 since the inception of OzTAM measurement in 2001, doing so for the first time in 2018 and second time in 2020. Prior to 2018, Brisbane provided an NRL grand final audience above 600,000 on 12 of 17 occasions, resulting in an average of 640,000 between 2001 and 2017. For the three finals between 2018 and 2020, the Brisbane audience has average 504,000. Even if one removes grand finals involving a Queensland team, Brisbane's average audience has shrunk from 603,000 (2001-2017) to 504,000 (2018-2020).

Whether Brisbane's AFL audience uplift will be sustained is yet to be seen. However, the circumstances of the AFL Grand Final in Queensland appear to have strong parallels to the timing of the Sydney Swans success and the Super League war in rugby league. As discussed in the previous section, the Sydney Swans rise from mediocrity to powerhouse commenced in 1996 and could not have been better timed given rugby league's commencing struggles with Super League. The Super League war particularly impacted rugby league interest in Sydney at a time when the Swans begun to rise in prominence. The concurrent timing of these two events undoubtedly accelerated the AFL's advancement in Sydney, and arguably rugby league has never truly recovered.

The AFL's successful foray into Queensland in 2020 should have NRL administrators concerned, given the State has been starved of local NRL success like never before. The impact of the Gabba AFL grand final upon shifting the code war in Queensland will most likely appear momentary, but AFL administrators will hope it provides a residual benefit at the community level. As metropolitan television ratings are calculated based upon the five mainland capital cities, and these are more commercially valuable than regional ratings, the NRL can ill-afford to lose the interest of Brisbane.

The state of play

When looking at aggregated popularity, the data suggests that about 39% of the national population is interested in Australian Rules, compared with 31% in rugby league. Soccer then follows (23%) with rugby union lagging (17%). My research is broadly consistent with that of Roy Morgan Research, which performs an annual survey tracking AFL and NRL club support. In their 2019 survey, they found the AFL clubs had a cumulative fan base of 7,870,000, compared with the NRL's 5,593,000 and the A-League's 2,750,000[83]. This equates to a national interest of 41% for AFL, 31% for NRL and 14% for the A-League.

In relation to the relative status of soccer and rugby union in the code war hierarchy, the above numbers overinflate the commercial gap between these two codes. Since the professionalism of rugby union in 1995, the local Super Rugby competition has been widely considered the world's strongest domestic tournament. The figures around rugby union interest therefore relate to fandom that mostly remains on Australia shores.

By comparison, the distinction between interest in 'soccer' from my data (23%) and Roy Morgan's surveying of support towards A-League teams (14%) is notable. Indeed, in my research of Sydney sport fans, among soccer fans, only 6% are uniquely fans of the A-League, compared with 34% who are interested in overseas competitions, with the remaining 60% of fans expressing an interest in some combination of both. This reveals the single largest, perhaps insurmountable, challenge for the FFA: converting fans of the sport to fans of the domestic league.

Simple division of the above national popularity figures would suggest that Australian Rules is about 30% more popular than rugby league in Australia. To many, this might seem like a surprisingly small difference. The significant disparity in attendance and membership rates as well as the far more national footprint of the AFL would have some suspecting a stronger dominance. Given the NRL has only one team south of the Barassi Line and has historically done incredibly little to expand the game's footprint, the NRL and its advocates could well consider this to be a relatively small margin.

Yet, Figure 5 revealed a significant difference between Australian Rules and its competing codes that is not immediately apparent when looking at aggregate level data. The AFL's significant advantage is that it does not share its fans nearly as much as its competitors do. Nearly half of fans interested in AFL (49%) are exclusively interested in AFL football. Only 30% of rugby league and soccer fans are solely interested in their respective codes. Only 11% of rugby union fans are solely interested in rugby union football. In real terms, there are about 3.4 million Australians solely interested in Australian Rules, followed by 1.7 million for rugby league, 1.3 million in soccer and only 351,000 for rugby union.

This key strategic advantage is a reflection of the AFL's successful northern expansion of the game. This has seen northerners become much more likely to be interested in a diverse array of football codes, whereas southerners remain single-mindedly attentive towards AFL. There are twice as many Sydneysiders and Brisbanites (13%) who are interested in three or more codes, compared with Adelaide (6%); with Melbourne (8%) and Perth (8%) only marginally more polyamorous. With no top-flight rugby teams of either persuasion located in Adelaide this millennium, as at least compared with Melbourne and Perth, the effect of placing expansion teams into new markets to drive fandom is particularly apparent.

From a sport culture perspective, it is particularly impressive to consider that, among people who are interested in only one code south of the Barassi Line, around 76% of people chose AFL as their sole football code of choice. The AFL are thus winning the code war because it owns the south-western states with an iron fist, while fragmenting football interest within the north eastern states away from a rugby core. This has occurred because the rugby codes remain transfixed with their own local markets, meaning the AFL has had to perform very little fortification of its own heartland markets. Aside from intermittent defence at the hands of soccer, the AFL has thus been able to focus its resources upon offence in northern markets. The AFL is therefore undoubtedly in a strong strategic position, but history shows us that this position cannot be taken for granted.

Part 2: Yesterday
Key moments that have shaped Australian football

"History is written by the victors and framed according to the prejudices and bias existing on their side."
George Graham Vest, 1891, Missouri Sen.

The above quote seems apt in a book that uses a war metaphor to describe the Australian football landscape, and it is perhaps an inconvenient truth that Australian football history is framed by prejudices. The state of affairs is perhaps best summed up by sport historian Ian Syson[84]:

"Most historians (amateur and professional) allow for the fact that a lot of the football played around Australia in the 1850s and 1860s was often an undifferentiated and usually locally 'flexible' set of behaviours... Sometimes a convenient look away allows Australian Rules to be there in place smiling innocently when the historian returns to the narrative...Other codes are excluded from historical consideration by the invention of a great Australian Rules tradition which, having acknowledged (or asserted) its contemporary social dominance, looks back over history and colonises the lot for itself."

Modern attempts by football codes to rewrite history according to self-serving narratives is perhaps best exemplified by the AFL's recent attempts to position itself as inspired by Indigenous culture.

At its most subtle, this agenda has been propagated by conscious efforts to regularly describe Australian Rules as the 'indigenous game'. This statement is factually true, in that the game originates from Australia, but it attempts to covertly conflate the game being indigenous to Australia with the game being invented by Indigenous Australians. These however, are two different statements of fact. As noted by vocal critic of such manoeuvres, prominent historian Roy Hay: "Historians including Bill Mandle, Geoffrey Blainey, Rob Hess, Robin Grow and Bernard Whimpress have demolished the anachronistic attempts to give the game Irish or Aboriginal antecedents"[85].

Such attempts became more overt in 2019, with the AFL adopting a new formal position around the origins of their game. In June of 2019, the AFL, through general manager of social policy and inclusion Tanya Hosch, attempted to rewrite history by inferring that the Aboriginal game of Marngrook informed the creation/origin of Australian Rules football. This change in policy was not supported by any new evidence since the AFL commissioned historian Gillian Hibbins in 2008 to explore the origin of the sport. Hibbins' essay concluded that it was a 'seductive myth' to tie Australian football to Aboriginal games. As noted by Ms Hosch in 2019:

"We are aware of this part of the game's history being contested and at some stage I hope the AFL will formally resolve this but as it stands, we now have a statement that acknowledges and accepts the link between Marngrook and Australian Rules Football…This gives us a good step forward in terms of acknowledgment in future historical records of the game"

This phrasing, that the AFL is entitled to control the framing of its history and such politically motivated policy represents a 'good step forward', speaks loudly to the overt attempts to impart prejudice and bias into history.

Roy Hay, again notable as the author of *Aboriginal People and Australian Football in the Nineteenth Century,* had this to say further on the matter: "That just simply is an attempt to rewrite history… The idea that [Indigenous football] was somehow a blueprint for the game that the white men developed in Melbourne around the late 1850s — I have searched high and low, and many other historians have done [the same], to find out if there is substantial evidence that supports that, and really we can find none". Dr Greg de Moore: "There is an evidence gap … I've seen nothing in recent years to change my view… I've found nothing that documented that he (Wills) saw the game (Marngrook). He never made reference to it, and no one ever else made reference to it"[86].

Retaining integrity and accuracy in the recounting of history is vitally important yet perhaps under-appreciated. At its worst, not valuing history enables disinformation to foster such things as Holocaust denial[87]. The historical record is also important in the sport context because sport is a key part of culture. Long and rich histories provide sports a form of cultural currency that can then be leveraged in the modern commercial environment. Indeed, the timing of the AFL's announcement was curious given a recent spate of incidents linked to racism towards both Indigenous and non-white AFL players had recently beset the league. Some consider this 2019 change an attempt to mitigate the public relations disaster that surrounded the treatment of Adam Goodes. However, as Syson describes, the broader history of football represents a contested battlefront between the codes.

Hence, here I endeavour to walk through the minefield of sport history to provide an agnostic insight into how our modern football preferences have developed. I focus on recounting incidents that have been particularly meaningful in shaping our football preferences today, many of which have received surprisingly little attention. This is because histories of the individual codes focus inwardly and thus often fail to consider the cross-code momentousness of particular events. Some of these moments speak more to history and sociology than football itself.

For instance, it is notable that if we compare the origins of where Australian Rules and rugby (pre splitting) were first played to where they are most popular today, the pattern is almost the exact opposite to what you would expect. Rugby was played before Australian Rules in both of Tasmania and Western Australia, while Queensland's first football club was aligned to Australian Rules!

If we were to simulate all the sliding door moments of Australian sport history, many of these alternate realities look far different, rather than similar, to the one we have today. In many alternate realities, we end up with two football codes in Australia by 2021. In another plausible alternate reality, we end up with five or possibly six codes. Most notably, the biggest 'what if' historical moment of Australian sports is one that few people are aware of. That is, Australian Rules and rugby league were on track to merge into one hybrid football code, only foiled by the outbreak of World War One. This merged code would have dominated the Australian sport landscape for the century that has followed.

As it stands today, Australian Rules is undoubtedly winning the code war. It is the financially largest, with the greatest number of supporters and holds the most prominent place in both media and culture. Only in terms of grassroots junior and adult participation is it not leading the football industry, but even here, is still on a far more positive trajectory than the rugby codes. Also notable is that the gap between the market leader (Australian Rules) and laggard (rugby union) has arguably never been larger, further exacerbated by the onset of COVID 19 in 2020. The gap between the codes may now be at a breaking point of no return, but was it always destined to be this way?

In the beginning

Several important factors framed Australia's colonial relationship to sport, setting in place the foundations to follow. When the First Fleet landed in what would become Sydney in 1788, they did so with 1,500 odd people on board. Significantly for the early development of sport, however, approximately half of those on board were convicts and over 80% were men. With these demographical statistics in mind, it is unsurprising that the early roots of Australian sport were characterised as 'likely to be found on the rougher edges of organised sport'[88].

Given this foundation upon which sport arose, it is easy to see why Australia was a fertile place to develop a strong football culture. Yet, this arguably also came with negative consequences which have haunted us in modern times. Early colonisation would see sport become synonymous with drinking and gambling, with the erecting of public houses (pubs) going hand in hand with sport infrastructure. This would set in motion the male dominance of sport that would follow for centuries. In this light, the modern day challenges sport is now grappling with around the inclusion of women and negative associations with gambling and drinking are perhaps easier to contextualise when viewed through a historical lens.

Although the nature and composition of our young population provided fertile building blocks for a football culture, it is the specific geographic features of what would become Australia that have had a profound impact on our specific football preferences. Specifically, the large physical distances between colonies and the non-federated nature of the continent prior to 1901 meant that each colony largely developed with autonomy from each other. Although many of our modern day sports were yet to be formally codified, an absence of regular, reliable transport between the distant colonies of Western Australia, South Australia, Tasmania, Victoria, New South Wales and Queensland in the early 19th century meant that there was little opportunity for inter-colonial sport contests. The first inter-colonial matches were cricket games at the newly established Melbourne Cricket Ground in 1856 and at Sydney's Domain in 1857.

The 1850s is generally attributed as a launching point for modern Australian sport. As noted by sport historian Richard Cashman: "organised sport before 1850 was a curious amalgam of more informal and violent pre-industrial games with some beginnings of commercialised and bureaucratic sport"[89]. Aside from these first inter-colonial matches, this period saw the Melbourne Football Club established in 1858 and the eventual formal codification of what would become Australian Rules football in 1866. In Sydney, the rugby football playing University of Sydney Football Club was formed in 1863 and played their first match in 1865. Rather than recounting every intricacy of sport history, the purpose here is to bring us to the real starting point of Australian sport. Critical moments in the time period between 1850 and 1920 have acted like flowing lava that, once set, have shaped the structure of the Australian football and sport industry in modern times.

While Australian Rules football now appears ubiquitous across south-west Australia, and the rugby codes retain the north-east as their heartland, this has not always been so straightforward. The decision on which football code to play in each colony (besides Victoria) was often highly contested, turning out to be a billion dollar decision. To some degree, this is attributable to unsuspecting individuals who merely held their own personal preference and could surely have never predicted how significant their decisions would become. However, common to the rise of Victorian rules through the span of history is a degree of orchestrated evangelism not matched by other codes. As described by Syson[90]:

> "The development of Victorian Rules around Australia in this time (1880) is not so much an inevitable development 'out of the soil' but is a product of patterns of politicised advocacy, evangelism and imposition. The fact that the game was being exported from 'neighbouring' Victoria made it no less a product of cultural imperialism in Tasmania or wherever else it was taken up."

With this in mind, we explore how football developed across the Australian outposts, specifically disregarding Sydney and Melbourne who have received adequate focus in part one, to instead consider the contested colonies. Note that the term 'football' is used here to typically describe pre-codified games or where the exact nature of the game played is ambiguous.

Perth

We start our exploration in Western Australia. Perth was first colonised in 1829 as the first free settler colony in Australia, an ironic fact given the city would struggle with meagre growth before becoming a penal colony between 1850 and 1868[91]. Football arrived in Perth aboard the last convict ship to arrive in Australia, upon the 14th Regiment *Hougoumont* on the 10th of January 1868. On board were 62 Irish Fenian political prisoners as part of a total of 280 convicts. Western Australia's first football match occurred on the grounds of Perth Collegiate School, played between the officers and men of this regiment and a team of Perth locals. We may never be sure of the exact nature of the rules (although tackling was involved), with the presumption of the game to be played under Victorian rules in the quote below perhaps reflective of Syson's observation that Australian Rules is guilty of colonising sport history. The description of this inaugural match is sourced from the historical research of Errington[92]:

> "After an hour the civilians scored a goal but at dusk, when no more goals had been scored, it was agreed to continue the match later. The following Saturday the Regiment scored the two winning goals. The match was presumably played under the Victorian Rules familiar to the soldiers, though the ground was rather small. Inspired by the Perth activity, on Wednesday 14 October the Fremantle Temperance Society played the Town on the Green — Fremantle's recreation ground at the north end of Cliff Street — winning two games out of three, and the brief football season was over. The visit of the footballing 14th had no lasting impact. They sailed away in February 1869, and seven more winters passed before football recommenced"

THE BATTLE FOR FANS, DOLLARS AND SURVIVAL

It is important to acknowledge both how small and isolated Perth was from the east coast colonies. By 1869, there were just under 5,000 people in Perth. By comparison, the population of Victoria was 690,000[93] and New South Wales 486,000 by this time[94]. Perhaps for these reasons, a football culture did not appear particularly high on the local agenda and thus little football was played between this first game in 1869 and 1880. Despite the modern day strength of the West Australian Football Association (WAFA) and powerhouse AFL clubs the West Coast Eagles and Fremantle Dockers, by 1885, Western Australia in fact became the last colony to establish Victorian rules football.

The real formalisation of football clubs commenced in 1881. In May 1881, Perth High School (now Hale School) officially adopted the laws of rugby for its football games, playing four games in that year[95]. Western Australia's first football clubs were in fact rugby union clubs and the following year (1882) would then see the formation of five clubs in Perth and Fremantle. Although a brief attempt was made to launch soccer in this period, this would not eventuate and the code was not officially established until 1896, almost twenty years later[96].

The catalyst for football's growth was the establishment of a central recreational ground, and so it was on May 24th of 1882 that Western Australia's first football (rugby) season began. I use the word 'season' loosely, as there was no controlling association for the sport, meaning fixtures were organised in a relatively ad hoc manner through the organisational skills of the honorary secretaries of each club. This would turn out to be one of the major downfalls of rugby in the State, as soon described. The Fremantle Football Club unofficially won the first rugby season, with a record of four wins and one loss and then winning a final match against a combined Perth team. In total, 18 organised games were reported to have been played this season, seven of which were between the three organised clubs.

Although rugby union was Western Australia's first football code, Victorian rules lurked in the background. Victorian rules success manifested in a relatively one-way flow in media narrative, in the form of commentary in the local newspapers. It is evident as far back as the 1880s that Australian Rules football had a knack for winning public relations battles and rugby losing them. In a thesis on the topic of West Australian football's origins by Sean Cowan, it was noted: "the amount of criticism, both overt and veiled, contained within the pages of these four newspapers provides enough evidence to suggest there was much dissatisfaction with the game (rugby) as played in Perth"[97]. In April of 1882, the *Daily News* appeared to pick a side, stating upon questionable factuality that Victorian Rules "is now generally adopted in all the other Colonies". A similarly dubious fact-check moment occurred in May of 1882 in the *West Australian*, where one commentator advocated a push for Victorian Rules, claiming it to have been universally adopted in the other colonies: "the Victorian or 'Bouncing' rules are those which are universally adopted in the other Australian colonies; why then should Western Australia be the exception?". The following week, an equally passionate rugby supporter replied by pointing out that NSW and New Zealand only played rugby.

Western Australia's second football (rugby) season began on May 24th 1883. The season was won by Rovers, who completed the season on July 28 by beating the Fremantle club by one try to nil[98]. Only six matches were reported as played this season, with the lack of central organisation between clubs beginning to lead to widespread dissatisfaction with the state of football. This would see advocates of Victorian rules begin to mobilise, although it would be a couple more years until they could complete their coup upon Western Australian football. In April of 1883, the Swan Football Club was established and aligned to Victorian rules, but nothing much came of the club. Later in May, the York club was formed and would be more successful at establishing itself. With a population of 29,708 in the whole of Western Australia at the 1881 census, it was evident that there were only enough people for one football code. While rugby had first mover advantage, Victorian rules had the more vocal advocates.

The third rugby season that commenced in 1884 would mark the code's last. It has been described as declining in quality, further fuelling the criticisms of Victorian rules football advocates. There is no record of Fremantle playing games in 1884, while mid-season, Rovers decided against playing other clubs to instead play intra-club matches. Reflecting upon this season in 1885 within the local newspaper: "Last year [1884] football had reached a very low ebb, the healthy and exhilarating rivalry of 1882-83 had been replaced by the lethargy of 1884. Those who, like myself are fond of the noble game were fearful lest it should go the way of all things athletic, lest its eager welcome should prove to be but the prelude to its early and complete abandonment"[99]

Rugby in Western Australia had its death warrant signed and executed in remarkable speed in 1885. It started officially on April 27th when both Fremantle and Rovers held their annual general meetings, with both voting to switch to Victorian rules. The Fremantle vote was described as an 'animated discussion' resulting in a majority vote, whereas Rovers, having been champions, were understandably reluctant to switch, but were evidently willing to go along with the majority.

The following day (Tuesday), *The West Australian* carried an advertisement calling a meeting to form a new Victorian rules club and by the following Saturday, the Victorian Football Club was formed. The club was founded by ex-pat South Australians, most notably Hugh Dixson. Only six days later, Dixson would seize the moment by calling the clubs together to form Australia's last Victorian Rules association. On the 8th of May, the WAFA was formed with Rovers, Fremantle and Victorian FC present and High School and Fremantle Unions' assurances of joining too. Within eleven days, Western Australia had gone from being a rugby union playing colony to establishing the groundwork of Australian Rules' dominance of Western Australia for the 140 years that have followed.

The colony's first Victorian rules premiership match followed on June 6th of 1885, whereas there was not another rugby game until the winter of 1887. The future significance of this change could not have been foreseen, and this was reflected in the relatively incidental nature of reporting the change at the time. The *West Australian*, covering the first round of Victorian rules matches in 1885 noted: "The football season was formally opened on Saturday by a scratch match player on the Recreation Ground under the Victorian Rules, which have been adopted by the majority of clubs here"[100]. Although rugby's presence in Western Australia would ebb and flow for the next 140 years, it is apparent that in 2021, the two football codes (and rugby league by extension) have had divergent fortunes in the state.

A key question, however, is whether it was inevitable that Western Australia would have embraced Victorian Rules. Historians view the switch to Victorian Rules with some degree of inevitability. Prolific sport historian Sean Fagan points out that Perth formed closer economic and cultural ties to Adelaide and Melbourne than to Sydney, Brisbane or New Zealand[101]. Relatedly, Errington and Cowan considered the western migration of South Australians pivotal in tipping the balance of the population enough to facilitate the switch. Yet it is notable that much of the early dissatisfaction with rugby was caused by a lack of administration, as much as anything to do with the on-field play. The two codes were simply not as different in 1885 as they are today. Had rugby been better administered from inauguration, for instance forming a State association, the code could have easily cemented its first mover advantage in Western Australia. Undoubtedly however, those in favour of Victorian rules certainly had the louder voices in their advocacy, while rugby did not ingratiate itself with good governance. In this sense, not much has appeared to change in the past 150 years.

How would the Australian sport landscape be different had rugby held its ground in 1885? Given rugby union stubbornly refused to surrender its amateur status until 1995, it is likely inevitable that Australian Rules would have gained power within the State over time. However, had Western Australia remained rugby orientated until at least the great schism of rugby union and rugby league in 1908, the adoption of Australian Rules may not have become so unilateral as history now shows.

Such is the pervasiveness of Australian Rules in Western Australia in the modern day that ARL Chairman Peter V'Landys has stated that the code should not bother attempting to expand rugby league into the region via a NRL team. Yet, the importance of Western Australia to AFL cannot be understated. Australia's modern football preferences divide along a relatively neat north-east and south-west divide. This results in the north-east accounting for 53% of Australia's population in 2018, compared with the south-west's 47%[102]. If Western Australia were a rugby state in 2021, rugby states would represent a 64% share of the modern population to Australian Rules' 36% share.

Adelaide

Similar to Perth, Adelaide's path to the current day setting of Australian Rules ubiquity conceals a unique start to football in the city. The first organised football club in Adelaide commenced in 1860 and while it would end up being an Australian Rules club, this is not necessarily how it started. Similar to other colonial settlements, the specific details of what football looked like during this time are vaguer than many readers would expect, with often contradictory reporting and dating. The colonialists at the time seemingly were far more interested in simply playing football than recording the intricacies of it for analysis 150 years later. Fagan[103] provides a detailed account of this historical vagueness:

> "All that is certain is that the game was played with a round-ball, had no (or very limited) off-side rules, commenced (and after each goal) via a kick-off from mid field, and that a goal only counted if it was kicked from the foot and went below a cross-bar... The extent of running with the ball and the permitted severity of tackling is not known. No mention is made in match reports of Melbourne style bouncing or hand-passing the ball, nor of rugby's tries at goal."

It is clear that Adelaide in fact played its own unique form of football, which had been quite popular in the city, and this was some agglomeration of Victorian rules, rugby and soccer. It wasn't until 1873 when the Kensington club initiated a conference to standardise rules of play that this would begin to change. The key moment though, would then come in 1876 when it was resolved to immediately adopt Victorian rules. This saw the round ball replaced with a rugby ball and the cross-bars removed from posts. The bouncing rule was adopted soon after to fully harmonise with Melbourne rules and allow for inter-colonial matches.

Although features of rugby rules were part of Adelaide football's formation, particularly in the briefly dominant Kensington rules of 1873 to 1876, rugby never really got a foothold in South Australia. The first rugby club "Rugby Union Football Club" was formed in 1885 but did not last, while matches were only intermittent and played against visiting teams. Similar to Perth, as identified by Fagan, local paper the *Advertiser* encapsulated the sentiment: "Established institutions have a great advantage, and the numbers available seem hardly sufficient to support in the colony two different forms of football"[104]. Victorian rules quite easily won this settlement, which is hardly surprising given the strong cultural ties between Adelaide and Melbourne.

Tasmania

Tasmania was Australia's second colony following Sydney, and similar to its fellow settlements, the nature of which football code was played during this early period is ambiguous from a lack of detailed recitation within local newspapers. Tasmania is a notable region for football controversy, for three particular instances that I recount here. First, although Sydney is credited as the starting point of codified soccer in 1880 in what would become Australia, matches in Tasmania in 1879 in fact pre-date this marker. Syson notes:

"Archivally buried and misremembered, their status as two of the very first games of organised soccer in Australia has been lost. And they remain lost because, their discovery has had little purchase".

Second, the narrative of Tasmania's football history represents a contested battleground, consistent with the quote which opens this section. Tasmania would not settle on a particular football code until 1879, prior to which it played predominantly rugby, soccer and other local hybrid variants. Victorian rules did not in fact arrive in Tasmania until 1878-79, brought by WH Cundy, who upon arriving found: "a mongrel sort of game, composed chiefly of soccer and rugby, with some local additions". This reality is different to that presented today, according to Syson:

"The received history is that Australian Rules (via Melbourne Rules and Victorian Rules) football was played in Hobart from the beginnings of organised football in Tasmania. It is historically inaccurate but remains a culturally powerful truism. It is an error that is repeated and compounded by mythologisers who have their purposes and historians who should know better"

WH Cundy was interviewed in 1931, reflecting upon his arrival to Tasmania fifty years prior. This was his recount of the landscape of Tasmania football:

"When I first came to Tasmania as a youth ... there was really no established code. Rugby, soccer, and a sort of hybrid game were being played, and it can well be imagined the chaos that existed. I had played what was then known as the Victorian code in Melbourne ... but at first was unable to induce other teams to adopt the Victorian rules. I had brought over a book of rules, and had 50 copies printed for distribution, and a meeting was later called at the old High School, now the University, to discuss the position. The ... meeting could not come to a decision to concentrate on one code, so it was decided that for a season the teams should play the Victorian rules game, soccer and Rugby... and at the end of the year decide which should be adopted, when all were fairly conversant with the codes"

While Tasmania is notable for being Australian football's first social experiment, this is not how history has remembered this period. Author of *Chronicles of Soccer in Austrlia - The Foundation Years, 1859 to 1949*, Peter Kunz notes that the Hobart press of 1859 reports 'a grand football match between two elevens, selected by G. Gregson and John Stockell, esquires for 10 pounds'[105], a description that rather neatly fits soccer. Syson, himself soccer-leaning in his research, is among the more openly critical scholars of Victorian rules bias that appears to, at least occasionally, pervade sport history. Again, he notes in relation to Tasmania's history:

CODE WARS

"Geoffrey Blainey's *A Game of Our Own* is one of the influential and most respected histories of Australian Rules football. Its section on early football in Tasmania, while acknowledging the uncertainty of codes in the colony, nonetheless constructs Melbourne Rules as the norm against which other codes butted... the important error here is the inadvertent deception of constructing Tasmanian football as Victorian Rules in embryo."

The final and perhaps most interesting controversy in Tasmania's football history therefore surrounds how the colony came to choose its football code. As described in the quote by WH Cundy above, at the end of 1878, it was decided that the 1879 season would see each code played in rotation to give all involved an adequate chance to compare them. After trialling each code during the season, there would be a vote surrounding which single code to adopt. This social experiment represented perhaps the most democratic approach to addressing the issue of football preference seen among all the colonies. On the ballot was not only Victorian rules, rugby and soccer, but also the local rules and a new set of rules that was a mixture of all games.

Ultimately, the Victorian rules won the ballot by one single vote. Having won this vote, Victorian rules would go on to become the ingrained code of Tasmania thereafter. Meanwhile, organised rugby would only re-emerge 50 years later in 1933 with the formation of the Launceston Rugby Club. The vote of 1879 however, raises many tantalising 'what-if' scenarios. Firstly, the NSWRU (rugby union) had been attempting to organise a British rugby tour of the colonies, and had contacted the Tasmanian association about the prospect of playing a match at each of Hobart and Launceston. The tour did not eventuate on account of the touring party demanding too high a financial guarantee, and likely would have been a year too late. However, a British tour under rugby rules playing two high profile fixtures in Tasmania could have perhaps been enough to sway this slender vote margin in rugby's favour.

Alternatively, what would Tasmania football look like today had the locals been stoic and instead voted for the adoption of their own 'Tasmanian rules' and rejected existing football codes as part of an anti-mainland philosophy? As we'll soon see in New Zealand, such a hypothetical was not implausible. Imagine a Tasmanian Football League today, a fifth code of sorts and a hybrid of Australian Rules, soccer and rugby. This may have looked something AFL's international rules, presumably with the addition of a try line.

In some ways, Tasmanians may have been better off in this scenario than their current situation. The state's loyalty towards Victorian rules since 1879 has arguably not been well rewarded, having been regularly rebuffed for inclusion in the AFL in the modern era at the expense of more strategically valuable outposts. This is certainly a key theme of Tasmania's AFL Licence Taskforce, who released their report and quasi-pitch document in late 2019.

The report noted that whereas two decades ago, Tasmania enjoyed the highest per capita rate of participation in Australian Rules across the country, the AFL will cede being Tasmania's favourite sport by 2030 based on current trends. Such trends refer to the fact that the number of Australian Rules football fans on the island had declined by 38% between 2008 and 2019, according to consultancy research[106]. Such figures suggest Tasmania to be a weak spot for AFL in the code wars battle map, with basketball (via a Tasmanian NBL franchise) and soccer (a prospective A-League bid) identified as the likely invaders.

Brisbane

As signposted in the introduction, the relationship between Australian colonies' early football preferences to what would become their ingrained football preference in 2021 is surprisingly misaligned. In the case of both Perth and Tasmania, the current day passion for Australian Rules conceals that Victorian rules was a late entrant to the two colonies by comparison to rugby and soccer. So too in Brisbane, where the current day passion for rugby, in particular the league variety, conceals that the state's first football club was aligned to Melbourne rules. The first football game occurred on Saturday, June 9th of 1866, which in the absence of a full scale league, was an in-house game.

Similar to the other colonies, it is difficult to know with certainty how strictly the Melbourne rule book was followed during this period. What is certain however, is that the Melbourne rules were the dominant rules for much of the period from inauguration in 1866 until 1886, which represents the marker for when rugby completed its ascendency in the state. This twenty year period in-between was similar to other colonies in that, in the absence of the formalisation of one set of rules, there was regular confusion within matches around the very rules of the game being played.

Similar to Tasmania, Brisbane also ended up playing what could be called 'Brisbane rules' around 1876, which was a version of rugby adapted to the personal preferences of participating locals. At this point, it was still no clearer which code would become dominant, although frustrations around the confusion various laws were causing had become apparent. As noted in *The Brisbane Courier* at the time (1876): "It is uncertain yet whether rugby or Melbourne rules will carry the day here, but some decision will have shortly to be come to on the subject, and the sooner the better."[107]

From an organisational perspective, two interesting events happened in Queensland that are relevant to the code wars and quite distinct from elsewhere in the country. First, in April 1880, four clubs formed the Queensland Football Association (QFA). What is notable about the QFA is that it was a dual-code body, playing predominantly Victorian rules but also playing rugby rules 'each fourth Saturday'. This balance reflected that, as noted in *The Brisbane Courier* in late 1979: "The Rugby game, however, is certainly not in favour here amongst either the majority of the players or with the public." [108]

Although the Melbourne rules were gaining ascendancy, the strategic intervention of the NSWRU from 1882 would help turn the tide and secure the state for rugby. In 1882, it was decided that Queensland would visit New South Wales and play the first interstate football match between the states. As part of the original plan, the NSWRU and NSWFA (Victorian rules) were to share costs so that teams would play under both codes. The NSWRU then offered to pay for all touring costs in return for only playing rugby matches. This offer was gladly accepted and is now the origin for what is recognised as the first rugby union match between the NSW Waratahs and Queensland Reds. New South Wales won this match by a score of 26/28-4[109] in front of approximately 4,000 spectators.

The tour was quickly reciprocated the following year, with NSW rugby touring Queensland for first time and playing in front of 3,000 spectators at Eagle Farm Racecourse. This game was momentous, with Queensland winning 12-11, providing the first of two particularly important on-field victories that would spark interest in the code and begin its dominance. In response, the QFA became an entirely Victorian rules association in late 1883 and introduced bans on players who participated in rugby. This moment was significant, as those with a rugby preference needed to decide whether to fall into line with Victorian rules, still a popular code, or go with rugby that had many more unknowns. In response, the Northern Rugby Union (NRU) was formed in November of 1883[110], which would later be renamed to the current day Queensland Rugby Union.

The creation of the NRU is the second interesting organizational feature of the code war in Queensland. Because the association was formed in response to rugby's exclusion from the existing QFA club structure, it was created without any member clubs. More typical in both Australia and globally, has been that clubs have formed first and then banded together to form associations (e.g. WAFA in Western Australia). It is a peculiarity of history that in this instance, the sport's association pre-dates its member clubs. Hence, the decision to form the NRU was put forward and seconded by individuals (Mr Hickson and Mr F Lea) rather than clubs. Notably also was the conciliatory tone of the meeting's discussion, with rugby wanting to seemingly avoid a code war: "Mr Hickson, without wishing to elight the Melbourne game, spoke strongly in favour of the game under Rugby rules. There was plenty of room for both games… Mr F.O Lea seconded the motion, and like Mr Hickson, would not disparage the Melbourne Game". Seven months later in mid-1884, Queensland's first dedicated rugby clubs: Fireflies and Wanderers, were formed.

The most significant movement however came in 1886 where once more, a significant on-field moment translated to off-field momentum. Queensland's 1886 tour of New South Wales saw them, for the first time, defeat NSW in Sydney. The effect of this would prove monumental for the local popularity of the code. By 1887, the NRU would have 25 clubs compared with the QFA's 4. Fagan pinpoints the following excerpt from the QRU's 1902 Annual report:

"The success of this team undoubtedly won the day for Rugby game in Queensland. The Victorian game supporters were struggling hard to uphold the premier position they had gained but after the brilliant performance of the 1886 team, who lost only one match through their tour, the Rugby game became very popular and the next season several new clubs were formed and the Victorian game began to wane"

New Zealand

Perhaps the most intriguing hypothetical historical scenario for the modern Australian football landscape, albeit a left-field one, is what may have eventuated if New Zealand had become Australia's seventh state during federation. New Zealand was in fact governed by New South Wales until the signing of the Declaration of Independence in 1835 and then the Treaty of Waitangi in 1840. As independent colonies, New Zealand had some sporting interactions with the pre-Australia colonies. In 1882, a NSW team made the first rugby tour of New Zealand, then reciprocated in 1884. The New Zealand Maoris team, returning home from touring Great Britain in 1889, had a layover in Adelaide and the opportunity to play either rugby or Victorian rules game against locals, but the opportunity was missed due to poor planning. Queensland would then make their first rugby tour to New Zealand in 1896.

Perhaps most notable in the early history of the colonies was New Zealand's non-consensual inclusion in Australia's federation plans. Upon Australia's federation, even without the agreement of New Zealand's government, Section 6 of the Australia Constitution Act included New Zealand as a prospective state:

"The States shall mean such of the colonies of New South Wales, New Zealand, Queensland, Tasmania, Victoria, Western Australia and South Australia, including the northern territory of South Australia, as for the time being are parts of the Commonwealth, and such colonies or territories as may be admitted into or established by the Commonwealth as States; and each of such parts of the Commonwealth shall be called a State."

It is important to note that there was never a strong public will in New Zealand to join the Australian federation, making the implications here far more hypothetical than within the Australian colonies. Theories for New Zealand's non-interest have included concerns the Maori would be treated similar to Australia's indigenous people, New Zealand's desire for their own South Pacific empire, a general cultural snobbery against Australia and a fear of a loss of power among existing leaders[111]. This last point being depicted in Figure 11 overleaf, from 1900.

Figure 11: A cartoon from 1900 depicting King Dick's snub

Yet, imagine how different the modern Australian and global sport marketplace could have looked today had New Zealand joined the Australian federation. New Zealand's dominance of international rugby union has seen the All Blacks become one of the largest and most valuable global sport brands. As a combined nation, it is difficult to imagine Australia ever losing a rugby match. This dominance would have been of such strength that it is difficult to imagine rugby union retaining the minimum necessary level of competitive balance between teams to create a legitimate World Cup. Of the ten men's rugby union World Cups since 1987, Australia or New Zealand has won five, and in only two has neither Australia nor New Zealand featured in the final (2007, 2019).

It may surprise some that the rugby league World Cup predates its union counterpart, having now had 15 'World Cups' since the inaugural competition hosted by France in 1954. Australia has won eleven and New Zealand one, for an even greater dominance than in union.

Competitive balance is said to be a fundamental requirement of sport contests, with the reasoning being that people do not enjoy sport contests where one team is too dominant. This has been called the Louis-Schmeling paradox, a boxing analogy that perfectly illustrates the peculiar economics of sport contests. The first criteria of sport economics is to avoid a market monopoly, as you need two participants for a boxing match (known as joint production). The second criteria is for a competitive match, as evenly matched boxers will generate bigger purses than mismatched ones. In a reality where Australia and New Zealand produced one national rugby team, the competitive balance of international rugby may have been weakened to such a degree that the Rugby World Cup would have never flourished to become one of the world's economically largest events.

Other hypothetical considerations also emerge. With New Zealand as a seventh state, one can wonder what rugby league State of Origin would have looked like in 2021. Given State of Origin is estimated to equate to around 20% of NRL revenue[112], would a tri-series State of Origin with the seventh state make the event bigger, or in fact take away from the very unique border tribalism on which the contest was founded? In 1997 during the Super League war there was in fact a Tri-series between Queensland, New South Wales and New Zealand that was hardly a resounding success. Given the disruptive nature of the Super League war at the time however, it is hard to read much from this series as a case study.

It is of course hard to predict what the sport culture of the two nations would look like today if they had federated as one. The 'cultural snobbery' offered as a motivating factor to remain independent from Australia may also reflect New Zealand's lack of interest towards Victorian rules. Notably, when the Australian National Football Council (ANFC) was established in 1906 as an early form of national governing body for Australian Rules, New Zealand was not only a delegate member, but an equal one amongst all the other Australian states. The ANFC even distributed funds to New Zealand to invest in the promotion of Victorian rules there. They were swiftly expelled after they stopped attending delegate meetings or explaining what they had done with the funding they had been given.

The strength of rugby union's cultural centrality in New Zealand of course provides a sharp contrast to the more fragmented Australian market. As one nation then, rugby union on the Australian mainland may have perhaps become stronger than the position it finds itself in today. Rugby Australasia would have been able to leverage the sport's immense popularity within the New Zealand state to try grow the sport on the mainland, akin to the NHL's relationship to Canada and the United States. It seems less likely that the evangelism that surrounded Victorian rules football would have seen it successfully propagated into the New Zealand state. Nonetheless, with the largest Australian capital cities all featuring an AFL team come 2021, the modern AFL competition would have likely included an Auckland team by now. Indeed Auckland's Eden Park is almost better suited to being an AFL ground than a rugby ground.

What could have been

Today's football landscape is largely a manifestation of significant historical moments influenced by some degree of chance. The embryonic relationship our colonies had with football in fact was closer to the opposite of today's landscape: Queensland first embracing Melbourne rules and Western Australia and Tasmania first embracing rugby. However, the codification of football rules and establishment of state associations typically around the 1870s/1880s acted like the settling of tectonic plates, resulting in the establishment of a locally dominant code that has largely perpetuated and been undisputed in the 140 years since.

Historical 'what-ifs' are evident throughout the histories of how the football codes fared during early settlement in each colony. Although each description is necessarily brief, and worthy of greater exploration, particular moments stand out. In Tasmania, the football referendum of 1879 was won by Melbourne Rules by a solitary vote. Had the establishment of rugby in Perth coincided with better initial governance in 1882, the root cause of much of the criticism that led to its overturning, the code could have easily cemented its first-mover advantage in Western Australia. In Queensland, had the NSWRU not intervened in 1882, Melbourne rules' early momentum would have likely seen Australian Rules become established the State's most popular code.

This brings us back to the lay of the Australian football landscape, as it landed and what could have been, as illustrated in Figure 12 (Australian Rules in blue, rugby in red). As events transpired, Australia's football preferences divide neatly along a north-east and south-west line. In another reality, however, the divide could have looked much messier, as illustrated on the right hand side of Figure 12. In an alternate reality, we end up with a 'Barassi boomerang' rather than 'Barassi Line', with Australian Rules states enclosing New South Wales.

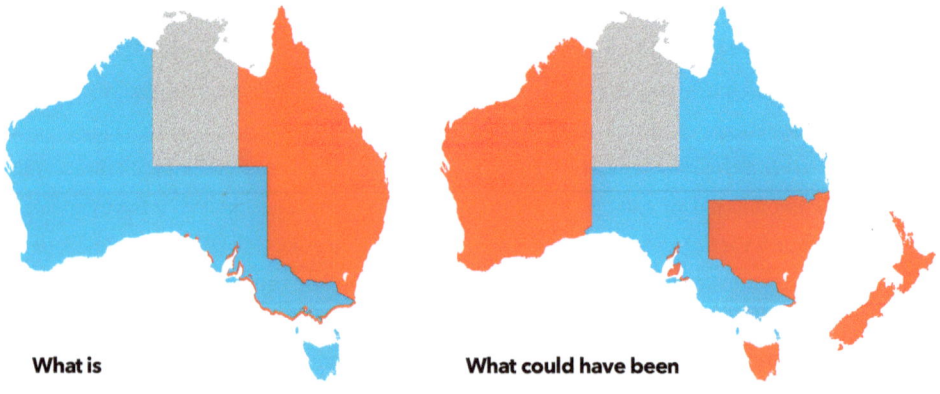

Figure 12: The 'Barassi Line' as is, and how it could have been

Hybrid games

The previous section described how football started in particular colonies to illustrate a number of 'what-if' scenarios that could have influenced the modern football environment.

THE BATTLE FOR FANS, DOLLARS AND SURVIVAL

One particular type of 'what-if' scenario is the numerous attempts to develop hybrid games that have littered the history of Australian football. This first wave happened during the colonial period prior to the formalisation and standardisation of football rules. The above section detailed how Tasmania could have ended up with a version of Tasmanian rules which combined elements of rugby, soccer and Melbourne rules. So too were there unique Brisbane rules of football. In modern times, our most famous hybrid games are perhaps the intermittent International Rules matches involving AFL and Gaelic players, and attempts to create a hybrid rugby between league and union.

International Rules is notable for appearing particularly unloved by the Australian sporting public. Australian crowds for the fixture hovered near the 10,000 mark for many of the Australian hosted series in the late 1980s and early 1990s. After an upsurge during the first decade of the new millennium, crowds have once again been on a diminishing curve. Just 25,502 fans attended the 2017 series opener in Adelaide, in a season where the Adelaide Crows averaged 46,650 attendees and Port Adelaide 38,136. Television audiences for the 2017 International Rules series were in fact smaller than an average regular season AFL fixture. AFL players have too appeared lukewarm in their desire to participate. The irony of this is that the AFL of course presents an annual 'All Australian' team, which is considered a highly prestigious accomplishment. Yet, players have often withdrawn their eligibility to actually represent Australia in International Rules fixtures. Despite this malaise, International rules has produced surprisingly even contests, with Australia having scored 48.4% of total points to Ireland's 51.6% over the totality of games.

Meanwhile former rugby league player Phil Franks has spent more than a decade trying to promote his Hybrid Rugby format, with little progress made. Hybrid Rugby has seen several trial games played (2011, 2015) and several false dawns in respect to blockbuster promoter proposals between the Australian Kangaroos and New Zealand All Blacks (2017, 2020). Yet, like International Rules, there appears weak political will to materialise the concept. So too is it worth noting that the gameplay mechanics of Hybrid Rugby do not appear to gel particularly well. Roy Masters, among the curious onlookers of a trial game described the sport not so much as a hybrid, but rather the sum of two distinct parts[113]. Despite the two rugby codes appearing similar to the untrained eye, the technical skills of union and cardio vascular requirements of league have caused the games to drift apart such that they no longer allow for easy reintegration.

For these comparatively unsuccessful recent hybrids, one particular historical attempt to create a hybrid game stands out as a moment in history that could have indelibly altered the path of Australian football history. This was the attempted merger of Victorian Rules and rugby league at the start of the 1900s, to create a new football called *Universal Football*. The gravity of what such a merger would mean for the modern Australian sport landscape is surely not lost on any reader of this book, and certainly wasn't lost to people at the time. As noted in the *Westralian Worker* (Perth) in February of 1915:

"It must be admitted that it stirs the blood, does the ideal of a big, powerful, unassailable national game, to be played on the big swagger grounds of Melbourne and Sydney and on the rough unkept reserves of the dry water famished interior of this vast continent".[114]

If it wasn't for the timing of World War One, it is highly likely that Australia's favourite football code across the entire country could have been something else entirely to what it is today, that being *Universal Football*. Additionally, while the Brownlow medal is the AFL's highest individual honour, and the JJ Giltinan Shield is awarded to the minor premiers of the NRL, both men advocated for Universal Football.

The history of Universal Football can be divided to three discrete time periods. First in 1908, the year of the first season of rugby league football in New South Wales. The game's founding administrator, JJ Giltinan, met with officials from the Victorian Rules Australasian Football Council, led by president Con Hickey, and the embryo of an idea was formed but left unactioned. Next came 1914-15 when a concrete proposal was put forward and momentum for change was high and merging seemed probable. Finally, a revisit of the idea in 1933 with a trial game played. These three time periods are detailed further.

In August of 1908, an interstate conference was held at the office of the Victorian Football League to consider establishing a universal Australasian game. The meeting was driven by Giltinan, who was chair of the NSW Rugby League and, by default, the Australian rugby league team who were soon to travel to England. In attendance were various state members of the Victorian rules ANFC[115]. The incompatibility of the prevailing mindsets of the two parties are easy to see, both through the minutes of the meeting and more broadly considering each code's strategic position at the time.

JJ Giltinan was rugby league's first entrepreneur, having provided the money to establish the game and compensate its players. Accordingly he entered the meeting from the perspective of an opportunity, to merge the codes to develop a stronger unified sport. Given rugby league had only just been created, Giltinan did not carry the weight of any existing cultural baggage, traditions or biases like his counterparts and could therefore enter the discussions much more open minded. Given he was about to board a boat to England, where the sport was also fledgling and capable of change, it makes sense that rugby league was malleable to change in this moment.

By contrast, it easy to see a pervading sense of elitism and institutionalism within the ANFC which made conceding any ground to rugby league an uphill battle. This was apparent in minutes of the meeting. Western Australia's representative Mr Symons stated that he considered it was "only a matter of time" until the Australian game would absorb all the other games, and hence a merger would have seemed unnecessary to him. Tasmania's representative Mr WH Gill stated: "The Australian game was made of the best points of other games, and after 50 years' experience was found to be nearly perfect". Admittedly, in a potentially hostile environment, Giltinan did not ingratiate himself to some of the ANFC members prior to the meeting. Giltinan had previously written to the secretary of the Victorian Football League stating that both Tasmania and South Australia were a "burden" to them, something their delegates naturally resented. Despite apologising, such statements probably didn't help the mood of the meeting.

The prevailing sentiment was that Australian Rules had much more to lose and far less to gain, although the merit of the idea appreciated. This was perhaps best echoed by New South Wales' delegate to the ANFC Mr Butler, who said that 'the present Rugby game [league] was 50 per cent better than the old [union], and it would require to be improved 50 per cent more before it would equal the Australian game'. The broader public sentiment was well captured in a quote from a Western Australian newspaper albeit from 1915, when the concept re-emerged:

> "There is something that appeals, but viewing the proposition as an admirer of the "best game on earth" [Australian Rules], will this amalgamation with the off-side, scrumbling, cross-bar Rugby compensate for the loss of those features which we all love so dearly"[116]

Being an adept entrepreneur, Giltinan attempted to overcome Australian Rules scepticism by offering the ANFC something otherwise unobtainable to them: international growth. With an impending tour of England, Giltinan suggested that "modifications might be arrived at to bring about an amalgamation of the Australian and Northern Union games", in essence suggesting an internationalisation of the game. Giltinan had at least partial support from the New Zealand delegate of the ANFC, who noted that rugby was entrenched in his colony and that 'a game could be evolved which would be the Australian game perfected'. The foresight of Giltinan at the time was impressive, with newspaper articles from the period suggesting the game could even be exported to America. Such an idea was not completely implausible. American football's genesis was not much earlier in 1880, while the National Football League did not start until 1920.

At the meeting, Giltinan suggested that 'in many points the Australian and rugby game were similar'. There was a willingness on rugby's part to abolish the scrum, while other matters could be settled. The main stumbling block was the off-side rule, which represents perhaps the most distinguishing feature of the two codes. The following excerpt of the meeting sums up the challenge:

Mr Tomlinson (ANFC QLD): 'Is there any prospect of the Rugby giving way with regard to the off side?
Mr Giltinan: 'None whatever'
Unknown delegate: 'That settles it'

Despite this seeming impasse, ANFC chairman Con Hickey was not one of the detractors of the amalgamation. He closed the meeting by stating that 'if the delegates could have seen the new Rugby game played here, it would have done more good than a conference. It was possible that modifications might be arrived at to bring about an amalgamation of the Australian and Northern Union games. Mr Giltinan deserved thanks for bring the matter forward and he hoped to see it brought to a successful issue'. Despite this sentiment, there was no action resolved from this initial conference.

The period of most promising progress towards Universal Football occurred in 1914/15 and coincided with two major football events in Sydney. The first was the British Lions rugby league tour and the second was the Australian Rules interstate carnival, both of which occurred almost concurrently in mid-1914. Incidentally, after the first two test matches of the Great Britain rugby league tour were held in Sydney, the third and final match was meant to be held in Melbourne. This would have been a fillip for the expansion of the game, exposing Victorians to the highest calibre of rugby league and indirectly addressing ANFC president Con Hickey's suggestion that the best path to unification was simply to expose the Australian Rules states to the quality of the new rugby league code. However, the NSWRL ensured the match was played in Sydney a third time, conscious that rugby union's All Blacks were playing in Sydney and the Australian Rules interstate carnival was to be held soon-after.

Given the choice between expanding the game or serving a heartland, it is evident that rugby league administrators will choose to defend a heartland. This appears just as true in 2021 as it was in 1914, with a second Brisbane team appearing more likely than Perth to be the next NRL expansion team. This can be viewed as either a sad lack of ambition or a commendably persistent insularity. In lieu of this aforementioned blockbuster clash in 1914, the NSWRL created a final tour game between NSW Firsts and Great Britain, that drew a comparatively paltry crowd of 13,000 to the MCG. The NSWRL seemed similarly unkind towards their northern partners in the Queensland Rugby League. The Chairman's report from the Queensland Rugby League's annual report of 1914 stating: 'Unfortunately, the action of the NSWRL in altering the fixture list without consulting either the English managers or the offices or the Queensland League rendered it impossible to play the Australia v England match, and the Englishmen had to be engaged by another Queensland team'.

The proximal timing of these two major events in July-August and their occurrence in one city most certainly helped put the idea of Universal Football back on the table by the time of the ANFC conferences in August and November of 1914. The three Lions matches at the SCG had drawn crowds of 40,000, 55,000 and 34,420. Meanwhile, the Australian Rules carnival was only able to recover about half its costs[117], representing a highly-visible but not unexpected failure for Victorian rules. The carnival provided a rare instance of fallibility for a code that had otherwise already established a culture of superiority. This is, in my mind, a vital but perhaps underappreciated contextual factor that catalysed discussion

THE BATTLE FOR FANS, DOLLARS AND SURVIVAL

of Universal Football. Had the 1914 carnival been held in Adelaide, played to huge crowds and been highly profitable, the idea of Universal Football may not have developed the required momentum to be discussed further.

The comparative success of the visiting Lions tour relative to the Sydney Australian Rules carnival was a topic of discussion at the ANFC's August 1914 council meeting. Here, some logic prevailed when it was suggested that a code war was in nobody's best interest. At this meeting, Charles Brownlow, of the medal variety, at this time the vice-president of the ANFC, stated what would become the prevailing logic of furthering Universal Football:

"Does it not seem madness... that two great sporting States like Victoria and New South Wales, friendly in all other branches of sport, should be at loggerheads over a code of football, and that thousands of pounds should be lost to each because neither side could agree?" [118]

Brownlow did not continue to be as strong an advocate for change as this quote would suggest, but no doubt he would still think it madness that in 2019, the AFL distributed $53 million to the Greater Western Sydney Giants and Gold Coast Suns, $20 million more than the average distribution of the remaining 16 clubs. Furthermore, the AFL also spent $58.8 million on game development, as did the NRL to the tune of $42.2 million in 2019. Combined, the two codes spent $101 million essentially fighting each other, soccer and rugby union. Had they merged, there would be little need to 'develop' the nation's most ubiquitous code[119].

Brownlow's quote speaks to the primary motivation to further Universal Football, worth clarifying here to juxtapose with the primary opposition. From the ANFC's perspective, and particularly the Melbourne perspective, an amalgamation would create the ultimate football monopoly, in turn improving profitability considerably. Firstly, each organisation (but particularly the ANFC as expansionists) would be able to stop haemorrhaging money from trying to expand their respective games into unwilling new markets. The logic of the merger, as written in the *Observer*, was prescient:

"Financially, the game has everything in its favour. Leagues, by adopting the proposal named, have increased revenues as the result of better interstate games, and through the reduction of the number of players clubs would benefit. There would be a big saving in the cost of propaganda work, and administrative charges would probably be less"[120]

Secondly, it would allow for an unfulfilled New South Wales versus Victoria football rivalry which undoubtedly would have been the most lucrative to foster. This is made obvious by looking at the attendances of Sheffield Shield cricket. When it commenced in

1892–93 as a tripartite series between New South Wales, Victoria and South Australia, NSW vs Victoria averaged 8,543 attendees per day. Meanwhile, NSW vs SA averaged 6,607 per day. Similarly at the MCG, Victoria v NSW averaged 9,613 compared with 7,375 against South Australia. In the summer of 1913/14, the SCG drew 15,249 against the Victorians compared with 9,800 for South Australia, while the MCG drew 32,736 for NSW and 28,279 for South Australia[121].

Although Giltinan's correspondence with the VFL in 1908 that South Australia and Tasmania were a burden to them was not particularly diplomatic, it most likely struck a chord of truth by reminding Victoria of the allure of the New South Wales rivalry. Similarly, it is worth mentioning that neither New Zealand Rugby League nor Queensland Rugby League were 'consulted or notified in any way'[122] by the NSWRL surrounding their amalgamation plans, reflecting its Sydney-Melbourne centricity.

The amalgamation had reasonable support amongst each of the codes' leading administrators, although by no means unequivocal. If sport were like any other business, however, the financial case for the merger would have been too compelling to ignore. This no doubt was the prevailing view of ANFC president Con Hickey, who was regularly cited as being strongly of the opinion 'that it is only a question of time when some arrangement will be arrived'.

But sport is not purely business and other influential administrators and particularly the media were against the idea on largely ideological grounds. Such ideological arguments were largely underpinned by ingrained parochialism that too much would be lost from a merger. Among the critics were prominent Australian Rules writers Jack Worrall and Reginald Wilmot, with the quote below from the former:

> "There is nothing in common between the two games, for the omission in one case of the off and on side and its existence on the other, forms the fundamental part of both pastimes. This difference is the rock upon which all unnatural innovations are likely to founder." [123]

Another suggestion, perhaps meant with some tongue in cheek, is that if there was truly a desire to play one unified game, then soccer had been strangely overlooked as the logical option:

> "In Melbourne, there are too many people devoted to the Australian game to allow of its being supplanted by a new code, half Rugby, half their own. In Sydney there are too many Rugby supporters- League and Union- to justify anyone being sanguine that a new game would catch the public fancy. Better for both sides, if they are keen on establishing a uniform code of football, to cast aside their own and take up Soccer, which has the world for its field."[124]

THE BATTLE FOR FANS, DOLLARS AND SURVIVAL

Not all views however, were dissenting. This quote from HW John:

"I see no reason why the proposed new game should not prove a success in Australasia. Perhaps not exactly as formulated at its present stage, be it said, but with further additions and improvements after the opening trial games… The playing rules as mooted will not be prove difficult to understand to either the Rugby League partisan or to the follower of the Australian game"[125]

While the August conference brought the topic back to the table, it was at the conference in November of 1914 that a preliminary code of rules was drawn up. Key features of the proposed rules can be found in Appendix 1 for those interested. In essence however, the game was to be played on an elongated rugby field, with scoring possible in both a Australian rules and rugby manner.

To what degree these hybrid rules gave a fair balance between Australian Rules and rugby league is a matter for subjective debate and personal opinion. Certainly, reporting at the time suggested that rugby league got the better deal from the compromise, although noting that sacrifices had been made by both parties. As Sydney's *Referee* publication put it:

"Though the scrummage is eliminated, it will be admitted that the adherents of the Australian game have given way to a far greater extent than those of the Rugby League. If a new game be evolved on the lines indicated, it will certainly be neither the Rugby nor the Australia, to which crowds in the two greatest cities in Australia are so attached. But it will be far more Rugby than Australian, for while a majority of the features of the Rugby League are retained in this draft, the features upon which the creators of the Australian game have always set so much store, are practically eliminated"[126]

Or the following excerpt from Western Australia's *Westralian Worker*[127]:

"To the average 'Australian' supporter probably a ground of this description [rectangular] would spell the adoption of Rugby purely and simply. The cross-bar, the method of scoring, the division of the playing area and the substitution of the oblong for the familiar oval breathe rugby. It is difficult on the face of it to figure out just where Australian would come in. But in fairness to the conference it might be stated Rugby is prepared to sacrifice certain features dear to the New South Welshmen… The methods of scoring are such that the Australian objective of quick passing and high-marking in front of goals would be entirely swallowed up in the desire to achieve the greater number of points on the Rugby system".

I believe this game would have certainly looked more like rugby than Australian Rules at a superficial level: rectangular field, rugby goal posts and no behinds, rugby passing and tries. However, had this become an entrenched sport, I am less certain that the game would be played in a rugby style today. Given a goal kicked from general play was worth 2, compared with a Rugby try worth 3 with a 1 point conversion, would game strategy have evolved such that winning was optimised by kicking goals or scoring tries? My suspicion is that Universal Football would today look more like AFL, with more regular attempts to kick goals than score rugby tries.

After the November conference, the prospect of moving towards hybridisation was strong. As quoted in the *Leader* paper in the week afterwards:

"The progress made in the direction of combining the two principal football codes in the Commonwealth- the Australian and Rugby Leagues games- is so encouraging that there is every probability of exhibition games being played next season. The New South Wales Rugby League has definitely approved the suggestions… and it is ready to give effect to them immediately [should] the Australian Football Council adopt the proposals. The interests of the council, however, extend over five States, and some time must elapse before the leading bodies of each State come to an agreement. It is significant, however, that prominent officials in Tasmania and South Australia have already given their personal views, mainly in favour of the proposed changes".[128]

On the 24th of November 1914, the NSWRL decided at a special meeting to adopt the amalgamation, contingent on the ANFC, proposing that a universal Australian game could be played by 1916. Ultimately, a more gradual hybridisation was later suggested as the most practical method of adoption. This resulted in agreed upon changes to both codes for 1915. Australian Rules football would disallow forward handpasses or knock-ons, adopt the stronger tackling rules and add a crossbar to the goalposts over which goals had to be kicked. Meanwhile, rugby league would require the try-scorer to take his own conversion kicks as well as replace the scrum with the ball-up and throw-in.

To a follower of football in modern times, it causes some bewilderment to review archival newspaper reporting of changes made to football in 1915, which were done quite so matter-of-factly. By today's standards there would be mass hysteria if the AFL and NRL attempted to merge, if the ACCC were to even allow it. South Australia was the first of the ANFC members to approve the changes, as described quite benignly in the following article from *The Register* in January of 1915:

"After discussion, the following alterations were agreed to by the meeting: Putting a bar across the goal at a height of 10ft. from the ground, throwing or knocking the ball backwards, and a very modified or strong form of tackle to overcome the present unsatisfactory rule of holding the man in possession"[129]

For the ANFC to adopt the change, it required a three-quarters majority to pass. At the time of voting, there were 14 votes evenly divided between the six Australian states and New Zealand. Notably, as Western Australia had two leagues (WAFA and Goldfields Football Association), each had 1 vote as equal representatives of Western Australia at the national council. Although hard to imagine now, until 1919, New Zealand essentially had more voting power than the WAFA and equal rights with Victoria, South Australia, as to how the game of Australian Rules should be played and governed.

South Australia was the first of the Australian Rules state leagues to approve the change in January, as quoted above (2-0). This was followed by New South Wales in February, who naturally voted in favour, having made little to no head-way in developing the code in the State (4-0). Next, the West Australian Football Association "very rightly" and "emphatically" turned down the proposal on March 3rd of 1915[130]. Remembering that WAFA retained only 1 delegate vote, this left the voting at 4-1 in favour. One wonders here if rugby not been so quickly usurped in Western Australia by Victorian rules in the mid 1880's, whether WAFA would have seen greater merit in the proposal by 1915.

Tasmania hosted their annual general meeting on March 29th of 1915. This meeting incidentally represented the retirement and honorary life membership of WH Gill to the ANFC. Yet, when Tasmania Football League discussed the proposed change in March of 1915, they deferred voting upon the matter due to the war. Tantalisingly, the following was announced at the AGM regarding amalgamation:

"Owing, however, to the way, such games will not be played this season, and the proposed amalgamation of the games is postponed for a season. Your committee favours the idea, and will, of course, fall into line with any action taken by the Council" [131]

Next came Victoria in April, a vital vote given the overall influence of the Victorians within the council. The VFL clubs voted on three changes that would commence bringing the two codes into unity the following season: placing a cross-bar on the goal posts, introducing a knock-on rule and no forward hand-passing, and allowing a tackle between the hip and shoulder. Collingwood, Essendon, Fitzroy, Geelong, South Melbourne, and St Kilda unanimously agreed to all three changes. Carlton and Richmond only dissented largely to the second rule (knock-on), resulting in passing all three resolutions. In return, the New South Wales Rugby League clubs, as previously outlined, agreed to get rid of scrums, introduce referee bounces of the ball, and ensure the men getting a mark or try will be the goal kicker. Adoption of Universal football was now tantalisingly near. As reported:

"Reports received at the Victorian football headquarters show that the Rugby League will fall into line, and that the South Australian League and West Australian Coastal League will agree, also that three-fourths majorities are assured in Queensland and Tasmania" [132]

Despite being within touching distance, this was as far as Universal Football would come in 1915. The outbreak of the war meant that the ANFC would not have the opportunity to put the rule changes to a formal vote of delegates, and hence while a three-quarter majority looked highly probable, was never formally voted upon. Meanwhile, the NSWRL's adoption of Universal rules was conditional on the ANFC holding up their end of bargain, and thus would eventually lapse. Both Australian Rules and rugby league continued to play their respective seasons during war time under their existing rules.

In the first meeting to occur post-war in December 1919, the ANFC discussed whether to revive the issue of amalgamation and decided against it. The war period saw rugby league's popularity grow, and the desire for amalgamation by the NSWRL too subsided. Incidentally, some scholars have attributed the war period as the moment where the shifting balance of power between league and union became fully entrenched, with union going into recess in 1916 while league continued on. By 1920, there was barely a mention of Universal Football or amalgamation within the press, appearing near instantly forgotten.

If World War One had commenced but a year later, there would have been enough time for the ANFC to legislate the three new amalgamation rules. This would have seen a cross-bar, backwards passing, knock-ons and rugby tackling introduced to Australian Rules. Rugby league would then have concurrently replaced scrums with ball-ups and throw-ins and try scorers would have had to convert their own kicks. If this process had been implemented for even a single year, adopted by the NSWRL/VFL and across the country in season 1915, the broader amalgamation of Australian Rules and rugby league would have been set in motion. Once in motion and even had World War One started, upon a return to peace time, the unification process would have likely continued to completion. But for a year's worth of bad timing, we would have likely celebrated 100 years of Universal Football sometime between 2015 and 2020.

The last attempt to develop Universal Football occurred in 1933, again spearheaded by Con Hickey of the ANFC and Harold Miller of the NSWRL, who had been long time proponents of the unification. Their advocacy for Universal Football is apparent from the page one spread below from the *Referee* publication of 20 July 1933 (Figure 13). Pictured in the top-left is Sir Joynton Smith, patron the NSWRL and the top-right, Dr McLelland, President of the VFL who both also speak positively of the unification within the publication.

The revisiting of the concept resulted in another conference between code officials. Using the code of rules developed in 1914, as listed earlier, only minor changes were then recommended, prior to a trial match being played. These included, the reduction in players from 15 a side to 14, knocking-on allowed from a ball-up (but not general play), a tweak to scoring such that all goals were worth two (conversions were previously worth one) and confirmation of the on-side versus off-side zones as was illustrated in Appendix 1.

A private trial match was played on the morning of August 11 at the Royal Agricultural Ground in Sydney, comprised of players mostly from the Queensland Australian Rules team and several rugby league players. The composition of players for this match can be considered thoroughly disappointing and undoubtedly was not the best endorsement for how well Universal Football could have been played. For a trial match attempting to absorb the best of both Australian Rules and rugby league, it is surprising a greater attempt wasn't made to facilitate a contest featuring a more even balance of players from both codes.

The reliance of lower grade quality Australian Rules players was never likely to provide strong advocacy for the new sport. The Queensland Australian Rules team were drafted as they had finished playing in the Sydney Australian National Football Carnival that was held between August 2nd and August 12th. At this carnival, they broke a 20-game losing streak, but only did so because they matched up against an even weaker minnow in Canberra, making their inaugural appearance. Given the NSWRL finals commenced only two weeks later on the 26th of August, and the VFL finals started on the 9th of September, it is disappointing that a match such as North Sydney versus North Melbourne couldn't have trialled the rules but a month later.

The game itself was played as a 12-a-side game instead of the intended 14, on account of the limited numbers available to play. This in and of itself does not speak highly to resourcing allocated to the trial. Despite the players having little understanding of the rules, those who witnessed and commented on the game gave positive, albeit qualified support to what they saw. The referee of the match called it "a cracker", but stated that it would require at least three or four years before the proposed merger could be accomplished as it was "too fast for human beings to maintain". That Universal Football was "too fast" would have surely delighted advocates at the time. The removal of rugby scrums and reduction in whistle blowing from technical penalties which had beset Australian Rules appeared to produce the desired outcome; a genuinely improved football code rather than a marriage of compromise.

Given the current criticisms of modern AFL surrounding congestion around the ball, and the need to introduce the 'six again' rule to speed up rugby league game play, it is a pity to think what we may have lost in Universal Football, given it was "too fast" for athletes of the time to play. Con Hickey, of the ANFC, said that the game "impressed everybody who saw it, I'm certain that the rugby people were greatly taken with the game they saw"[133]. Harry Miller of the NSWRL said: "At the moment it is even too fast, and no human being could survive it. At the next trial the game will be slowed down, and I expect it to be even more satisfactory. Trials will be continued until the rules are 100 per cent satisfactory".

The language of all involved in the conference and proceeding trial game was certainly courteous and harmonious, and is almost hard to imagine today. As stated by Hickey of the ANFC: "One thing the conference has done is to bring two great bodies together. Arrangements for the fusion of the two football codes have been carried out harmoniously". Or his counterpart Mr Miller of the NSWRL:

> "we have not got perfection in our own regular game… In Victoria, they have things in their game no one wants. Well, why should we not try to create a game common to all, which all will want to play?... Now I say, if both bodies have been able to achieve these things in their own games, why should not the two in concert achieve something still greater, that is a game to appeal to every footballer in Australia?"[134]

As the trial was positively received, and certainly the language of both Hickey and Miller intimated a desire to further the project, it was decided to submit the set of combined rules used in the trial game to the various State leagues for discussion and report. Yet only three days after the trial, Universal Football was killed off by the NSWRL and has never been spoken of since. For this we have Mr S.G Ball, after whom the NSW Under 18 Rugby League competition is named, among other conservative board members to thank. Ball moved a motion that the report be received and no further action be taken. The Eastern Suburbs representative Quinlan countered that "they had been appointed as a body and clubs had the right to know what they were doing"[135]. The motion was seconded by the Western Suburbs and matter closed. Ultimately, rugby league regressivism won at the ballot by 15 votes to 10, and so ended the dream of Universal Football.

It is impossible to comprehend how popular Universal Football would be today had attempts, particularly in 1914, been successful. Relative to its competitors, Universal Football could well have been as popular among Australians as soccer is amongst the British, Europeans or South Americans. Individually, Australian Rules is Australia's most popular sport, with 39% of the population interested in the code and 52% interest among those with a self-identified interest in sport. Rugby league being Australia's second most popular football code, holds a 31% rate of interest amongst the general population and 41% amongst self-identified sport fans. Importantly however, there is a comparatively small overlap between these two fan groups, explained by the Barassi Line dividing them geographically. The small cross-over between Australian Rules and rugby league fans is in fact scientifically small, as explained by marketing theory's duplication of purchase law[136]. When combining the two fan bases then, the amalgam of Australian Rules and rugby league has a combined fan base of 56% of the general population and 74% interest among those with a self-identified interest in sport.

Having genuine interstate contests between NSW and Victoria was among the primary objectives in the negotiations between the NSWRL and ANFC, perhaps almost more so

THE BATTLE FOR FANS, DOLLARS AND SURVIVAL

Figure 13: Front page of the *Referee*. Sydney, NSW. 20 July 1933.

than unifying the game nationally. Here, estimates of viewership for a NSW-Victoria Origin match make the appeal of Universal Football immediately apparent. I estimate that a 2019 Universal Football Origin match would draw a national audience of 4.4 million viewers, far exceeding State of Origin Game 1 (3.23m), AFL grand final (2.96) and NRL grand final

(2.64m). This audience would be larger than any State of Origin game in the NRL's history, surpassing the 4.195 million who viewed Game 3 of the 2013 series.

Universal Football ratings for the weekly club competition would also have likely been 50% to 75% larger than the AFL or NRL currently achieve individually. This would add to Universal Football's monopoly of Australia's top rating programs. Consider that of the top 20 programs of 2019, the AFL and NRL already own the top five. If we exclude News telecasts from our discussion, this leaves the Men's Australian Open final (6th- 2.11 million), Married at First Sight (7th- 1.95 million), Lego Masters (9th-1.89 million), Ninja Warrior (13th- 1.44 million), The Voice (15th- 1.42 million), the Block (16th- 1.41 million) and The Masked Singer (19th- 1.34 million) as illustrative of strongly rating content[137]. Universal Football telecasts, with a Friday Night Football audience circa 1.5 million in addition to finals and Origin, could have singularly accounted for approximately 15 of the top 20 highest rating programs on Australian television annually. Nearly every Thursday night or Friday night fixture would make the annual top 50 programs. Perhaps the only semi-accurate comparison to Universal Football's Australian media dominance is that of American Football upon American television ratings. American football retained 20 of the top 50 broadcasts of 2019 and 13 of the top 16 telecasts[138].

The power Universal Football would therefore wield upon both the Australia sport landscape and media landscape would have been remarkable. If the AFL's $2.5 billion and NRL's $1.8 billion dollar deals are a barometer (totalling a combined $780 million per annum), Universal Football would have likely achieved at least a $600 million per annum rights deal. Universal Football would have had greater market power than the AFL and NRL individually, but would of course had produced less overall content than the AFL and NRL combined. Central revenue would have likely reached $1.2 billion in 2019, making Universal Football about ten times bigger than either the FFA or Rugby Australia.

However, it is highly doubtful whether rugby union in Australia would have become an elite commercial sport had Universal Football taken hold in 1914. Eighty years of Universal Football being ubiquitous across all of Australia, coupled with rugby union's amateur nature, could have easily seen the code completely eradicated before the global professionalisation of the sport in 1995. Soccer, in the face of an even more ubiquitous competitor, at least would have remained part of the subverted culture shared by foreigners and migrants. Making life more difficult for soccer and rugby union is that a Universal Football would have also had profound impacts on sport infrastructure. A single dominant winter and summer code across the whole country, that could both be played on existing oval fields, would have resulted in a prioritization of infrastructure development benefiting cricket and Universal Football. In this hypothetical reality, there could well not have been a rectangular stadium in Australia of a capacity greater than 20,000 in 2021.

The implications of Universal Football would be similarly significant for Australia's media industry. Retaining access to top-flight sport content has been shown to be vital to the success of free-to-air television networks the world over. This is perhaps especially so within Australia, where the value of associating with the AFL, NRL or cricket extends beyond their quantifiable ratings and into the halo effect they have on the broadcaster and their suite of other programming. Television broadcasters do not so much compete at an individual program level, but rather compete in terms of overall viewing share. Having two major football codes and three commercial broadcasters not only means just enough competitive tension to keep inflating the broadcast rights balloon of the AFL and NRL, but also that the structure of the media market will result in one inevitably weaker commercial network.

In some ways however, we could have been worse off through the advent of Universal Football. It would be great to have one truly national football code with an embedded culture and history that brings all of Australia shared meaning. Yet the downside to this would be turning on Fox Sports in winter to find only one football code to watch. The great benefit of our Australian sport culture is that for much of the year, we can channel surf and have at least three alternatives to watch between AFL, NRL, Super Rugby or A-League. The presence of so much football, i.e. supply, is also what keeps the price of attending football so reasonable as compared with other parts of the world. A ubiquitous Universal Football with 16 to 20 clubs could have easily seen the cost of supporting a team head the direction of the NFL. The average ticket price to a Los Angeles Chargers NFL game in 2019, as previously mentioned, was $165 USD.

The 'sleeping giant'

Australian soccer for much of its history has been metaphorically called the *sleeping giant* of Australian sport. Even FIFA itself has leaned on this metaphor in the past, with one such article titled "A sleeping giant is slowly awakening", describing Australia's improving performances in 2000[139]. Twelve years later and in announcing their new rights deal in 2012, FFA CEO David Gallop stated "the former sleeping giant of Australian sport is awake".

There appear to be, however, many such sleeping giants. The United States has also long been considered a *sleeping giant* of soccer, but similarly to Australia, is distracted by other codes. Roy Hay rightfully points out, however, that in America's case, soccer has been America's top women's code for a significant period of time[140]. India too has also been called a *sleeping giant* of soccer. Common, but not universal, to many of these sleeping giants is the presence of more dominant local sports that buck the trend of soccer's otherwise apparent near-global ubiquity. In this respect Australia is not unique, and Hay notes that 'none of the white dominions of the old British Empire has soccer as its main code'. Scholars Majumdar and Bandyopadhyay succinctly summarise both the frequent and tired use of the metaphor in relation to soccer:

"There is still a temptation to classify this, the world's second most populous nation, in the familiar category popularly and vaguely known as 'sleeping giants'. The term has been applied, with varying degrees of justification, to many other countries, especially to those in Africa, where the giant has woken and has startled others into doing so. In China, to take another example, the giant appears to be awake but is seemingly incapable of getting out of bed. The Indian colossus remains mostly in slumber, despite intermittent bouts of insomnia, reacting to the occasional attempts to rouse it. But such awakenings have seldom had sufficient effect as to transcend regional frontiers" [141]

The common interpretation of the meaning of the term *sleeping giant* suggests it involves having significant but unrealised power or potential. Yet, the term *sleeping giant* appears to have a divergent connotation depending on whether it is applied to a dominion in which soccer is the main code, or not. When a country such as China or a region like Africa is referred to as a *sleeping giant* of soccer, the metaphor generally intends to infer that such countries have unrealised power or potential to become a high performing national soccer team. In the case of Africa, they are a *sleeping giant* not because of a lack desire or interest in soccer, but the untapped potential from a lack of critical infrastructure and support. The size of the giant is therefore measured by the disconnect between current, potential and future performance. This is the interpretation applied by FIFA in the abovementioned article about Australia, as can be seen from the first paragraph:

"Runners-up in the FIFA Under 17 World Championship New Zealand 1999, South Melbourne SC taking part in the FIFA Club World Championship Brazil 2000 as Oceania champions, and over 200 players engaged with overseas clubs - Australia has made striking progress as a footballing nation"

How the *sleeping giant* metaphor is applied in the context of countries such as Australia and America, where soccer represents a threat to culturally entrenched and dominant market competitors, is very different. In such countries, the metaphorical *giant* represents a powerful, uncontrollable source of danger for those who must co-exist with it (other sports). Their *sleeping* represents a form of safety and status quo and their awakening a source of peril for those who cohabitate with it. This may sound like an academic over-analysis of a simple phrase, but language and phraseology are among the most powerful components of culture. If you are sceptical, consider some of these references to Australian soccer in reference to other football codes. A column in Melbourne's *Sunday Age* from 2014, titled 'Sleeping giant looms over footy's fragile web', inferring that support for AFL in Australia is somehow fragile and vulnerable to soccer: 'as the long-time sleeping giant of

THE BATTLE FOR FANS, DOLLARS AND SURVIVAL

football codes in Australia gradually awakens'[142].

Irrespective of whether headlines like the above come from a place of journalistic neutrality, clickbait strategy or reinforced football allegiances, they speak to a fundamental challenge that handicaps Australian soccer: being positioned as an outsider and threat to existing order. That's a problem because social identity theory illustrates that being perceived as an outsider never tends to work out well for the group in question. Historian Roy Hay considers soccer to have been Australia's sporting outsider essentially from day one.

> "As a predominantly working-class game, soccer did not receive support from British elites seeking to influence their colonial brethren. Nor did it appeal to colonial elites… the greater availability of open space and grass militated against the development of soccer compared with cricket and Australian Rules, which were more suitable to societies with more land. There is obviously a class dimension to the status of football in Australia. As a general rule British officials and teachers did not promote soccer and the process was left to seamen, engineers, artisans and the like." [143]

Of the competing codes, the AFL both as an organisation as well as its media advocates, are undoubtedly the strongest aggressor against soccer. This is true both in historical terms and contemporary times. The AFL was intransigent in giving up some of Melbourne's stadiums for the FFA's FIFA 2022 World Cup bid, and by the time a bid was produced for the Women's 2023 World Cup, the AFL states had to be near-excluded from the event due to a lack of co-operation on stadium availability.

However, attempting to suppress soccer's rise by attempting to block their access to infrastructure has been part of the Australian Rules, rugby and cricket playbook since day one. As noted by Hay:

> "The popularity of the early established codes of football was reinforced by some explicit antagonism exhibited by these codes as they fought for their patches. In this they were regularly backed by the domestic media and local authorities. Examples abound from Australian experience as soccer clubs were pilloried in the press and refused permission to use football and cricket ovals or banished to remote areas within municipalities at the behest of established sporting bodies."

It would seem unfair to criticise the AFL or any sport league for not wanting to help its competitor, given this reflects a logical business strategy. We would never expect Apple to share a factory with Samsung, or Coke with Pepsi, just because it would help the latter. The difference, however, might be, that sport is treated somewhat like a social good and when our sport leagues don't cooperate, it is sport fans who lose out. With a lack of cooperation between the codes fair game, until it suits everyone (e.g. stadium building), it may be the more overt commentary of journalists that is particularly telling of the aggression found between the codes. As anthropological researcher Dr Buck Rosenberg notes in his work on the Australian football wars:

> "AFL journalists/commentators are not shy to describe the potential of soccer as a 'threat', where the 'local' code needs to be defended, implying that soccer will be forever foreign, forever un-Australian. This focus upon the threat of soccer to their 'local' game barely masks insecurities about the potential loss of AFL's 'essential' role in shaping national identity."

A key reason why we love sport and sport teams so much as previously mentioned is that they can form powerful components of our social identity. Key to social identity theory, as pioneered by the great Polish social psychologist Henri Tajfel, is that such identities create respective 'in groups': people we identify as 'like us' and we become favourable to, and 'out groups': people not 'like us' and we become unfavourable toward. While supporting the Collingwood Magpies makes Richmond Tigers fans such an out-group in the context of barracking within an AFL game, consider that both Collingwood and Richmond fans belong to a greater and arguably stronger in-group of Australian Rules supporters. For this greater in-group, rugby league, rugby union and soccer supporters are an out-group.

It is worth noting, as was explored in part one, that only half of those interested in football support only one code specifically while the other half of football fans support two or more codes. One can therefore support multiple football codes, and indeed, many do. However, each code has its own particularly identified tribe who most loudly advocate for it and this drives the in-group/out-group dynamic between codes. Consider the following quote by AFL columnist and radio host Graham Cornes, in response to the Australian Soccer Federation rebranding itself Football Federation Australia in 2005 (bolding for emphasis):

> "**We Aussie Rules fans**, are sitting blissfully unaware that **our great game** is about to be challenged seriously by soccer. For heaven's sake, **they're** already trying to call it football."[144]

Such in-group/out-group mentality is apparent beyond the media and at the level of fan. Rosenberg's analysis of fan commentary on the AFL website 'bigfooty.com' and soccer fan forum website 'melbournevictory.net' reveal this dynamic at play[145]. Consider the following quote from one AFL fan 'harmesy37' in regards to soccer (bolding for emphasis): "[soccer] could challenge AFL unless we **stand up** to the power of world power culture [sic]". By contrast, 'Garzi' from the melbournevictory forum states 'well hate to say it AFL but the GIANT is AWAKENING'. Rosenberg draws the following conclusion from reviewing the online commentary of AFL and soccer fans:

> "AFL fans are arrogant about the present strength of their code, but are equally fearful of the (future) threat posed by soccer. Soccer fans are just as arrogant. Many express disbelief that soccer has not taken off in Australia, but combine this with a sense of injustice in the manner in which the mainstream media has ignored it. Their arrogance relies on the global popularity of soccer and they put faith in the 'inevitable rise' of the 'sleeping giant'"

Using a social identity lens, it becomes apparent why being labelled a *sleeping giant* could be considered disadvantageous for soccer in Australia: it positions soccer fandom as an outgroup that threatens the existing order of football. Given 63% of people who are interested in football support a code other than soccer, the emergence of the *sleeping giant* represents an out-group threat to nearly two-thirds of Australian football fans.

Australian soccer's *sleeping giant* moniker is thus a double-edged sword for the sport as it positions the sport as a threat to the other football tribes, which encompasses the majority of the domestic football supporting population. A key question is therefore why the expression has such considerable traction amongst the soccer tribe. Much like the fan tortured by supporting a team with a long history of under-performance, the answer to this may in some degree reflect that it serves as a beacon of hope for Australian soccer and its tribe. That despite a history of marginalisation, miss-starts and restarts, the sport retains some innate unrealised potential that will eventually see it rise to glory. However, if disregarding soccer's global prosperity to focus on the domestic setting, one needs a long memory to recall a moment where the sport appeared to be living up to its perceived potential.

Australian soccer's best chance at awakening

Soccer's best chance of becoming embraced by the mainstream occurred in the 1970s, with the Socceroos making their first World Cup in 1974 and the establishment of the National Soccer League in 1977. Soccer's biggest historical failing was its inability to convert this first-mover advantage in developing a national football league into longer term success.

The relaunch of the A-League in 2005 perhaps obscures the notable historical fact that soccer was in fact the first sport to develop a national league in Australia, with the launch of the Philips Soccer League (NSL) in 1977[146]. This pre-dated the VFL's expansion into Perth and Brisbane by ten years and the league's rebranding to AFL by 13 years. The AFL in fact was not even the second league to nationalise. This accolade goes to the National Basketball

League, which followed the NSL shortly after in 1979. Meanwhile, rugby league remains ambivalent towards achieving the 'National' part of its moniker to this day and would more appropriately be called the Tasman Rugby League.

As detailed within Joe Gorman's account of Australian soccer history, the NSL represented a golden opportunity to break from soccer's historical subjugation, yet simultaneously was doomed from inception. The NSL introduced new concepts to football that had largely yet to emerge in Australia. For instance, the introduction of Canberra City to the NSL could be argued to have represented Australian football's first 'franchise' team. Canberra City was essentially the first commercial football franchise, devoid of either a previous team connection (e.g. South Melbourne to Sydney in the VFL in 1982) or connected to a community or club association (e.g. all prior VFL, NSWRL and NSL teams). They in fact pre-dated the Canberra Raiders, with the NSWRL adding them and the Illawarra Steelers in 1982. The West Coast Eagles then joined the VFL in 1987. Canberra City and then Newcastle KB United the following year were in essence, the first attempts to develop franchises in Australian football, precipitating the wave of football expansion that would soon follow.

Although both the Canberra and Newcastle NSL teams had limited success on the field, they were a relative success off the field in the early seasons by comparison to the rest of the teams in the league. In respect to Canberra, the emergence of the Raiders and later the Brumbies may leave people unaware of the fact that the Canberra City NSL team were the foundational tenants of Bruce Stadium, after it was constructed in 1977 for the Pacific Conference games. Canberra City's first game in the new stadium drew a crowd of 6,000 before peaking at 7,450 attendees in round 10 of 1978. While this may appear small by today's standards, consider that the Canberra Raiders' first game in the NSWRL (at Seiffert Oval) drew an attendance of 6,769. Perhaps reflecting the absence of any other established code in the capital at the time, Ian Turner's 'Barassi Line' ran through Canberra, dubbed Australia's "soccer city".

In a similar vein of 'what could have been', Newcastle KB United's debut in the NSL in 1978 drew a crowd of 15,067 to Newcastle's International Sport Centre, with the team pre-dating the entry of the Newcastle Knights to the NSWRL by 10 years. While Newcastle has a rich rugby league history, in fact being one of the foundation teams of the 1908 rugby league competition, it's noteworthy that the Newcastle region was overrepresented by early Scottish and north-east English migrants, and hence too had soccer advocates. Soccer purists should be left wondering to what degree a more broadly successful NSL competition would have shifted the balance of football interest in this region. Here, the 3rd June of 1978 is particularly notable with elite soccer and rugby league having been scheduled for the same day. A total of 6,789 people attended Newcastle's NSL match against the Western Suburbs, compared with only 3,500 for a rugby league match between a Newcastle representative team and the touring New Zealanders[147].

THE BATTLE FOR FANS, DOLLARS AND SURVIVAL

With the exception of Canberra and Newcastle, the majority of the remaining teams involved in the NSL drew from the existing state competitions, resulting in the participation of teams with strong ethnic identities. History would show that this was among the primary causes of the league's downfall, its inability to grow support beyond core soccer fans and into the general population. In this respect, Australian soccer faces the exact same fundamental challenge today that it had more than 40 years ago: how to harness the passion for soccer found amongst ethnic minorities without alienating the mainstream majority?

The involvement of pre-existing teams with ethnic ties turned out to be a strategic error on both a marketing and operational level. In respect to marketing, the ethnicised nature of clubs only reinforced long-held negative perceptions of soccer as being a foreigner's sport. The lack of support for such ethnicised NSL teams was particularly apparent when contrasted to the national team, the Socceroos, who have been warmly received by media and public alike since their 1974 World Cup appearance.

It is a sad reality that Australia has a long and shameful history of manifesting xenophobia via overt vitriol towards soccer. In 1953 for instance, three soccer grounds were vandalised in Adelaide with large signs reading: 'Down with the soccer. Play Australian Rules you bastards'[148], again illustrative of the strong social identities that can be tied to sport. In Melbourne's *Argus* newspaper in 1951: 'People who come to this country and accept all the advantages should support Australian Rules football instead of furthering their own code'. Such examples certainly speak to why Australian Rules football would become compared with a religious cult. Such sentiments were not just the views of extreme individuals but part of the collective mainstream. Writing in the *Sporting Globe* in 1950, JO Wilshaw noted:

"The whole question of these new Australians being allowed to form national clubs should be the subject of special investigation and although one does not advocate a boycott of these recent arrivals from the playing fields it certainly would be much better if they were assimilated into the ranks of teams mainly of British stock and thus became better 'mixers' instead of keeping to themselves"[149]

The retention of previous state teams in the new national competition would turn out to be an error at an operational level also, perhaps the greater of the two errors. The increased expectations of clubs in terms of professionalism and commercialism could not be matched by most clubs in terms of administration, grounds, facilities and marketing. This shouldn't have been surprising to the game's administrators, given these clubs had subsisted at what at best can be described as a semi-professional level prior to the NSL. Gorman's account of the rise and fall of soccer would reach this conclusion, pointing to a prescient quote by prominent soccer pundit of the time, Andrew Dettre. After witnessing what would eventually be the short-lived success of the North American Soccer League, Dettre observed in 1979:

"We are on completely the wrong track. We had the chance when we created the Philips League - but blew it. Instead of creating an entirely new structure on new foundations, we thought it would be enough to throw out the "ballast" (unfashionable clubs) and continue in the same vein. The effects of this mistake are still felt, especially in Sydney and Melbourne."

Soccer's initial error of including pre-existing teams would continue to compound as it expanded upon its fragile base. By 1987, every participating club was supported by an ethnic community and only one team (Adelaide) came from outside of Sydney or Melbourne. Ultimately, while soccer had gained the opportunity to be the first football league to go national, the existing clubs weren't well positioned operationally to execute the opportunity.

Other strategic errors were made along the way. For instance, the televising of the competition on SBS only further perpetuated the perception of soccer as a foreigner's game. This is because the SBS's core identity could not have been more multicultural, or 'ethnic', as would have been perceived at the time. Founded in 1978, SBS was established by the Federal Government of the time, led by Prime Minister Malcolm Fraser, in response to the Ethnic Television Review Panel of 1979 to promote multiculturalism and shift away from the prior assimilation and integration practices.

Ironically then, despite the NSL representing soccer's single greatest opportunity to make significant advancements in the Australian sport marketplace, the competition arguably did the code more damage than good. The competition perpetuated the negative perceptions of soccer for 30 years, arguably causing more damage to the public perception of soccer than had the sport remained in relative obscurity by retaining a focus on state premier leagues. Yet, this period of time is tantalising for considering what Australian soccer could have become today had it set more sustainable foundations for its national league in 1977. With a ten year plus first mover advantage in forming Australia's first national football league, could better strategy have led to the awakening of the sleeping giant?

Empirical research on the value of first mover advantage in the business world is mixed, with the idea that it leads to automatic success a seductive myth. For the many publicised successes (Gillette, Sony, Xerox, Coca Cola), there are many more failures (think MySpace or Alta Vista) that by nature we don't recall because they failed. Consider also however, that people are creatures of habit. The QWERTY keyboard was developed in 1868 and remains the default structure of our modern keyboards in 2021. The QWERTY layout is in fact so durable that it has remained the default layout on mobile phones, despite one-handed typing dictating a completely different layout optimisation to the two handed type writer of 1868.

Research on first mover advantage suggests it is based on three factors: 'firm-level enablers' (a firm's resources and capabilities to cement their advantage), 'isolating mechanisms' (how the advantage is consolidated) and 'environmental enablers' (the pace of market change in response to the first mover)[150]. Applied to the context of the NSL in 1977, had the league been run to its optimal, it is apparent that becoming an embedded and stable commercial league was indeed possible although market dominance was improbable.

First we consider firm-level enablers. In the first year of running the national competition in 1977, the FFA (then ASF) made a $14,305 profit on non-NSL operations and a $40,000 loss on running the NSL. The NSL made about $200,000 in revenue against $240,000 in expenses. The organisation had $236,000 in assets against $144,000 in liabilities to retain equity of about $92,000 to end the financial year. It therefore did not commence the NSL from a position of financial strength in terms of cementing their advantage.

The challenge of resourcing was made more difficult by the NSL embracing existing clubs of questionable administrative capacity, rather than taking what would become the A-League approach of new baggage-free clubs in 2005. Having de-ethnicised club franchises from inception in 1977 would not overcome the prevailing Australian public opinion of soccer as a foreign, wicked, ethnic game. But with a decade and a half until the AFL and ARL would emerge, there was time to slowly shift consumer perceptions towards a more favourable light. Even at the time, the FFA certainly seemed somewhat aware of the tremendous mistake they were making, as made evident in their 1978 annual report:

"Many of the administration problems of the League could well be avoided if the administration of the Phillips League clubs were more professional. It is wrong for P.S.L clubs to be spending well in excess of $100,000 in expenses but to be still relying on part-time administrators."

In respect to 'isolating mechanisms', or how a first mover advantage is generally consolidated, these have been categorised into: a technological/technical edge, monopolising access to scarce-assets or capturing early customers and retaining with high-switching costs. Ironically, it has been Australian Rules, rugby and cricket that have used their access to sporting facilities to historically subjugate soccer from the mainstream. The NSL's best opportunity to cement its first mover advantage was therefore in respect to capturing early customers. To do this, their missed opportunity was to not better leverage being Australia's first national league, positioning the NSL as transcending the Australian Rules versus rugby league divide of the country. Indeed when talks of a Universal Football code were in full force to unify Australian football in the early 1900s, it was rightfully pointed out that soccer was this very alternative.

This represents a considerable missed opportunity as there were certainly pockets of the community not enamoured with their respective entrenched football codes. Sport historian Dr Matthew Klugman recounts how in the 1960s, an organisation called the 'Anti-Football League' emerged in Melbourne who actively sought to reject the dominant rituals of Australian Rules[151]. The Anti-Football League was launched by two Melbourne journalists: Keith Dunstan and Douglas Wilkie, by virtue of a full-page column in the *Sun*'s weekend magazine on Saturday 17th June 1967. The organisation was a somewhat tongue-in-cheek manifestation of their exasperation towards the dominance of Australian Rules football within local culture. The response from the public, as Klugman's research details, was overwhelming:

> "In the first of the day's two mail deliveries Dunstan received 104 letters from people so desperate to join the Anti-Football League they had posted their letters on the weekend immediately after reading of the league. In the next few days an application for membership came in from Darwin, and a Sydney *Daily Telegraph* columnist, Ray Castle, formed the New South Wales chapter of the Anti-Football League for those Sydneysiders against rugby league. Soon memberships were numbering in the thousands, reaching a high of 7,000 – which was considerably more than the number of members for many of the 12 individual Victorian Football League clubs".

For many of these Anti-Football League members, their rejection of the dominant local football code was likely part of a broader rejection of sport culture. Hence, such members were not all likely ripe consumers for a NSL or a NBL. Nonetheless, they illustrate that potential fans existed at the margins of existing dominant football cultures. Furthermore, given how much historical resistance has faced both Australian Rules and the rugby codes on the opposing side of the Barassi Line, one can't help but wonder if the NSL over time would have increasingly been perceived as a palatable second-choice league by comparison.

Had the NSL been successfully established in 1977 and remained a going concern until the current day, irrespective of fluctuations in popularity over time, Australian soccer would today be in a far better state. This would be the case in two important respects. First, the effect of not having a stable competition is apparent when reflecting upon the iconography our four football codes embrace in their marketing. Australian Rules and rugby league regularly lean on imagery fifty years and older to reinforce their cultural and historical significance. The NRL trophy itself exemplifies this, officially called the Proven-Summons Trophy, with the image of the two rugby league legends embracing after the 1963 NSWRFL grand final cast in iron. In the case of rugby union, it is insightful that the game's go-to imagery often reverts to the golden period prior to professionalism between 1980 and 1995, featuring iconic moments and athletes such as David Campese and Mark Ella.

Undoubtedly, Australian soccer's most iconic image is from 16th of November 2005 at Sydney's ANZ Stadium, seconds after qualifying for the 2006 World Cup while being arm-in-arm during a penalty shootout. The photo captures the very first moment of jubilation amongst what would become a golden generation of Socceroos, who appeared destined to coax the sleeping giant from its slumber. Yet beyond this moment sits a comparative vacuum of iconography between 1977 and 2005 to remind the average Australian of soccer's historical existence, let alone significance.

Additionally, whereas Australian rules and rugby league can rely on an overwhelming history of domestic imagery, soccer's scant inventory is strongly international. This leaves the modern A-League comparatively devoid of cultural meaning. There will be no equivalent to Gary Ablett's playing in the same jersey for a while yet, let alone third generation Silvagnis. Rivalries are built from scratch, relying somewhat more artificially upon geography (think the 'F1 derby') rather than history or significance (think 'fibros versus silvertails').

Becoming an A-League club's most capped player, or top goal scorer, represents a less remarkable achievement owing to its shorter existence. Had the NSL been built on stronger foundations, with clubs now in the competition for almost 45 years, becoming Sydney FC's top goal scorer would have more significance if it involved surpassing Robbie Slater's record, for example. A 44 year old NSL in 2021 would still have an asset base of iconography and cultural currency, irrespective of whether the competition had existed on the margins for much of its existence.

The second major implication from the absence of a stable domestic competition is the generational impact it has had upon consumer interest towards domestic professional soccer during a period of rapid globalisation. More than ever, international leagues and particularly the EPL, are siphoning consumer interest away from domestic soccer leagues and concentrating interest towards the world's largest leagues. The future implications of this are explored in more detail in part three, but it's important to note that while media globalisation has accelerated this leakage, international fandom predates the 1990s. In Scandinavia for instance (like many places), support for English clubs on the modern scale can be traced to the late 1960s when Scandinavian TV began weekly coverage of English football[152].

In distant Australia, our European and particularly British dominant migration also meant that English soccer supporters were arriving literally by the boatload. The United Kingdom dominated Australian migration, representing between 50% and 70% of migration until 1960, before commencing a period of decline. However, the United Kingdom accounted for 40% of Australia's migrants in the 1961 (718,345 people) and 1971 (1,046,356 people) census. Accordingly, there was no shortage of potentially imported fans of soccer by the time of the NSL, even if such migrants had to rely on newspapers and radios to follow their home teams. Illustrative of how much our migration patterns have changed, as of 2016, the United Kingdom accounted for only 16% of migrants, followed by New Zealand (8%) and China (8%).

While our British DNA means that Australia has likely always been home to a decent amount of English soccer fans, the creation of the EPL in 1992 and its coalescence with media globalisation has fundamentally changed soccer fandom. The transformation in media in the mid to late 1990s and its impact of opening the global sport economy cannot be understated. For sport teams in the world's most prominent leagues, the period between about 1990 and 2000 was undoubtedly the best possible moment in sport history to be experiencing a period of on-field success. This is because for the first time, such success was witnessed by an ever larger part of the world, creating the first generation of global fan bases.

Netflix's recent documentary 'The Last Dance' surrounding the NBA's Chicago Bulls illustrated how the team's popularity during the Jordan era (1990-1998)[153] transcended into global culture, and arguably, this still provides a halo effect for the team's brand in the modern day. Similarly, among the Scandinavians mentioned earlier, the Liverpool Supporters' Club doubled from 10,000 members in 1994, to 21,634 by 1998 on the back of reducing technological barriers to foreign fandom.

In essence, the globalisation of sport and the growth the EPL coincided with a period where the NSL was approaching a low-ebb, to be soon disbanded and replaced in the early to mid 2000s. The timing of this can be argued to have created a fandom vacuum, particularly among younger Australians, who are now of prime age. At a moment in which technological barriers were falling and the EPL becoming increasingly accessible, nascent Australian soccer fans had little compelling domestic alternative to invest even a portion of their soccer fandom. Even if not setting the sport market alight, had the NSL been built on more sustainable foundations, a new-found curiosity or passion for soccer borne from globalisation would have been more convertible into domestic soccer interest. Instead perversely, the domestic A-League is the one that now appears alien, while a suite of established and successful international club teams like Liverpool are the ones that appear familiar to many Australian soccer fans.

The NSL was undoubtedly a missed opportunity for Australian soccer. The sport may not have realistically had the financial clout or organisational capacity to convert first-mover advantage such that soccer surpassed Australian Rules or rugby league immediately, but so too can it be said that it fluffed a golden opportunity which came at a cost of 30 years progress. The price paid for this lack of progress was not so much that soccer became more oppressed by stronger domestic football codes, as this largely remained the status quo for a century. The price for this lack of progress was that Australian soccer failed to establish a domestic cultural relevance prior to globalisation, resulting in foreign leagues becoming far more important to the average Australian soccer fan than anything that occurs on domestic shores.

Perhaps among the most frustrating elements of Australian soccer's story is that, to understand the strategic decisions and non-decisions made by the game's administrators over the span of time, is to study history repeating itself. To this day, Australian soccer chiefs continue to wrangle with the same structural and organisational issues that beset the game more than 40 years ago and even prior. For instance, the early 1980s saw national league chairman Frank Lowy advocate for the complete autonomy of the NSL from the Australian Soccer Federation, mirroring the exact furore that engulfed the A-League and FFA in the period from 2015 to 2018. Ironically, 30 years later, it was Lowy as Chairman of FFA who resisted the separation of the A-League from the FFA, in sharp contrast to his previous stance. Similarly, this period saw an internal ASF marketing report recommend a need to introduce summer soccer, move away from promotion/relegation to franchises and begin de-ethnicising clubs. While all these recommendations would eventuate in the A-League by 2005/2006, Australian soccer looks to be flipping once more back to winter soccer and towards promotion/relegation in 2021, and with yet another organisational name change to FA from FFA.

Australian soccer fans have perhaps leaned on the sleeping giant metaphor as a way to provide hope that better times for the sport lay ahead in the future. Yet it can at least be questioned whether better times indeed lay ahead. Whether Australian soccer is a sleeping giant, or a deceased giant, is further explored in part three.

Rugby union: Has professionalism been worthwhile?

Two interesting topics emerge from the professionalisation of rugby union. First, the way in which the sport became professional is unique, both in the Australian and international setting, and worthy of revisiting. Australian rugby's path to 2021 has been completely different to the remaining football codes and the events of 1995 make for an interesting yarn in terms of the history of sport. Second, whether 'professionalism' has been 'good' for rugby union in Australia is worth critiquing, given the state of the sport come 2021.

Rugby union is in many ways a unique sport, not only because it officially declared a transformation from being 'amateur' to 'professional', but also because this happened in 1995. Accordingly, while rugby league started compensating players around the time that radio technology was introduced, rugby union did so (officially) after mobile phones and the internet had been invented. That over half a billion dollars was injected into the game in 1995 (via broadcast rights) sounds like a positive outcome for the game, and professionalism may have been inevitable, but it is not necessarily a foregone conclusion that rugby union in Australia is better off today because of it.

A slight oddity in the history of rugby union in Australia is that the game in fact committed to a half billion dollar broadcast deal while still technically an amateur sport. SANZAR (South Africa, New Zealand and Australia Rugby) entered a USD$550 million dollar broadcast rights arrangement with Rupert Murdoch's News Corporation on 23 June 1995, yet the game did not officially become sanctioned as professional until two months later at an International Rugby Board (IRB) meeting on 27 August[154]. This created an awkward situation whereby the Australian Rugby Union had committed to a half billion dollar undertaking without having any players signed to contracts, given their amateur status.

While the Super League war was the headline story of Australian football in the late 1990s, what is less known is that concurrent with rugby league's war, rugby union too only just avoided a commercial breakaway scenario. Rugby union's global commercialisation and professional status was most likely inevitable, but the Super League war also pushed along by rugby union's proceedings in way that could have drastically changed the way that rugby union is governed today.

In 1995, a rival organisation called World Rugby Corporation (WRC) was established. Formed by lawyer Geoff Levy and former Wallaby player Ross Turnbull and funded by Kerry Packer, WRC intended on signing 900 leading world-wide players to create a new global professional rugby union competition.

Given the amateur status of rugby union at the time, it was in some ways an easy target that was ripe for overtaking by a media conglomerate. This was evident in a press release from leading All Blacks players at the time, who expressed confidence in the WRC proposal by stating: "If another option was not on the table, more than half the current All Blacks would have been lost to rugby league". For a period of time, WRC appeared to be gaining ascendency, having claimed to have signed 453 players, including the entire South African Springbok squad. In Australia, the ARU and WRC entered into a battle for the signatures of players. As Dr Braham Dabscheck noted:

> "While individual players may have waxed or waned, signed with one organisation in preference to the other (or with both), they made a crucial decision which was to have a lasting impact on Australian rugby union. They decided to act collectively. On August 10, 1995, 70 players attended a six-hour meeting held at the Park Royal Hotel, Darling Harbour, Sydney, to consider which of the rival organisations they should join." [155]

Australian Rugby players would eventually side with the ARU, as did most players globally to their respective home unions. The WRC released signed players to allow them back to their home union, once realising that the battle for the sport was lost to the traditional hierarchy. In sport history, it appears invaders rarely beat out traditional incumbents.

In an alternative reality, however, and ignoring the real threat of a corporate takeover, rugby union could have stayed stubbornly amateur and followed the path of Ireland's GAA in trying to uphold their traditional values. As time has since shown us, this appears to have merely delayed the inevitable for the GAA, now in the midst of "professionalism creep" that is seeing the organisation and its stakeholders increasingly act professional, but avoiding to officially acknowledge it so. Consider the GAA situation described by local commentator Kieran Galvin in 2019:

> "Anecdotal evidence suggests the following things are happening right now in the world of inter-county GAA - free cars, clothes, fuel and food, unvouched mileage expenses, cash bonuses from benefactors for trophies won, phones, holidays and rent paid for. And there have been stories of "appearance fees" of up to €1000" [156]

The description above is reminiscent of the very behaviours seen in rugby union before it ceded to the inevitability of professionalism. Yet, Gaelic Football and the GAA in this grey area of amateurism-professionalism have been able to maintain a perhaps surprising dominance of the Irish sport marketplace[157]. The GAA as an Ireland-only institution however is able to control its own destiny in a way Australian rugby never could, given it was World Rugby that decided to turn the game professional. Yet the GAA provides an example, albeit rare, that an amateur logic does not necessarily have to be an inferior one. With fears that rugby union appears to be sliding back to potential semi-professionalism, it is worth exploring the roller coaster the sport has taken since 1995.

Rugby Australia has made many commercial mistakes between 1995 and 2020, and a whole book could be written to cover this topic fully. Indeed Geoff Parkes' *A World in Conflict: The Battle for Rugby Supremacy* largely does this, providing an admirable synopsis of Australian rugby's problems as part of a discussion of the greater global context. Criticism of Rugby Australia by Parkes, the media, and among those within the game, can be broadly demarcated into two buckets: poor strategic and financial decision making, and weaknesses in governance. While these are naturally interconnected, I briefly summarise them here.

Strategically, the decision to expand the number of Australian domestic Super Rugby teams has been considered a grave mistake. While on face value, having elite rugby played within as many major Australian capital cities as possible seems a logical objective, the benefit of hindsight shows that expansion has had perverse outcomes. This was because, concurrent with an increasing leakage of players to Europe, domestic expansion contributed to a dilution in local playing talent which saw our domestic teams become less competitive against SANZAAR rivals. This appears to have culminated in 2017, when Australian club teams won 0 games in 25 attempts against New Zealand opposition during the regular season.

This decision would have an ensuing financial impact, as the poor performance of club teams then contributed to what appears a terminal decline in Super Rugby attendance.

The NSW Waratahs recorded their worst ever attendance in 2020, with only 7,191 fans attending their fixture against Auckland in Newcastle before the onset of COVID-19. Never before had less than 10,000 fans attended a home game in New South Wales, and perhaps the restart of the competition with COVID-19 crowd limitations was merciful for the Waratahs. In Canberra, an average of only 8,509 people attended each Brumbies' fixture in

2019, the lowest in the club's history. Perversely, the club was anticipated to incur a financial loss from hosting a quarter-final fixture in 2019, when it was only able to draw a crowd of 11,112, equating to 44% of the stadium's capacity. As Brumbies' coach Dan McKellar noted in 2019: "If we continue to play in front of 6,000 or 7,000 people, the Brumbies won't be around for too long. That's the harsh reality."[158]

Rugby Australia's willingness to support an expansion of the competition into Japan and Argentina, has also been credited as a major strategic blunder. The inclusion of these two teams acted to create an even more unwieldy competition that further alienated the fan base. Wallabies great Mark Ella succinctly summed up the problem in an *Australian* article in 2017:

> "Australian rugby let itself down by expanding too quickly and is now paying a dreadful price. From the moment Super Rugby went from 15 teams to 18 last year, fans have constantly vented their anger on any available forum to let the game's administrators know that what they had created was confusing and uncoordinated. Barely a year on, the governing body SANZAAR and the host broadcasters have come to their senses and decided the format is unruly, too costly and alienating key audiences, particularly in Australia where the fan base is much more diverse." [159]

The other main strand of criticisms of Rugby Australia stem from what can be considered issues of governance. Rugby Australia, like many Australian sport organisations, have had historical struggles shifting from a federated structure of national governance to a more modern form that typically promotes the use of independent, diverse and expert boards. Therefore Rugby Australia, like other national sporting organisations, have historically had issues of alignment between the national body and the state unions. This is made worse in rugby's case by a particular concentration of influence between the New South Wales and Queensland unions relative to the rest of the country. This, however, is not necessarily all that remarkable a challenge within the Australian sport sector, and is indeed so too a challenge in soccer.

What has been the particularly unique governance challenge has been Rugby Australia's alliance with SANZAAR that has effectively ceded considerable control of the domestic game to a larger alliance of nations. Parkes describes the problem with this structure eloquently: "The line between what the ARU can control and fix by itself, and what it is under SANZAAR's control has become inextricably blurred, and the ARU isn't afforded the luxury of parking one to the side while it addresses the other." [160] This sentiment was echoed elsewhere by Wallabies great Rod Kafer:

> "If we sat down today with a blank piece of paper and we said 'let's draw up the model that works best for Australia, a model that would give us sustainable success

for rugby at all levels', there is nobody except those condemned to an insane asylum, who would choose the model we have today. Given that we can recognise that, it's totally frustrating that we seem unable to collectively make decisions that would positively change outcomes for Australian rugby."

In fairness to Rugby Australia, external market forces have been detrimental to Australian rugby. The most significant has been the comparative strengthening of rugby in Europe that has seen the leakage of Australia's best union players increase from a trickle to a stream (but not yet a flood). This is significant because, much like its AFL and NRL counterparts, Rugby Australia has thus far been able to market Super Rugby as the world's premier rugby union competition for much of its existence. One only has to look at the difficultly the FFA has in convincing informed soccer fans to support an A-League team, when such better quality soccer can be found offshore. The accolade of rugby's best competition is now at least contested with England's Championship, with the French Top 14 also growing in leaps and bounds in the last decade. If Super Rugby is still the world's best rugby union competition, it is arguably so despite Australia's involvement. Hence, Australian rugby is increasingly at risk of drifting in consumer perception towards an A-League rather than an AFL or NRL in terms of relative quality.

Rugby Australia has been stuck in what appears a paradoxical cycle in which it has been earning more money yet finding it harder to sustain itself. This reflects upon the financial management criticism some have levelled against the organisation. Specifically, there have been criticisms of the organisation's 'top down' approach of focussing on Wallabies rather than junior development. Citing corporate expenditure of $19 million to community rugby's $4.3 million share of expenditure, former Wallaby, Eastwood President and strong critic Brett Papworth used the following metaphor: "[Rugby Australia has] chopped all the trees down and been a fantastic logging business and they've built massive timber mills, but they've forgotten to plant any new trees".[161] Other financial criticisms have centred on the dissolution of RA's $45 million dollar 2003 Rugby World Cup war chest, for seemingly little tangible return today.

The overall growth in Rugby Australia's revenue from 1980 through professionalisation to 2019's controversial annual report can be seen below, with expense data added from 1992 onwards. The conclusions here derive from a study I co-authored in 2020 with my colleagues from the University of Technology Sydney, analysing Rugby Australia's financial performance. Our study concluded that between 1980 and today, during which time the transformation of the sport industry to a professional logic is captured, Rugby Australia experienced four distinct phases.

The first phase is the 'purely amateur era', spanning from 1980 to 1985, during which revenue grew comparatively slowly and match day revenue accounted for 35% of cumulative income. The data illustrates the shifting financial structure of professional sports. In 1980, match day revenue was 54%, the highest it would be in 40 years. By contrast, sponsorship accounted for only 9% of revenue, the lowest it would be in 40 years.

The second phase of the amateur era spans nine years from 1986 to 1994, which we called 'embryonic professionalism'. What is interesting here is that scholarly research into the concept of professionalism of sport organisations has found it to typically be a transitionary, rather than a transformative, process. In rugby union's case, the fact it officially changed from an amateur to professional status suggests it should have been a transformative process, but this was not the case. Despite maintaining an official amateur status, the period from 1986 to 1994 was characterised by a marked acceleration in revenue, catalysed by the hosting of the inaugural Rugby World Cup in 1987. If we adjust the numbers for inflation, there was a 17 fold increase in revenue in this period to rugby union's last amateur year in 1994. Match day income was beginning to become a less significant driver of revenue, decreasing to 28% of total revenue for the period. What is apparent is that Rugby Australia did not commercialise because of professionalism, but commercialism led to professionalism.

The third phase was the 'growth phase' of the professional era, spanning 1995 to 2007. The significance of News Corporation's broadcast rights deal becomes immediately apparent, with revenue nearly doubling from 1994 ($5.09m) to 1995 ($9.97m). From total revenue of just over $5.09 million in 1994, Rugby Australia was generating nearly $35 million only four years later, resulting in an annualised growth rate of 61% in gross terms. Contributing to this period was hosting the highly successful Rugby World Cup of 2003 as previously identified. The 2003 RWC resulted in a one-off $220 million spike in revenue, contributing to a record $45 million revenue surplus. This was the one year in Australia's modern football history that another football code made more money than the AFL.

The growth phase of rugby union in Australia is particularly apparent when evaluated against the revenue growth of soccer, as arguably the most financially comparable pair of football codes. Figure 14 displays the annual revenue of the two code's national body, averaged over a three year period to reduce volatility. Although these periods don't align perfectly to rugby's identified phases, they do illustrate the particular significance of rugby's growth phase.

In the late 1980s, with rugby union officially amateur but in embryonic professionalism, the code generated an average $1.69 million in revenue. Soccer was financially bigger ($1.96m), being a decade into having established Australia's first national league (but now uprooting and changing it). A decade later, rugby union went from being 14% smaller financially to nearly three times larger than soccer. This period saw rugby union hold an average annual revenue of $28.17 million, to soccer's $9.98 million. A decade later once more, which marked the end of rugby union's unabated growth and the start of their volatility phase, soccer had caught up in revenue terms. Having adopted findings from the Crawford report and disbanded the NSL to introduce the new A-League in 2005, the FFA reached an annual revenue of $77.75 million, to be just shy of rugby union's $78.35 million.

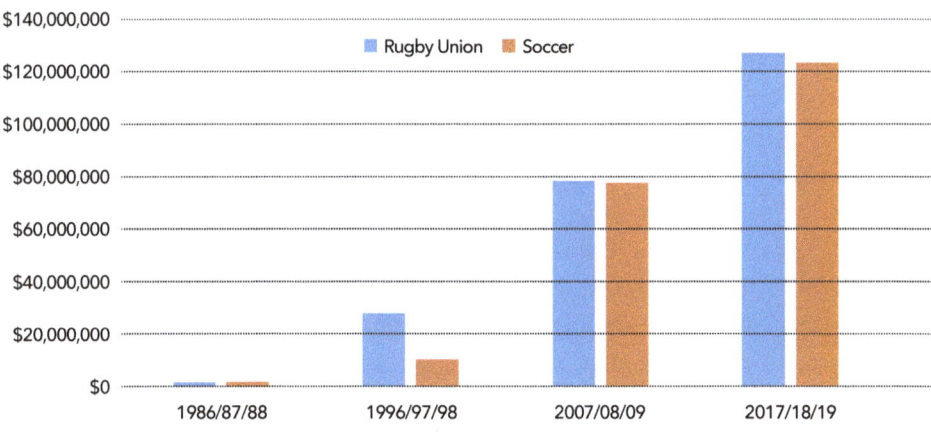

Figure 14: 3 year rolling average total annual revenue.

The fourth and final period can be described as the 'volatility phase'. As the name suggests, this period between 2008 and 2019 saw Rugby Australia revenues become increasingly volatile. During the 40 year period of analysis. Rugby Australia made eight operating losses, of which five were derived from this phase. This period however, also saw the organisation's second and third largest operating surpluses (2017 – $20.2m, 2013 – $27.9m).

Figure 15 illustrates a broader point about the financial management of organisations, including sport organisations. That is, that making money is inevitably tied to spending money. This might seem a truism, but it is worth remembering that wealth derives only

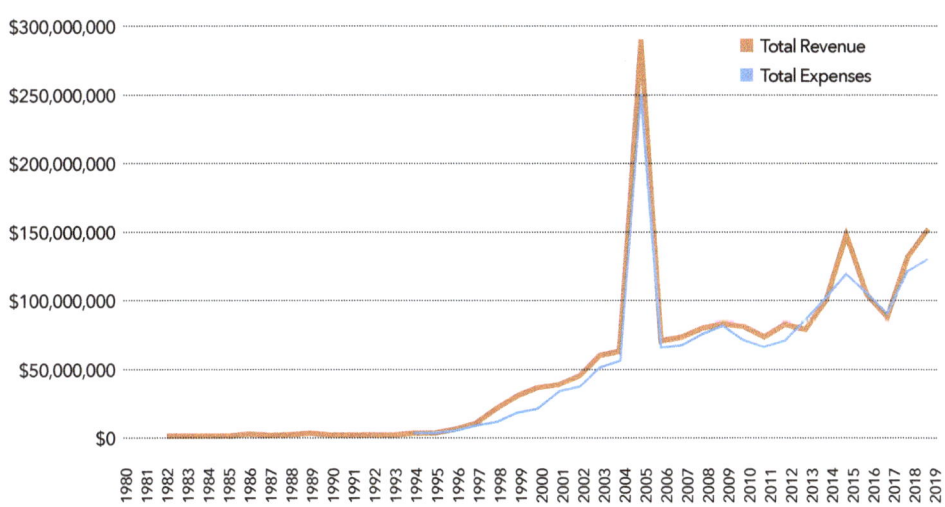

Figure 15: Rugby Australia revenue and expenditure: 1980-2019.

from the differential between earning and spending. The significance of this point is particularly apparent in 2021, with broad criticisms of the NRL that the governing body had not managed to grow its underlying wealth despite a decade of billion dollar broadcast deals. As can be seen in Figure 15, revenue and expenditure are closely tied over the span of rugby union's history.

Despite achieving record surpluses (at the time) between 1994 and 1997, the national body ended up with a weaker balance sheet than it did before professionalism! This was due to the financial distributions over the time period made to state unions. Rugby Australia generated $23,967,585 in profit between 1994 and 1997 but distributed $26,071,271 to its state member unions. While many sports budget on a quadrennial basis to account for World Cups or Olympic participation, it is nonetheless ironic that despite the national governing body's new-found professionalism, it ended up in a poorer financial position. This would see total equity decrease from $2,160,594 in 1994 to negative $113,780 at the end of 1997.

Becoming a 'professional' sport comes with clear consequences for how you invest your organisational resources. For instance, only 15% of Rugby Australia's expenses in 1993 pertained to administration ($1.37 million), with no line item allocated to marketing expenses. By 1998, administration and marketing had grown to $8.11 million and accounted for 41% of organisational expenses. This observation ties back to Papworth's and others' criticism of the seemingly growing disregard of grassroots rugby within the national body. To this point, it is hard to argue on the basis of longitudinal financial analysis that community rugby has been deprioritised by Rugby Australia over time[162].

This is illustrated in Figure 16, which tracks the longitudinal change in community

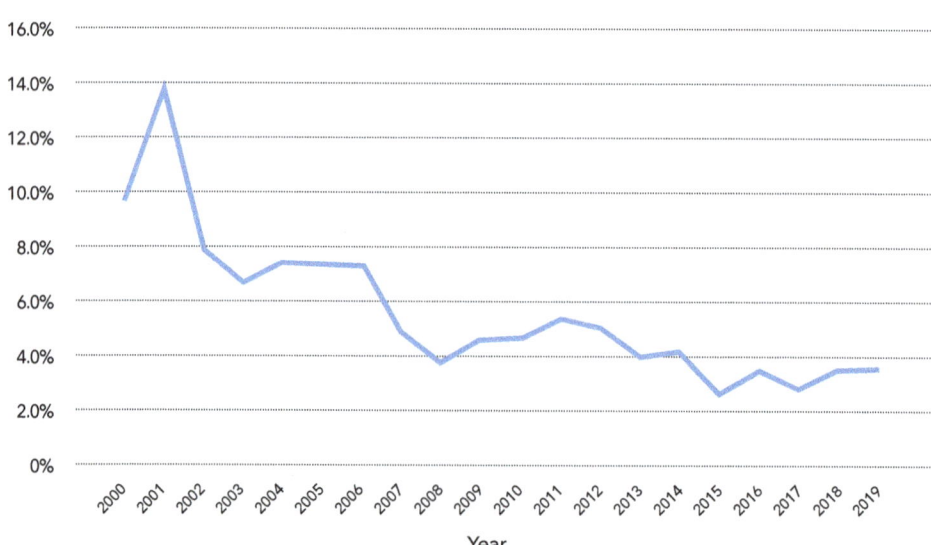

Figure 16: Proportion of total annual expenditure allocated to community Rugby.

rugby spending from 2000 to 2019 as a proportion of overall expenditure. From a peak of 13.76% of expenditure in 2001 ($7.06 million), spending on community rugby has declined in waves over the past 20 years. Year 2015 is the record low, with only 2.64% of total expenditure relating to community rugby ($2.37 million), which happened to also be the lowest aggregate spend on community rugby this millennium. After dipping under 3% once more in 2017 (2.86%), community rugby spend has stabilised to account for 3.6% of total RA expenditure in 2018/2019. Earlier periods are not discussed here due to changes in how expenses are reported in annual reports that have created ambiguity, but it would appear that even the 13.76% peak expenditure in 2001 is low relative to pre-millennium investment levels in community rugby.

For the sake of scale, however, while rugby union spent $4.3 million (3.59%) on community rugby in 2019, the AFL spent $58.8 million on game development in 2019. This represented 13.7% of their overall expenditure. Similarly, the NRL spent $43.3 on game development in 2019, accounting for 8.2% of their expenditure bill. While each organisation is likely to categorise community/game development expenditure in slightly different ways, the scale of both the absolute and relative differences should provoke thought around just how many 'trees' each code is planting for the future. Even when accounting for the absolute size difference between the AFL and Rugby Australia, the AFL is still proportionally investing nearly four times as much into their community development than does rugby union.

Although the above-mentioned strategic and governance matters receive the lion's share of attention when it comes to criticising Rugby Australia, I consider another issue to have been perhaps a greater historical failing of the organisation: its broadcast strategy. Specifically, the single biggest mistake the code has made since it went professional has been its inability to get Super Rugby broadcast on free-to-air television.

In strategic terms, choosing an appropriate mix of subscription platforms and free-to-access broadcast platforms is a little like a person deciding whether to spend (subscription) or save (free-to-access) their pay cheque. Subscription rights will always be tantalisingly larger than free-to-air rights, but come at the expense of widespread exposure to the Australian public. Spending will, therefore, give you an immediate pay-off (financially), whereas savings will accrue to give a bigger long run pay-off (exposure). Hence, it appears no coincidence that generally speaking, successful sports retain a blend of both, much like a successful person retains a mix of consuming and saving their money.

Australian Rugby has had only four broadcasting contracts in its professional history up to 2020, and at each juncture largely maintained existing terms with News Corporation. The inaugural contract in 1996 spanned ten years. The second deal with News Corporation spanned five years from 2006 to 2010 at which point Western Force were added to the competition. The third deal with News Corporation spanned 2011 to 2015 and saw the Melbourne Rebels introduced. The most recent five year deal with News Corporation spanned 2016 to 2020, with the final season impacted by COVID-19.

Rugby Australia's error has been a historical inability to refuse the vast sums of money from pay television, upon which the contractual value proposition was conditional on content exclusivity. In essence, it has spent 25 years taking the largest possible offer, unwilling to make the financial sacrifice necessary to obtain the exposure of FTA television.

To illustrate how damaging adopting a near-exclusive subscription television broadcast strategy can be, British rugby league provides a near-perfect comparison case study to Australian rugby. British rugby league not only retains a highly similar contextual environment but has also mirrored Rugby Australia's broadcast strategy, and their deterioration has been even starker. Come 1996, both sports were:

1. Domestically popular and among the larger sports in the market (when you consider all sports), but still considerably smaller than the absolute largest market participants.
2. Heavily regionalised. British rugby league popularity was and remains concentrated to pockets of northern England. Australian rugby union popularity concentrated to north-east Australia and specifically within particular pockets of Sydney and Brisbane.
3. Underpinned by support from specific demographic segments: the working class in the case of British rugby league, and the upper class in the context of Australian rugby union.
4. Entered into near-exclusive broadcast agreements with a subscription television provider that introduced a record amount of money into the game.
5. Created a new competition to facilitate their new broadcast agreement.
6. Experienced failed expansion beyond traditional markets between 1996 and 2020.

Rugby league had been broadcast on FTA in Britain since the 1950s, but the 1996 restructuring of rugby league saw the game accept an £87 million investment from News Corporation to shift near-exclusively to their subscription television platform. This saw the creation of Super League, the weekly league competition, broadcast exclusively on BSkyB, with only some Challenge Cup matches (equivalent to soccer's FA Cup) and a highlights show broadcast on the FTA network BBC.

Prior to reaching this agreement, British rugby league had been at its zenith, with a cumulative audience in 1995 five-fold larger than in 1992, as seen in Figure 17. Rugby league was still by no means a big sport, but BBC coverage had increased from 6.5 hours in 1992 to 26.5 hours in 1995. In 1990, rugby league received a 5% share of BBC coverage behind soccer (44%), cricket (41%) and rugby union (10%). As noted by scholars Chris Gratton and Harry Solberg, from whose case study these figures are derived:

THE BATTLE FOR FANS, DOLLARS AND SURVIVAL

"The extent of televised coverage was increasing alongside that of the other three professional sports and at the same time television support for the game was also on the increase. Rugby League was enjoying a period of healthy audience viewers, which suggests that televised demand for the game was expanding" [163]

Although the move to BSkyB was both a financial windfall and increased the total amount of hours dedicated to rugby league, it was a disaster in terms of the sport's exposure and audience size. In the period between 1992 and 1995, an average of nearly 5% of the televised viewing population watched rugby league. During the BSkyB period of 1996 to 1999, this dropped to less than 1%. A British market research agency determined that in just six years between 1996 and 2003, interest in rugby league in Britain halved, declining from 20% to 10% of the general population[164].

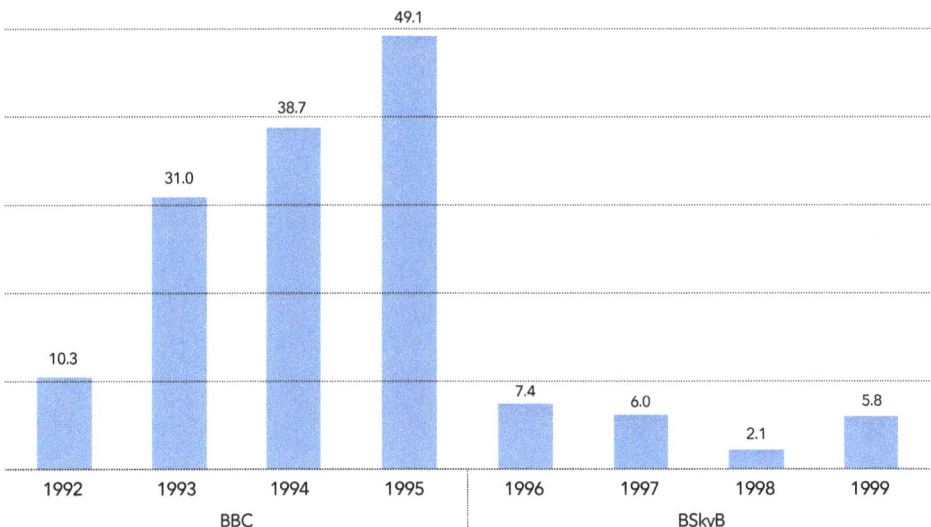

Figure 17: British Rugby League Cumulative Audience (million): BBC vs BSkyB.

While in 1990, rugby league received a 5% share of BBC coverage, by 1998 rugby league's share of coverage on the BBC declined to 2%, trailing Football (70%), Cricket (24%) and rugby union (4%). It is impossible to know if British rugby league would have fared any better with a different broadcast strategy, or whether the rise of the EPL would have inevitably come at the expense of all competitors. However, at a moment where the sport's profile was growing and needed to continue growing, its administrators decided to remove it from public view in exchange for a large financial windfall. Tragically for British rugby league, this windfall would prove to be both an illusion and a curse.

The first contract was renegotiated with two years remaining, and the new five year contract for 1999 to 2003 was reduced to £45 million, down from the initial £87 million intended for the five years from 1996 to 2000. Given the initial contract had two years remaining with £34.8 million attached to it, and the new contract totalled £45 million with an additional three years, these additional three seasons were essentially valued at £3.4 million per annum. This equated to an 80% discount on the original annual valuation and arguably, British rugby league has never recovered. The sport in Britain now relies on a diminishing trickle of subscription television funding, and is commercially too weak to secure a greater FTA coverage component. The sport's decline in Britain was comically illustrated in mid-2020, when it was revealed that Super League had entered a sponsorship agreement with pizza chain Papa John's that saw the organisation provide teams with free pizza, instead of cash, for their league sponsorship[165].

The similarities between British rugby league and Rugby Australia's context and broadcast strategy decisions should be apparent. Australian Rugby, during each of the four moments (besides perhaps the initial contract) needed to carefully consider sacrificing money for greater exposure. In each case, they chose the money instead of making the necessary financial sacrifice to obtain greater FTA coverage. Here, the comparison to the AFL broadcast strategy is stark.

The AFL, who admittedly are wealthy enough to make financial sacrifices for strategic gain, have a history of leaving money on the table to ensure northern markets receive maximum FTA exposure. Every single game involving the Swans, Giants, Lions and Suns is broadcast into their respective home state on FTA television. These teams, and even more so games that do not involve these teams, generate such small television audiences in northern markets that they're not of a commercial scale. They are telecast because of the AFL's desire for exposure as contractually obliged, not because Channel 7 achieves a particularly strong return on investment from this spectrum use.

Given the earlier case study of British rugby league, it is worth unpacking further exactly why Australian Rugby's broadcasting deal, as part of its broader establishment of professionalism, has been a disastrous strategy.

The key to a brand's popularity, irrespective of being a confectionary product, breakfast cereal or sport team, is its availability to consumers[166]. This availability has a physical and mental component. In respect to physical availability, products that are physically easier to buy for more people in more situations achieve greater market share. In typical product categories, increased physical availability can be achieved through improved distribution channels that facilitate greater product exposure for consumers. For example, consider that you can purchase Coca-Cola from literally every supermarket, service station, most fast-food outlets and vending machines. If you live in a capital city, you are probably no further than 500 metres away from a Coca-Cola. Mental availability is achieved by developing genuinely distinctive brand assets, such as colours, logos, tone and fonts, which are uniquely linked in the mind of the consumer to the brand in question.

Super Rugby has historically failed to maximise physical availability in several important respects, starting with physical attendance availability. Although the code is underpinned by a high quality club competition in both Sydney and Brisbane, at the pre-eminent Super Rugby level, there have simply been too few local teams playing too few local fixtures.

In 2018 for instance, the NSW Waratahs played nine Super Rugby fixtures in Sydney, equating to only 10% of the comparative supply of NRL fixtures. The Waratahs' nine fixtures were also fewer than half of the total AFL fixtures held in Sydney in 2018 (19), and nearer to a third of the total A-League matches played in Sydney in the calendar year. There are simply far fewer opportunities to watch top-flight rugby union matches in our major population centres than there are AFL, NRL or A-League.

The second half of the physical attendance availability relates to the dispersion of matches. Prior to 2018, the NSW Waratahs had barely played a regular season fixture away from the Sydney Football Stadium. The one exception was the signing of a deal in 2009 to play at least one fixture at ANZ Stadium until 2015. Otherwise the team has almost exclusively played fixtures in the eastern suburbs-based Sydney Football Stadium, only once relocating a fixture to the Northern Beaches in 2018. In practice, the Waratahs may play too few matches to be splitting their fixtures across venues, but their near exclusive scheduling of fixtures in the eastern suburbs creates fundamental barriers to the accessibility of the code.

This stadium barrier acts as a double-whammy in conjunction with limited supply. Rugby union is already far more popular in the north-east of Sydney and far less popular in the south-west. Accordingly, by playing all its fixtures in the east, the Waratahs make themselves most accessible to people who are more likely to be fans already, and least accessible to potential new customers in the south-west who are less likely to be fans. The club's nomadic existence from 2019 onwards due to the redevelopment of the Sydney Football Stadium provided a brief opportunity to experiment with the team's physical footprint, although curtailed by COVID-19.

The parallels to the NSW Waratahs physical availability problem is evident in the broadcast strategy of Rugby Australia. Most pundits who have criticised Rugby Australia's reliance on subscription television have focussed on the fact that Australia's Foxtel service has historically struggled to break a 30% penetration rate among the Australian population.

Yet, this does not articulate the full historical problem for Australian rugby. The bigger problem is that Foxtel customers are more likely to already be rugby union fans, while non-Foxtel customers are the cohort rugby union needs to be converting into fans but cannot reach. Rugby union is more popular in higher socio-economic areas of Australia, which include Sydney's northern and eastern suburbs. According to the ABS Socio-Economic Indexes for Areas, seven of New South Wales' ten most socio-economically advantaged suburbs are within Sydney's North Shore or Eastern suburbs region[167]. By matter of comparison, there are only four Sydney regions among the state's twenty most socially disadvantaged, and all are west or south-west suburbs.

Subscription television is a luxury good and hence, the target market and subscription base of Foxtel is overrepresented by affluent households and underrepresented among working class and disadvantaged households. This explains why rugby union has historically represented attractive content for Fox Sports: its fan base aligns very neatly with Foxtel's customer base. But this alignment between rugby union's existing fan base and Foxtel's customer base has been the code's big broadcasting weakness. Broadcasts of Super Rugby are mostly reaching households of people likely to already be rugby union fans, rather than new households where new fans might live.

For those 300,000 people in the eastern suburbs who are a short commute away from the football stadium and more likely to have a Foxtel subscription, Super Rugby has been highly accessible. For the near 3,000,000 people in west and south-west Sydney, who are less likely to have a Foxtel sport channel subscription, there have been nine opportunities per year to physically access Super Rugby by driving over one hour to the eastern suburbs to attend a fixture.

Compare this to the AFL strategy of ensuring all Swans, Giants, Lions and Suns games are telecast live on FTA. Any viewer from New South Wales who has their television on during a Swans or Giants match could stumble upon the respective AFL fixture and become enthralled by what they see. Similar, too, the channel-hopping Queenslander during a Brisbane Lions or Gold Coast Suns game.

As a final point of illustration of how the professional structure of Super Rugby has not worked for Australian Rugby, I present some Google Trends search data (Figure 18). What this reveals is that the AFL, NRL and A-League have never had greater Google search volume than in 2019.

Google search volume of the NRL tripled (306%) between 2004 and 2019, closely followed by A-League growth (266%) and AFL (259%)[168]. Each of these three codes has

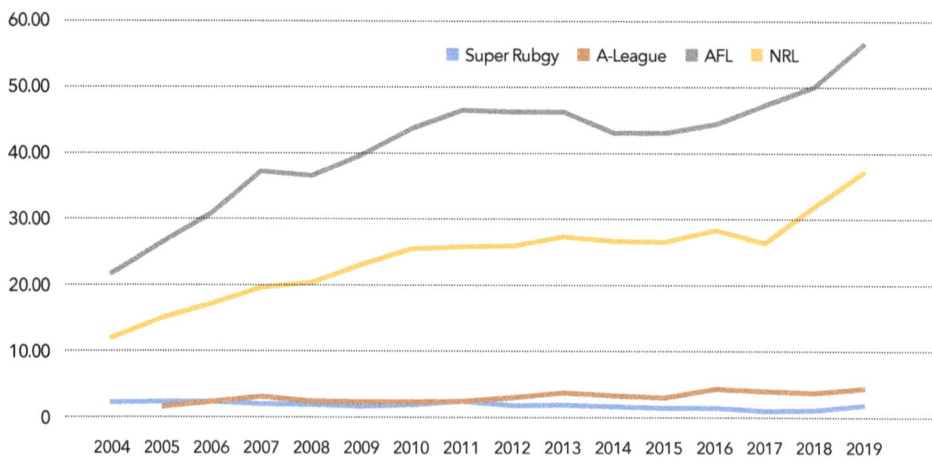

Figure 18: Relative football code search volume, annualised and over time.

experienced a generally positive slope in search volume over time, with the exception of the A-League, which is more volatile because of being a new league in 2005. Meanwhile, Super Rugby had nearly 30% less search volume in 2019 than it had in 2004. Its peak was in 2011, coinciding with the Queensland Reds winning the competition. However, this was only marginally higher (11%) than in 2004 when the ACT Brumbies won the competition. At Super Rugby's lowest ebb in 2017, search volume was only half of what is had been in 2004. After 2011, Super Rugby drifted to a distinct fourth position among the codes in terms of search volume, as it began to ebb downwards and A-League upwards. In 2019, Super Rugby generated only 3% of the relative search volume of AFL on Google.

The evidence that rugby union has now drifted to a distant fourth in the Australian football hierarchy since professionalism is now overwhelming. Admittedly however, this section perhaps unfairly focusses on the considerable gloom and skips rugby union's brighter historical moments.

Most notable, of course, was when Australia hosted the highly successful 2003 Rugby World Cup with Super Rugby interest and crowds flourishing. In this brief window in the early millennium, the Wallabies were perhaps on par with our national men's cricket team as the flagship Australian team, and there was genuinely belief that rugby union could supplant rugby league as Australia's number two football code. In this respect, the negotiation of the second broadcast deal for 2006 to 2010 was the most fatal strategic error for the code. Planning and negotiating this broadcast deal in the years immediately following the 2003 RWC, when the sport was at peak popularity, should have been a catalyst to leverage a FTA broadcast component for Super Rugby. This opportunity as we now know, was missed and the game has gradually regressed since.

Has professionalism been worthwhile for rugby union in Australia? The most pragmatic answer is that remaining amateur was an implausible scenario, given the game was at the precipice of a corporate takeover and vulnerable to continued player raiding by rugby league. Yet the question of whether the professional period has been more prosperous for the code than the preceding amateur era is a different one, to which the answer may in fact be no.

There have been few bright spots for Australian rugby since professionalism, and negative sentiment towards the code has continued to grow, perhaps culminating in 2020. Rugby Australia went within a whisker of being declared insolvent, requiring the provision of a $14 million dollar emergency loan from World Rugby to help convince auditors KPMG to sign off on the 2019 financial accounts and declare the business a going concern[169].

The 2019 accounts showed a record $9.4 million dollar loss, attributable to reduced match day revenue from participating at the RWC and the Israel Folau legal saga. Potentially of more concern, however, as noted by KPMG, is that RA's financials showed a net deficiency in current assets (versus current liabilities) of $6.7 million at 31 December. In other words, Rugby Australia's balance sheet is incredibly weak. As of 1 January 2020, it had net assets of

$18.3 million, but this included $21 million of 'intangible' assets such as trademarks, software and leasing rights, as well as $1 million of memorabilia. It has laid off a third of its workforce in response to the required organisational restructuring with a view towards a post-pandemic environment, as discussed further in part three.

Super League and the knee-capping of rugby league

In the mid to late 1990s, a commercial dispute between a league's stakeholders saw a sport ripped apart. In the process, fans became disillusioned by a sense that greed and commercialisation had poisoned their beloved sport from the pastime they loved and cherished. Fans were lost to the game, with many pundits wondering if the game could recover, let alone ever be the same.

Although the above paragraph could easily summarise the Super League saga, it also describes a sport management catastrophe that pre-dates the Super League war by just a couple years.

In 1994, in the middle of their season, America's Major League Baseball Players Association commenced what would become a seven month strike, or 'lock-out'. This resulted in the cancellation of the 1994 World Series, the first time there had not been a World Series since 1904 and the first time a North American sports league lost a post-season due to an industrial dispute. It would take 232 days to reach a resolution, which spilt over into the 1995, resulting in a shortened season (from 162 to 144 games … per team!). Evidently, rugby league does not hold a monopoly on calamity. This was MLB's Super League saga.

The lockout is notable for marking the end of baseball's reign as America's dominant past time. Although Gallup polling suggests American football overtook baseball in the late 1960s, according to ESPN's internal behavioural data, American football surpassed baseball as America's favourite pastime in the autumn of 1994 because of this strike[170].

The effect of the lockout on baseball's popularity was clear and profound. Average attendance during the 1994 MLB season was at near record highs (31,285). Upon returning the following season, despite a scarcity of baseball that could have increased crowds, average attendance decreased by 20% to 25,034. It would take 12 years for MLB average crowds to recover to their 1994 levels.

The drop in attendance was also reflected in the sport's broader popularity. According to Gallup's survey, 21% of people cited baseball as their favourite sport in 1994. This was in fact the highest this figure had been in nearly 20 years, illustrating that baseball was riding a wave of momentum. One year later, baseball was the favourite sport of only 16% of the American population, the lowest it had been to that point. Within seven months, approximately 10 million adult Americans had dropped baseball as their favourite sport. By 1997 and in the midst of Michael Jordan-mania, basketball (17%) would overtake baseball (14%) as America's second favourite sport.

The parallels to rugby league and the Super League war are in some ways uncanny. In a fiercely competitive sport market, MLB had momentum in 1994 but lost it in a bitter dispute between stakeholders over finances. The timing of their strike was particularly inopportune, given it coincided with the rapid rise in popularity of the competing NBA in particular. In the case of MLB, club owners were losing considerable money and therefore wanted to introduce a salary cap with other amendments to improve profitability.

Similarly in rugby league, it can be argued that Super League was able to manifest because of both the financial insecurity of clubs and financial imbalances between them. Yet unfortunately, perhaps the greater parallel is how Super League derailed rugby league's momentum at a time that allowed its competitors to profit. Between 1988 and 1992, rugby league crowd attendances grew 65% and television ratings rose 70%[171]. Yet by 1996, rugby union was able to professionalise and started pinching back players for the first time in 88 years. Meanwhile, the Super League period represented perhaps the single moment from which Australian Rules firmly accelerated ahead of rugby league as the undisputedly most popular football code in Australia.

Rugby league fans old enough to have witnessed Super League first-hand hold overwhelmingly negative experiences from the period. However, the purpose of this section is not to recount how or why Super League happened[172]. Rather, it is to illustrate how Super League derailed rugby league at a critical moment in history. In particular, I want to focus on two important and interrelated issues that illustrate how Super League impacted rugby league and football more broadly: fan base changes and the distribution of clubs.

Football fan base changes between 1994 and 2010

One particular public dataset provides us an opportunity to see, in real terms, how fan support towards rugby league changed during this period. Between 1994 and 2010, the ABS ran five surveys around spectator attendance at sporting events, providing a comprehensive longitudinal dataset during this vital period of sport commercialisation and the Super League war[173].

The data displayed in Figure 19 and in Appendix 2 reveals something that I would myself confirm in my own more recent research; the AFL is able to achieve such comparatively exceptional crowds because of two factors that require distinguishing. First, **more people** within the population attend AFL games (penetration) and second, these people attend games **more often** (frequency). Yet, much like a bike sprint where the cyclist chooses their moment to break from the pack, the ABS data reveals a notable acceleration in the AFL's market dominance between 1994 and 1999.

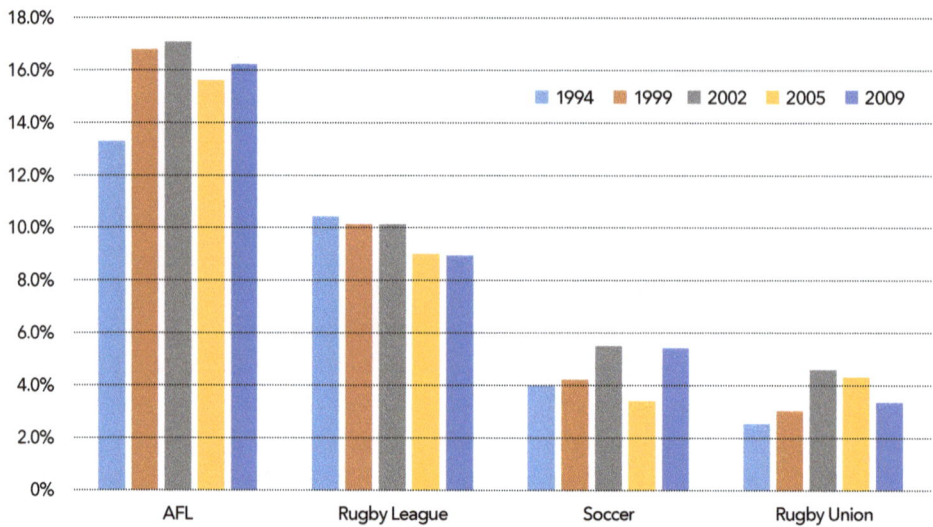

Figure 19: Proportion of adult population attending at least one game in preceding 12 months.

The closest rugby league came to matching the AFL's attendance penetration was in 1994, where rugby league achieved an attendance penetration rate 78% of the AFL. By 2009-2010, nearly half as many people (55%) had attended a rugby league match compared with an AFL match. This represents a 30% decline from 1994. The trends illustrated here should be alarming for rugby league administrators and enthusiasts, with attendance penetration appearing to be on a terminal declining trajectory. Attending rugby league is undisputedly becoming a less popular leisure activity, more so than every other football code, no matter what excuse is provided by the code's administrators or admirers.

Rugby league's response to poor crowds has typically been that it's a 'television sport', but this is an illogical defense, akin to admitting that rugby league fans aren't passionate enough about the sport to leave their house. It is hard to reconcile that on the one hand, Roy Morgan research suggests that the Manly Sea Eagles and Penrith Panthers held a combined fan base of 513,000 people in 2017[174], yet on the other hand, these two clubs were only able to attract 15,408 attendees to Allianz Stadium for their finals match that year[175]. Ignoring the likely crowd contribution of SCG trust members who attend as neutrals, at best these figures suggest a conversion rate of only 3% of 'fans' attending a finals match featuring their teams. Typical of many Sydney-centric rugby league administrators and pundits, Penrith Panthers' General Manager at the time, Phil Gould, came out in the aftermath of this match and found a way to blame the NRL for the crowd rather than reflect on his club's own deficiencies:

"I often wonder if the NRL cares about the Sydney clubs... My feeling has been for over a decade that (the NRL thinks) as long as Melbourne and Brisbane were doing well, rugby league was doing well... You might think that's a biased view from a bloke who grew up in Sydney, but the figures sort of back it up" [176]

The figures do indeed 'back up' that rugby league has performed poorly compared with rival football codes in the past 25 years. Rugby league was the only football code whose attendance rate in the population went backwards between 1994 and 2010. In 1994, 10.4% of the population attended a rugby league game. By 2010, this had declined to 8.9%. By contrast, the Australian Rules attendance rate increased from 13.3% to 16.2%, soccer from 4.0% to 5.4% and even rugby union grew from 2.5% to 3.3%.

To make matters worse, while the other codes each experienced a growth in the number of people attending six or more games a season (soccer +25%, rugby union +17%, AFL + 8%), rugby league managed to record a significant decline (-9%) in the number of fans attending six or more games per year. Rugby league is truly the outlier in the worst possible way, having seen a decline in both their attendance penetration and frequency. While every other code has more people attending more often, rugby league had less people attending less often in 2010 compared with 1994. Yet the broader question of who is at fault; clubs, players or the NRL central administration, is a controversial one we return to in part three.

The ABS attendance data provides several other notable insights into how football attendance changed between 1994 and 2010 (Figure 19).

The most notable is that patronage by women accounts for a large portion of the overall attendance growth in football. In 1994, women represented 33% of the audience for rugby league, union and soccer and 37% in AFL. By 2010, this was 36% in union, 38% in league and soccer and 41% in AFL. Evidently, the codes have been successful in growing their accessibility to women.

Remarkably, although rugby league has remained dogged by the actions of some its players towards women, it has in fact been women who have saved rugby league attendances from declining even more sharply. An extra 100,000 women attended rugby league games in 2010 compared with 1994, a 22% growth in absolute terms. Alarmingly for rugby league, fewer men attended rugby league fixtures in 2010 (969,000) than did in 1994 (976,000), despite a growing population.

By comparison, the AFL has been an absolute success story during this period. Between 1994 and 1999, the AFL experienced a 34% surge in the number of people attending AFL games, undoubtedly aided by the fortuitous timing of the Swans' success. Indeed the AFL attendance rate in New South Wales jumped from 1.8% to 4.3% between 1995 and 1999, just as rugby league was on its knees.

The AFL's overall attendance penetration grew 51% between 1994 and 2010. What is notable is that despite growing the base of its audience during this period (+51%), the AFL was also able to get more people attending more regularly (6+ games growing 8%). The contrast with rugby league could not be sharper.

The ABS data also provides valuable insights into the progression of soccer and rugby union over this period. The 15 year period of 1994 and 2010 are arguably equally significant to these two codes as to rugby league. The launch of Super Rugby in 1996 provides a pre and post period to compare attendance behaviours with the professionalisation of the game. Similarly, the launch of the A-League in 2005/2006 provides data comparisons to the prior period of the NSL[177].

In respect to rugby union, it is clear that the mid-2000s represented a watermark period for the game. As illustrated in Figure 20, which plots the comparative attendance rates of the codes to AFL, the 2002–2005 period marked the smallest differential between the rugby codes in terms of attendance popularity. In 2005, this was aided by the introduction of the Western Force but in 2002 this was no mean feat given there were only three domestic teams in Super Rugby. With the current doom and gloom surrounding rugby union, it may be hard for some to recall that in the mid-2000s, the NSW Waratahs averaged 30,000 fans and the Brumbies 20,000 fans for their fixtures. From this watershed period, the decline in rugby union attendance in 2009 was the beginning of a trend line for the decade to come.

In respect to soccer, the impact of the A-League can also be seen in the data. Come 2009, soccer reached its highest attendance rate (33%), relative to the AFL. This saw soccer approach the attendance levels of rugby union for the first time since the rival code turned professional.

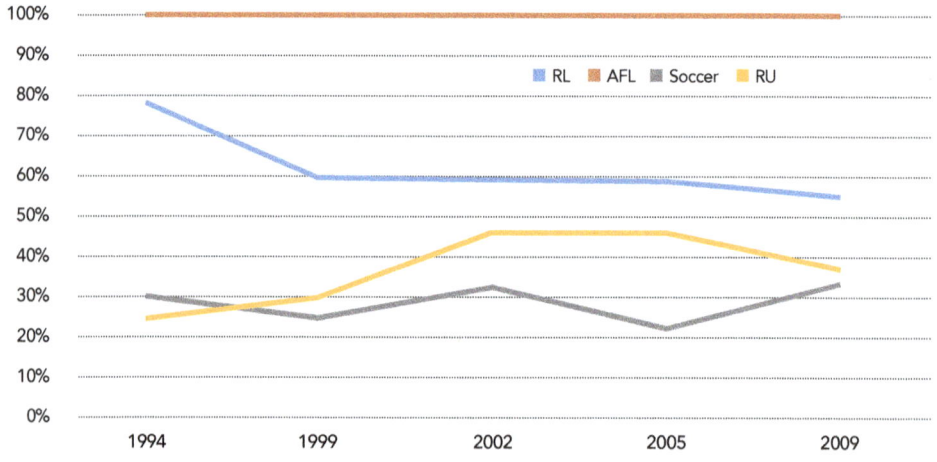

Figure 20: Football code attendance standardised against AFL attendance rate.

Rationalising rugby league clubs with no strategic vision for the future

The most lasting impact of the Super League war on rugby league in Australia has been how the post-war rationalisation of clubs would go on to dictate the physical footprint of the

THE BATTLE FOR FANS, DOLLARS AND SURVIVAL

NRL since. At the time of rationalisation, there were in essence 22 potential clubs between the ARL and Super League competitions as well as the soon to be formed Melbourne club. If all these clubs existed today, the NRL would have clubs in nine of Australia's ten most populated cities (plus Townsville in 13th). Instead, the NRL currently operates in only six and half[178] of Australia's top ten cities.

How rugby league reached a fourteen team competition by 2000 was perhaps brought to public attention by the plight of South Sydney's expulsion and reinstatement into the competition. Their legal battle is most remembered by the iconic rally in late 2000 that saw an estimated 80,000 protestors march for the Rabbitohs against News Limited. However, their litigation against News Limited also brought to light the process by which the 14 team goal was set and the inclusion criteria for NRL clubs measured. This admission criteria document arguably remains among the most important documents ever produced in rugby league, being responsible for setting the parameters for which the future footprint of the game would be determined.

Despite the critical role of the admission document in setting the future footprint of rugby league, the criteria for evaluating clubs was exclusively focussed on past performance. Nothing in the evaluation criteria focussed on the future strategic contribution of teams or regions to the long-term growth or positioning of rugby league. This did not necessarily decide the fate of the NRL, as most of the expansion clubs folded before reaching the criteria phase, but it speaks volumes about the strategic orientation of the NRL as a new governing body.

The selection criteria to assess future admission, had there been too many applicants, was based upon assessing clubs on past performance rather than future direction. For example, how many competition points a team had accrued over the previous four seasons was included in the criteria[179]. Hard to comprehend is that on-field results were weighted in such a way that more recent seasons were more important than earlier seasons. For example, performance in the 1999 season was four times more important to the admission calculation than performance in season 1995. Given teams naturally move up and down the competition ladder from season to season, this admission criteria around on-field performance was essentially a lottery that rewarded those who were currently experiencing success. If this had happened more recently (2016–2019), the North Queensland Cowboys, whose best two seasons were 2016/2017 and worst two were 2018/2019, would have come out 14th in the calculation, despite being tied for 8th in overall performance if applying an equal weighting.

The absence of strategic measures in the criteria was a conscious decision by the new league's administrators to provide objectivity, as outlined in the notes of Judge Finn's ruling. Within the draft admission criteria circulated in May 1998, the introduction section of the selection criteria outlined the mechanism to differentiate between competing tenderers as "intended to provide an objective basis for ranking tenderers through a calculation of measurable criteria, appropriately weighted"[180]. Yet, the absence of consideration towards factors like population catchments or the growth potential is hard to comprehend.

Despite attempting to form objective criteria, after a consultative process with clubs, feedback was provided that "The vastly different histories of the competing clubs together with the different existing facilities, locations etc. means that the playing field starts out being far from level with respect to all of the suggested draft criteria".

Selection criteria designed to achieve a level-playing field is mind-blowingly counter-intuitive. The purpose of a selection criteria is to help distinguish and rank alternatives, not make the alternatives look as equally appealing as possible. It would be akin to saying that everyone should have an equal chance to play in the NBA and therefore characteristics like height, shooting accuracy, and physical ability should be disregarded because they create a 'far from level playing field' among prospective NBA draftees.

Given important strategic metrics like existing facilities, team locations and club histories would result in an uneven playing field upon a selection criteria, they were unsupported by clubs as evaluation metrics. Instead, the feedback concluded that recent on-field success was the best way to decide the future footprint of rugby league: "Actual performance on the field is least likely to be manipulated and has the benefit of being readily identifiable".

In May 1998 the merger that would become the NRL was executed. With it was a merger agreement that stated the organisation's priorities which was to implement the agreement such that: *"public interest and support for the game of rugby league is maximised"*. Yet, it is difficult to reconcile the NRL's adherence to this principle given the significant rationalisation which followed, including major metropolitan city team Adelaide. Clause 7 of the agreement provided the definitive structure of the competition, enshrining a 14 team competition by 2000 and beyond.

At this juncture, how the number 14 and the rules around its composition were determined is worth revisiting. Put simply, it was a compromise made in June 1997 between News Limited who wanted 12 and the ARL who wanted 16.

In the Memorandum of Understanding (MoU) signed at the end of 1997, it was decided that these 14 teams would contain no less than six and no more than eight teams from Sydney and conversely no less than six and no more than eight from outside of Sydney. The MoU also stipulated the order of inclusion among prospective club applicants, vitally important for how the NRL's club composition would manifest. This order was: (1) merged Sydney clubs, (2) regional clubs (i.e. any non-Sydney club) and (3) stand-alone Sydney clubs. Following this, the abovementioned selection criteria would apply if there were more applicants than positions, given the structural limitations on the competition and the six-eight split. With that, the boundaries of what the NRL could become were set, created through compromise rather than designed via strategy.

The composition of the NRL was essentially left to chance rather than any concerted strategy or design, given that the Sydney clubs had autonomy to determine whether to

THE BATTLE FOR FANS, DOLLARS AND SURVIVAL

merge or stand alone. Given Super League was predominantly composed of regional clubs and the breakaway was wholly premised upon expanding the boundaries of the sport, it is surprising in some respect that there wasn't greater intervention in determining which clubs would form the NRL. Given how damaging the Super League war had been, however, the non-interventionist nature of forming the new NRL may have reflected a desire to not create further warring and controversy. One can also only presume that after a short but financially costly battle, the growth appetite of News Limited to retain outposts in Adelaide and Perth was diminished despite the Merger Agreement clearly stating a key objective of the new entity was to maximise interest in rugby league. As the ABS sport attendance data between 1994 and 2010 showed, rugby league certainly failed to achieve this objective.

The NRL made two critical mistakes during this period. The first is that it did not push harder in pressuring Sydney clubs to merge. This might seem obvious now, but consider the golden opportunity this period provided. From an original pool of 12 Sydney teams[181], the NRL ended up with nine, only a 25% reduction. It's not as if the league didn't understand that there were too many teams in Sydney and too few elsewhere.

In 1992, the Bradley report had been commissioned to review the Australian Rugby League and in fact concluded that a 14 team competition was optimal! To reach this number, it was suggested that there should only be five Sydney teams and nine elsewhere: "Sydney based clubs are going to have to move to new areas, merge or be relegated from the League". It was never going to be a particularly easy task to reduce Sydney teams, but there was also never going to be a more opportune moment to pull the much needed trigger.

The big catalyst for the NRL's failure to merge more Sydney teams was that five of the ten pre-existing regional teams were dissolved by the end of 1998, leaving little pressure on Sydney teams to merge. With the addition of Melbourne in 1999, there were only six regional teams left, guaranteeing eight spots for Sydney teams. Remembering that regional teams took precedence over unmerged Sydney teams, had two additional regional teams (such as Adelaide or Perth) remained in existence for 2000, unmerged Sydney teams would have been competing for only six franchise slots. This would have created greater competitive tension to merge and rise from last to first in the inclusion hierarchy.

History would therefore suggest that News Limited's decision to shut down Perth in 1997 and Adelaide in 1998 was therefore a huge strategic loss from the game's perspective. Given how much money had already been lost, perhaps only a few more million dollars into Adelaide and Perth could have at least pressured Sydney clubs into better mergers. Twenty years after Super League, former CEO John Ribot said that Adelaide 'was closest to making a dollar'[182], despite entering the competition the same season as the Adelaide Crows won their first AFL premiership and only a year after Port Adelaide also joined the AFL competition.

The second critical mistake during the rationalisation process was that the desire to facilitate mergers appears to have been more important than ensuring the <u>right</u> teams

117

merged. The design of the inclusion criteria incentivised teams to merge not because they made for logical partners, but out of shared necessity. Here is where game theory helps to explain why suboptimal mergers occurred. Essentially, there was little incentive for strong teams to merge with a weaker team (to become even stronger) because they were readily assured of survival by the selection criteria. Nor would it make sense for two strong teams to merge. The only combination of teams for which merging was a logical strategy was two weak teams who, by merging, would automatically be included in the NRL competition.

Perhaps the best example of how a good potential merger was ignored for a bad one involves the Western Suburbs club, a weaker team (commercially and on-field performance wise) of outer south-west Sydney. Their most logical merger partner was the strong Canterbury-Bankstown club (inner south-west Sydney) who, despite sharing a geographic boundary, were not particularly fierce rivals. This merger would have created one club to represent the entire south-western corridor of Sydney, which is now among the fastest growing regions of Australia. Doing so would have provided the stronger Canterbury a growth outlet, being geographically boxed-in between the Parramatta Eels and St George Dragons in the west and inner south-west suburbs respectively. For the Western Suburbs club, it would have ensured a presence in the competition with a partner that would have kept the team relatively local. Notably, Wests did in fact first approach Canterbury to merge, only to end up with Balmain as their second choice.

While the West Tigers appears an amicable partnership, it is not an optimal merger combination. This is because the club grapples to form a unified identity given their two catchments are 50 kilometres apart and represent distinct social and demographic populations. The club has to spread itself thinly in representing two distant regions with no central stadium which could equally please both catchments.

Other failings from the mergers are apparent in the footprint of Sydney teams. Part one illustrated that close to 1 million people in northern Sydney remain unrepresented by a local NRL team in modern times. Despite the opportunity to grow a broader northern catchment, the Manly-Warringah Sea Eagles continue to position themselves as a niche northern beaches peninsula club. The outcome of this strategic positioning can be found in the club's attendance rate. Manly recorded an average attendance of 10,493 at Brookvale Oval for the four years between 2016 and 2019, a decline from the pre-Super League era (1995; 12,519, 1980; 12,420). In 2018, when Brookvale recorded an average crowd of 8,630, it was the lowest season average attendance since 1966 (6,080).

In reality, there were few 'perfect' merger combinations given most neighbouring teams retained large rivalries. Yet the way the cards have fallen offers some clubs little room for growth, while other areas are critically underrepresented. This is a crazy outcome for a league that commits nine of its 16 licenses to one city.

How do the Cronulla Sharks, already a small club, grow as a brand when their catchment is literally enveloped by the St George-Illawarra Dragons? How do the Eastern Suburbs

Roosters grow, while being essentially fenced in by the South Sydney Rabbitohs? How does the NRL service northern Sydney and the outer south-west? These challenges stem from poor strategic decisions caused by a laissez-faire merger approach that will haunt the game into the foreseeable future. This future is now explored.

Part 3: Tomorrow
The Golden Goose, served medium-well

Australia is home to many reasonably wealthy sports. Among sports within the Coalition of Major Professional and Participation Sports (COMPPS), which includes the four football codes plus cricket, tennis and netball, the average revenue was AUD $330 million in 2018/19.

Of these, Netball is the straggler with $29.3 million in revenue in 2018, the only member below $100 million. Tennis Australia gets close to the big three, with $374 million in revenue in 2018/19 compared with cricket ($486m), rugby league ($500m) and the AFL ($668m). Until 2020, Australia's largest sport organisations had experienced a period of prolonged commercial prosperity. As mentioned earlier, the 'big five' of the AFL, NRL, RA, FFA and CA saw their collective central revenue nearly double in seven years, from $1.1 billion in 2012 to a touch over $2 billion by 2019. This of course was up-ended with the onset of COVID-19 in early 2020.

Even prior to the pandemic however, there had been a growing chorus of experts and commentators who believed that the Australian sport market could not sustain both the number of market competitors and their current scale into the future. Australian sport consultancy Gemba, themselves reliant on a vibrant domestic industry, led the calls in 2017 when Andrew Condon stated "Ultimately we have too much sporting content relative to our size…It becomes fragmented and a very competitive landscape in terms of broadcast and sponsorship dollars."[183] To make matters worse, according to their research, the proportion of Australians fanatical towards any sport had declined by 13% between 2007 and 2017 (down to 69%). In essence, Gemba were suggesting that more teams and leagues were competing for a shrinking amount of interested people.

A second reason for concern, again prior to COVID-19, was the market signalling that the value of sport broadcasts had peaked. In May 2019, Foxtel signalled cuts to 'non-marquee' sporting content after recording a $417 million dollar loss in 2018. Notably, sport rights and their production accounted for more than half of Foxtel's $1.6 billion of programming costs. In July 2019 both Seven and Nine, who do the vast majority of the heavy lifting in terms of sport broadcasting, also flagged to the market that the good times were coming to an end for sport leagues. Channel Nine's director of sport Tom Malone made the following comments to Mumbrella at the time:

"There has to be a pretty significant reset in the sports rights model in Australia. I would argue that the current sports rights model is broken. Sporting bodies and broadcasters have to get together to find a model that's going to deliver a commercial return for the sport and for the broadcaster... It's very hard to persuade someone that the model is broken until it breaks. So you might see one or two sports fall over in the next 12-24 months as their rights models come up for renewal because there just won't be the appetite to pay the same amount in fees" [184]

Channel Seven's director of sport sales Pat Moloughney, echoed this sentiment:

"We can't simply just prop up the rights owners, so moving forward there has to be a recalibration. Short-term gain often isn't about growing the sport, if you look at sports that have gone behind a wall, they've taken significant cash upfront, but they've actually killed the participation. We've done a great job competing and growing the pie for rights owners, but it has hit a tipping point."

Malone's comments in particular appear prescient, given what has transpired since. However, it's worth noting that media commentators and pundits have been predicting 'peak-rights' for decades. In this respect, the commentary from 2019 could have easily been interpreted as media organisations attempting to posture in preparation for future sports rights negotiations. They were hardly ground-breaking and Foxtel had previously used hard-ball scare tactics negotiations before ultimately reaching new deals. However, even as early as the 2017 NRL Annual Report, it was noted that "Responding to the structural decline in broadcast television by working with its media partners" was a key future imperative[185].

We'll now never know if a reset of the sports rights valuations would have occurred organically, because COVID-19 ensured the sport landscape was thrust into a recalibration that the media landscape appeared to be calling for.

The effect of the pandemic on the sport broadcasting landscape was near immediate. Since at least the turn of the millennium, every sport broadcast deal negotiated in Australia has come with considerable fanfare. The standard formula has been a formal press conference to trumpet the significant financial uplift in rights achieved, followed with infographics illustrating how much wealthier the sport had just become.

My personal favourite was in 2015, when the NRL successfully annoyed Rupert Murdoch, enough for him to attend the AFL's press conference to state: *"We've always preferred Aussie Rules and we've always believed this is the premium code in Australia"*.

Upon hearing this, many NRL fans were no doubt puzzled as to why then, Murdoch couldn't have therefore tried to ruin Australian Rules with a Super League war instead of rugby league.

It was therefore telling that unlike the now customary broadcast rights celebrations, the AFL and NRL's revised broadcast deals negotiated in 2020 have been kept in commercial confidence to little fanfare. As best as we know, the AFL and NRL appear to have taken approximate 20% reductions on their broadcast deals. This hardly seems disastrous when compared with the FFA which accepted a revised deal with 50% discount upon a final season, or Rugby Australia's final season token $9 million for a shortened five team Australian competition in 2020. Rugby Australia too has been circumspect in detailing what proportion of their new deal with Channel Nine for 2021 onwards is cash and how much is contra.

At the most commercial end of the sport landscape, there remains an incredible emphasis and focus upon broadcast rights as the ultimate barometer of sport league success. The narratives that surround the future prosperity of sport leagues also tend to focus on the prospective value of broadcast rights. This focus is somewhat misplaced, but understandable when we see broadcasting's share of total revenue among our major sport leagues.

In the case of AFL, Channel 7's broadcast deal for 1992 represented 14% of the league's $42.7 million in revenue in what was the last year before the television broadcast rights explosion. By 2019, the league's $397 million in broadcast and media revenue accounted for an exact 50% share of total revenue. The NRL are the most leveraged to broadcasting among the major leagues, given broadcasting accounted for 61% of league revenue in 2019, down from 64% in 2018 and a record high of 67% in 2013. Whether the NRL's relatively high reliance on broadcast income can be explained as an over-performance in media rights, or an under-performance in non-broadcast revenue, is certainly a question the game's stakeholders should be asking.

The degree to which prolonged austerity eventuates is still largely ahead of us, and prognosticating about the medium-term impacts of COVID-19 on the sport industry risks quickly rendering this book outdated. However, it is already clear in early 2021 that even in the best case scenario of virus containment or quick eradication, that the opulence our wealthiest sports have enjoyed will likely shift to a mindset of efficiency for the foreseeable future. This came to view within months of the onset of COVID-19, with our largest sporting organisations having either initiated or flagged major plans to streamline activities beyond the immediate staff furloughs of March to May of 2020.

The AFL announced in July of 2020 that the 'soft cap' on football department spending amongst clubs would be slashed from $9.7 million to $6.2 million for 2021. Multiplied across 18 clubs, this equates to $63 million dollars in spending withdrawn from the AFL ecosystem. Given football department spending includes a number of unavoidable non-staffing costs (capital expenditure on equipment, nutrition, technology), it is labour costs which are likely to wear a larger proportion of this 33% cap reduction. Accordingly, it is many of the assistant coaches and other support staff, already furloughed for much of 2020, who are expected to be lost from the AFL ecosystem. Centrally, it has been reported that the AFL intends to reduce its own costs by up to 40% by trimming its 'bloated' wage annual bill of $115.6 million to an estimated 600 staff[186]. Internal reporting obtained by the *Herald Sun* noted:

> "We will have a leaner structure with less roles…Many roles will be impacted based on changes to what programs, products and services we continue, do differently or stop…While we will keep some specialist roles there will be more generalist roles – with multiple responsibilities"

On the one hand, the AFL and its clubs have had the most to lose during the crisis, given reduced broadcasts and lost revenue from league-wide regular season attendances of 35,122 in 2019, compared with 15,030 in the NRL. Yet being Australia's financially strongest league helped ensure the AFL a $500 million line of credit against Marvel Stadium during the first crest of the crisis. The foreshadowed streamlining of the AFL can, to some degree, be therefore viewed as more of a proactive measure to strengthen the league's future as much as it is about surviving the present. As quoted by the *Herald Sun* from the internal AFL document flagging changes:

> "The necessity of operating differently has given us an incredible opportunity to understand what we can do and what we are capable of… We want to rebound from this unprecedented time on the offence."

While COVID-19 will undoubtedly negatively impact the entire sport industry in the short to medium term, there is some truth to the above quote. It may further widen the gap between the 'haves' and 'have nots' of the sport industry, providing the AFL an opportune moment for offence while others are on the defence.

Although the NRL from a revenue perspective represents one of the 'haves' of the Australian football and broader sport landscape, the code's inability to convert strong revenue into assets has been a testament to poor governance. The zenith of this mismanagement was perhaps agreeing to provide clubs 130% of the players salary cap in 2015, perpetuating a hand-out culture among NRL clubs first established by a long-standing reliance on poker machine money. In 2012, when the NRL became independent of News Corporation, the game had $36 million in non-current assets. In 2019, non-current assets grew to $47 million, but included $11 million in intangible assets. By comparison, the AFL had $247 million in non-current assets on their balance sheet in 2019. When the AFL's independent commission was established, in the mid 1980s, the AFL had total net assets of $3 million and half its member clubs were bankrupt. The importance of this asset base difference would manifest during the pandemic, with the NRL reportedly unable to secure a loan from domestic finance lenders[187].

In contrast to the AFL, the guiding mindset of the NRL during the COVID-19 crisis has clearly been one of survival. After navigating the NRL back onto the field during the pandemic, the first sport league in the world to do so, ARLC Chairman Peter V'landys reflected that: "When I used the word catastrophic I was thinking this was bad enough to send five or six clubs broke". Like the AFL, the NRL is going to endeavour to reset the cost structure of the game. In mid-2020, it was flagged that $80 million of the organisation's annual $180 million in operating costs would be stripped from operations. Later in 2020, it was flagged that 25% of NRL staff would be made redundant. In the case of the NRL, a cost base restructure has been perhaps 20 to 50 years overdue.

The game itself appears primed for a broader reset, and the pandemic merely brought to the surface simmering frustrations long-held by many of the game's stakeholders. The introduction of an independent commission has not been the panacea many expected, and perhaps the success of the AFL's independent commission set expectations around improved governance too high. Advocates of the NRL may have started to suspect an independent commission was not a likely cure-all by 2018, when embarrassing media gaffes by the code's chairman beset the game in a manner that would be unthinkable in the AFL.

The difference in governance was perhaps most apparent to Graeme Samuel, the sole individual to have served as a commissioner for both the AFL (an inaugural commissioner in 1984) and NRL (2013–2017). He describes the AFL's governance as "impeccable" and "highly professional" and the NRL as "weakened" and "clearly not in the same position" as the AFL. He resigned from the ARLC because of the lack of true independence, being "largely controlled by clubs". Samuel confirms what many sport industry insiders are aware of, that rugby league still remains thirty years behind the AFL in many respects: "The [ARL] commission is still one that has some of the relics of what the AFL had pre-1992, which is a commission which is largely controlled by the clubs and so you know it's still got to get to the stage of being a professional governance structure"[188].

Linked to poor governance is a widely-held perception that NRL management has underperformed, both in KPI terms and relative to the financial cost of the central administration. Consider some of the more easily measurable objectives set out in the ARLC's inaugural strategic plan for 2012 to 2017, relative to eventual performance:

- *Club membership will reach 400,000 in 2017* (210,677 in 2012). Membership reached 316,000. Aiming to achieve 90% growth over four years, the NRL achieved 50% growth.
- *Average attendance at NRL games will increase to 20,000 (16,423 in 2012).* The average regular season crowd in 2017 was 14,919. Aiming for 20% growth, average regular season attendance declined 9% over the period.
- *700,000 people will play in competitions (growth of 12.5%).* Roy Morgan estimates

suggested rugby league participation declined by 8.7% between 2013 and 2017 to 327,000 participants[189]. An alliance/integration between the highly participated Touch Football Australia and the NRL in 2013 masks a decline in full contact rugby league participation.

- *84% of all NRL players will be engaged in education or career training.* The NRL's 2017 annual report cites 87% engagement but this includes under 20s players (half the population) who by being aged 18-20, are considerably more likely to be in education or training. An ABC report in 2017 put NRL player education rates at 80%[190].
- *Central revenue will have doubled to more than $300m.* The NRL successfully grew their revenue from $182m in 2012 to $354m in 2017.

Despite broad criticisms of the NRL that appear likely to trigger a reset of the administration, the NRL's clubs have appeared to have largely avoided scrutiny, despite being vocal critics. The Brisbane Broncos have been the only club to have historically made regular profits, more recently joined by the South Sydney Rabbitohs.

Graeme Samuels considers COVID-19 not to be rugby league's second financial crisis after Super League, but rather its third. The second came in 2016/2017, when the NRL central administration, at the behest of the game's commission, exhausted its growing sustainability fund to support broke NRL teams[191]. This is telling when considering the contribution of clubs versus the league to overall game revenue. While AFL clubs contribute closer to 50% of all of the game revenue (through attendance, memberships, sponsorships, etc), NRL clubs contribute nearer to 30% of total game revenue[192]. Such statistics reveal the financial fragility of rugby league heading into the future: the NRL is the most reliant on broadcast revenue among all of Australia's major sports (61% of total revenue) and its individual clubs contribute comparatively little to total revenue (30%). The NRL, more so than any other Australian sport, is a bad broadcast deal away from implosion. Inconveniently then, the NRL's television ratings in season 2020 were underwhelming by comparison to the AFL.

For those sports that had existing question marks around their existing commercial models, most certainly including the Rugby Australia and FFA, the timing of the pandemic could not have been worse.

Rugby Australia was in the midst of negotiating their next broadcast deal when the pandemic commenced. The timing was truly unfortunate. In an attempt to create competitive tension, Rugby Australia rejected what was perceived as an initial low-ball offer from Foxtel during their exclusive negotiating period. This strategic play involved taking the sport to open tender in February 2020, involving Foxtel, Optus, Amazon, Rugby Pass and Australia's three commercial free-to-air networks. Yet barely a month later, broadcast negotiations would be put in hibernation and the trans-national nature of Super Rugby would see the code's competition model blown up for the foreseeable future and perhaps beyond. Rugby

Australia has appeared to escape their peril with a reasonable rights deal with Channel Nine, that provides the code the necessary FTA exposure it requires, but the deal is not without risks.

More broadly in succumbing to financial pressures which have built up within the sport, Rugby Australia at the national level has let go of one-third of its work force, 47 of 142 staff in 2020. At the state level, NSWRU has made redundant a quarter of its workforce, 15 of its 50 odd staff in order to "protect the long-term financial viability of rugby" in New South Wales[193]. Notable at the state level is that all 12 of the organisation's development officers were among those made redundant, further eroding the sport's grassroots infrastructure. NSWRU chief executive Paul Doorn attempted to put forward an optimistic tone: "Just because we have to cut 12 development officers, we will continue to provide support to community rugby". Yet, it was previously illustrated how Rugby Australia at a national level already commits a paltry 3.6% of total expenditure to community rugby, a minnow by contrast to AFL ($59m, 13.7%) and NRL ($43m, 8.2%) in both absolute and relative terms.

The importance of grassroots development, and the failures of rugby union, were perhaps best summed up by Sydney Swans chairman Andrew Pridham in June 2020. He urged the AFL not to abandon the northern junior development academies as part of future cost cutting within the AFL, stating: "I think it's a very high priority, because if we don't continue the grassroots development eventually you could become rugby union"[194].

The FFA also enter 2021 significantly more affected by COVID-19 than its larger football rivals. Foxtel had long been rumoured to be agitated by the poor return on investment the A-League had provided for its $57 million per annum investment. With the interruption of the 2019/20 season in March, Foxtel was able to walk away legally from this existing commitment, which was due to expire after the 2022/23 season. In its place is a deal to broadcast one further season in 2020/21 for $32 million, to run between December 2020 and July 2021. From a financial perspective, this naturally represents a significant retraction for Australian soccer. Yet from a strategic perspective, the sport appears to be making the most of the opportunity provided, using the disruption as a catalyst to shift the A-League to becoming a winter competition for 2022. As noted by FFA chief executive James Johnson: "The shift in the timing of the next A-League season is a strategic decision to enhance the alignment of our top tier professional men's league with the grassroots playing season of the largest community sport in the country"[195]

This change will have profound impact on the commercial footing of the game. On the one hand, it is said to be supported by A-League powerbrokers by improving the alignment of participation in the game, therefore also removing a key obstacle to introducing a promotion and relegation system. Yet the A-League (and the NSL before it) shifted to summer to try to avoid direct competition with other football codes and maximise its chances of publicity in the less contested summer period, as well as align the domestic season with the international football calendar.

THE BATTLE FOR FANS, DOLLARS AND SURVIVAL

Since starting the summer A-League in 2005/2006, the Big Bash Leagues (2011/2012, 2015/2016) and AFLW (2017) have increasingly crowded the summer landscape, as has the resurgence of the NBL. Despite the increasing intensity of summer sport league competition, research by media monitor Streem illustrated that the A-League's share of media coverage across the big six leagues/events[196] peaked at 16.9% in December 2019, and declined to about 5% in July/August 2020. Such data provides cautionary evidence of the likely publicity impact of competing in the heart of winter. More broadly however, it is telling that Australian soccer seems to be grappling with the exact same issues in 2021 that they have been dealing with since the 1970s and prior. I asked Joe Gorman for his reflections upon Australian soccer:

"The current 'debate' around a national second division and promotion and relegation is quite a niche conversation. It is not a concern to the tens of thousands of regular Australians who play soccer on the weekend or have a child involved in junior soccer. And it is even less relevant to the mainstream sports fans that the A-League wants to convert. It seems the game is destined to go round and round in circles. We're back to thinking Australian soccer must look like it does in Europe, rather than the national league being tailored to tastes and behaviours of the local market."

The A-League's future value to Fox Sports appears obviously even more diminished in winter, given the broadcaster is far less concerned about losing subscribers in winter (thanks to AFL and NRL content) than in summer. What commercial value the A-League offers Foxtel is not in the relatively small five-figure ratings it generates, but rather the content hole it fills in the summer schedule. This winter/summer dichotomy also explains why Foxtel invested so heavily to obtain cricket content. A shift to winter soccer will certainly burn the bridge to Foxtel, and the FFA will undoubtedly have to look to broadcast alternatives.

Soccer pundits have also regularly criticised the surface quality of Australia's multi-purpose stadiums as a major explanatory variable for poor domestic match quality. How east coast A-League teams will fare sharing grounds for the entirety of their season with rugby league and union teams during cold and wet winters could prove problematic. With declining broadcast revenue inevitably reducing investment into the professional game, it is somewhat difficult to envisage how the A-League competition can advance toward future prosperity. Indeed the first signs of stress caused by reduced revenue appeared in late 2020 with the players' association and association of professional clubs unable to easily reach an amicable salary cap for the league moving forward. Indeed the A-League salary cap looks likely to be slashed by approximately one-third from its previous value of $3.2 million. Yet when I posed these challenges to Simon Hill, esteemed soccer commentator and journalist, his response was simple:

"New CEO James Johnson came out saying that he wanted the FFA to become a 'football first' organisation and I absolutely support him. To hell with what's best for Australian Rules, rugby league and Foxtel. We've got to start doing what's best for us. We've got to stop worrying about the mainstream casual fans and win back our core supporters".

While commentary surrounding the future of sports tends to inevitably tie into comparisons of broadcast rights, a singular focus on broadcast rights is too simplistic a mechanism to evaluate the future prospects of each football code. What is often unspoken in the discussion of sport broadcast rights is that the value of rights is itself just a proxy for the underlying popularity of a sport product. The key to increasing broadcast rights is really quite simple, if not difficult to then execute: get more people, more interested in the sport product. With this in mind, sport administrators must remain conscious that large broadcast rights are in fact **an outcome of success**, rather than an input to success. The error made by some sport practitioners has been to frame their broadcast rights thinking around the wrong question. When taking the necessarily long view of strategic planning, the question of 'how do we increase our broadcast rights?' is actually the wrong one. Rather the more fundamental question should always remain 'how do we become a more popular sports league?'

The distinction between popularity and revenue is probably best illustrated by the trajectory of Australian rugby union. While 25 years of Super Rugby spent exclusively behind Foxtel's paywall has been reasonably effective in maintaining a return on broadcast rights, it has been terribly ineffective in helping the sport become more popular in Australia. Usually when catastrophic mistakes occur, criticism must be tempered by the fact that things appear more obvious in hindsight. Yet in rugby union's case, it had been foreshadowed for at least a decade that change was needed and the game's popularity was eroding.

The success of all the football codes, and all sports, is therefore predicated upon their underlying popularity.

The 'code war' is therefore really just a collection of battlefronts that take the form of popularity contests. Here, however, sport is somewhat different from a typical consumer product. For a confectionary product or carbonated beverage, popularity is relatively unidimensional; factors like product features, positioning, pricing and availability all feed into sales, which feed into market share. Hence, Coca-Cola (40.2%) can be said to be more than twice as large as Asahi (Pepsi, Schweppes, Solo) (15.2%) in the Australian carbonated beverage market[197].

In contrast, there is no one single sales or market share figure that can capture the hierarchy of Australian sport. Instead, battlefronts of popularity include junior participation, corporate sponsorship, government support, media coverage and consumer interest. Many of these battlefronts are interrelated, but these individual battlefronts each contribute to the overall code war. Importantly, these battlefronts are shaped by social, cultural and commercial trends, which are likely to influence the prospects of each code as we look ahead to the future. Having looked at the present and past of our four football codes, we now look forward to consider what the future may hold.

Urbanisation and generational change in junior participation

The decline of baseball in the American psyche previously mentioned exemplifies how slow moving environmental shifts can lead to drastic generational changes that may not seem evident in any one discrete moment. At baseball's zenith, Hall of Famer Jackie Robinson was responsible for breaking the Colour Barrier in 1947, which had excluded players of African American descent from playing in baseball's Major and Minor Leagues. His success was a catalyst for an explosion in African American talent in MLB, and further increased interest in the sport which had been built upon local Negro leagues. By the 1970s African American representation was at an all-time high, accounting for 25% of MLB players despite representing 12.5% of the population[198]. Yet by 2001 this would decline to 13% and then 8% by 2018. As Dr David Ogden and Dr Michael Hilt's research put it:

"There was a time, right after Jackie Robinson, when everybody was interested in the game of baseball… you had sandlot ballclubs everywhere … I think the African-American community loved the game, but somewhere along the line we lost interest in appearing at Major League games and Minor League games"

Several practical lessons can be learnt from baseball's long-term decline as America's favourite sport, both among African Americans and more broadly within American culture. First, baseball fell victim to structural change in the distribution of America's populous, in the form of urbanisation. The 20th century had seen populations across all western nations increasingly drift from regional areas to metropolitan cities. In 1900, 39.6% of Americans lived in urban centres. By 2010, this had doubled to 80.7%. Baseball has been a net loser of urbanisation because of the comparative amount of space needed to play the sport, while basketball has been a comparative winner for inverse reasons. Basketball therefore offered functional advantages over baseball: greater accessibly of courts and being comparatively cheaper and easier to play socially.

Urbanisation had a flow-on effect that further contributed to baseball's decline and basketball's rise. Basketball's superior accessibility within inner city neighbourhoods, where a greater proportion of populations resided, resulted in a particularly radical change in the cultural preferences of African Americans with basketball becoming central to their collective identity. Racial scholars noted that, like jazz or hip-hop, basketball "belongs to an African American, whether she likes it or knows anything about it, because it is culturally marked as black"[199]. This observation once more reflects that sport can be a powerful contributor to people's social identity. By 2012/13, 45% of NBA viewers were African American compared with only 9% of MLB viewers[200]. By 2015, 74% of NBA players were African American compared with 8% within MLB. The influence of NBA players, and the NBA organisation overall, in response to the Black Lives Matter movement of 2020 is also testament to this.

Urbanisation is also significant because of where most professional athletes are produced. As previously discussed, regional towns and smaller cities overproduce athletes, while larger cities tend to under produce athletes. This is true in Australia and around the world, but is wonderfully illustrated by research from the American context. Approximately 50% of the US population resides in cities with over 500,000 people, but only 13% of NHL and PGA and 15% of MLB athletes derive from these large cities. Notably this statistic increases to 29% among NBA players, which while still an underrepresentation, is significantly less[201]. With urbanisation set to continue, the NBA stands to continue to benefit from structural changes in how populations are shifting in the American context.

Although the above examples are American-centric and particularly pronounced, it is possible to observe an urbanisation effect in Australian sport. This is significant because the continued urbanisation of western populations will have profound implications for the future production of athletes.

As of the 2016 Census, 71% of Australians live in major cities (population 100,000 and over), up from 61% in 1966. Only 2.3 million people lived in small towns (less than 10,000 people) in 2016. By 2040, our capital cities are projected to account for 71% of our population, with non-capital cities bringing the total to more than 80%[202].

The potential impact of this slow moving shift of populations to major cities will affect sports in various ways. For example, 40% of current W-League players were born in regional centres[203]. Cricket (38.0%) and tennis (37.8%) for instance run neck and neck in competing to be Australia's second favourite sport. Yet, these two sports split along a clear regional versus urban divide similar to baseball and basketball in America. Cricket is far more popular than tennis in regional areas (42.4% vs 34.4%), while tennis is more popular in metropolitan areas (39.2% vs 36.3%). This divide manifests in where these sports get their athletes. Major cities have produced a comparatively respectable volume of our tennis champions, given the general dominance of small cities and towns in athlete production, Samantha Stosur (Gold Coast), Nick Kyrgios (Canberra), Lleyton Hewitt (Adelaide), John Newcombe (Sydney), Ken Rosewall (Sydney) and Mark Philippoussis (Melbourne) to name a few[204].

THE BATTLE FOR FANS, DOLLARS AND SURVIVAL

Rugby league's State of Origin provides another good example of the metropolitan vs regional effect and its corresponding implications for player pathways. One analysis found that Sydney produced only 25% of New South Wales' rugby league State of Origin players between 1980 to 2015, despite the city accounting for 57% of the state's population. Similarly, Brisbane was estimated to have produced 18% of Queensland's Origin players, despite the city representing 45% of the State's population[205].

Counterbalancing the decline of rugby league and union athletes from Australia's regional centres has been the rise of Pasifika athletes[206]. For context, Pasifika players accounted for 9% of the NRL in 1998, only growing to 12% by 2008 before then reaching an astronomical 46% by 2018[207]. Consider that while 12% of NRL players are indigenous and account for 2.8% of the population, 46% of NRL players are Pasifika compared with just 1.4% of the Australian population having a Pasifika ancestry.

From a value judgment perspective, it is neither 'good' nor 'bad' that such a considerable proportion of NRL athletes are from Pasifika ancestries, with strong parallels to the ascent of African Americans in the NBA. From a statistical perspective, however, it is at least curious that 1.4% of the population produce 46% of a workforce, while a further 12% derive from 2.8% of the population. In total then, 58% of NRL athletes derive from about 4% of the Australian population[208]. Considering the NRL also features both a small proportion of imported Englishmen and a not insignificant number of non-Maori New Zealanders (who are not included in *Pasifika*), the remaining 96% of Australia's population don't appear to progress through the rugby league pathway to the elite level anywhere near the statistical levels one would expect.

The same is true in rugby union. It was reported in late 2018 that 55% of players within the premier Auckland Rugby competition identified as Pacific Islander, despite representing 14.6% of the city's population. Conversely, Aucklanders of European descent account for 24% of Auckland Rugby players despite composing 60% of the population[209]. Players identifying has holding an Asian descent accounted for just 2% of participants.

In the context of rugby, this demographic shift in elite participation has previously been called "white flight"[210], a somewhat uncomfortable expression and topic generally to grapple with in the modern climate around race. The expression, in relation to the idea of a tipping point, perhaps gained most recent prominence from Malcom Gladwell's *The Tipping Point*. In his book, Gladwell illustrates the effect of white flight in the racial composition of American neighbourhoods and how upon reaching a tipping point, rapid changes occur in such composition. The athletic composition of the rugby codes appears to have already passed the tipping point, contributing to white flight, which could prove disastrous for the prosperity of the rugby codes into the future.

Given basketball is a non-contact sport, the African American dominance of the sport at the NBA level does not necessarily significantly discourage non-African Americans from participating in basketball. The underlying base participation rate of basketball is therefore not harmed by the dominance of one demographic group at the elite level.

The same cannot be said in the rugby context. The introduction of size-for-age rules in junior rugby, which introduced bands around allowable height and weight limits within each age group, can be seen to have both an operational and marketing component. From an operational perspective, it attempts to help junior participants better develop by placing them at the most appropriate playing level for both their age (and hence cognitive level) and their size. Arguably however, it also serves a marketing purpose. These rules can also be seen as a form of signalling to safety-concerned parents, particularly of non-Pasifika background, that rugby remains a sport their children can participate in.

Yet, rugby is losing the battle to have their sport appeal to a wide demographic of people at the participation level. Roy Morgan research indicated that rugby union participation declined 29% amongst Australians aged 14+ between 2013 and 2017, well over and above the overall decline amongst all codes (-12.1%)[211]. Rugby Australia disputed these numbers, and large declines are not evident between 2016 to 2019 in Sport Australia's preeminent AusPlay participation data. Yet the AusPlay data is hardly positive, and speaks to significant chasm between the codes in terms of participation. Among children aged 15 and under in 2019 who played sport in an organised capacity, only 77,000 participated in rugby union and 112,000 in rugby league. For context, more children participated in 'DanceSport' (97,000) than union, while Karate (149,000) chopped both codes. With 429,000 child participants in 2019, Australian rules retains a healthy participation base in relation to soccer (748,000)[212].

Does the NRL or Rugby Australia require diversity amongst their junior participants and elite athletes to appeal to a wide commercial audience? I suspect it certainly helps, although there may not be a definitive answer. It is unquestionable that Australian Rules and soccer not only have wider participation bases, but likely more diverse ones (AusPlay sport participation data does not capture ethnicity). This is a significant strategic advantage. Not only does growing the base of junior participants increase the quality of talent that will eventually progress to an elite level, but it also has implications on the commercial value of those participants as eventual adult consumers. This is what Figure 21 suggests, as it divides Sydney sport fans into three columns depending on whether they have played their respective sport, and plots it against their current day television consumption. Appendix 3 does the same but with attitudinal interest rather than behavioural outcomes.

The conclusion is obvious: people who participate in their sport, become more attitudinally passionate about the sport and consume more of it at the elite/commercial level. This relationship also holds true for attendance. Of course, it could be the case that people who view a lot of games are then encouraged to participate in the sport. This is the classic causation versus correlation problem, and hence the relationship could be the opposite to what is being proposed. Yet, when we look at the relative consumption rate of adults who participated in their sport as child, we see that playing a sport as a kid corresponds to higher consumption rates of that sport as an adult. Additionally, this data only includes Sydney residents who spent 'the majority of their childhood (0-18) raised in Sydney'. This controls the risk of surveying Sydney adults raised elsewhere (for example Melbourne), who may have played and loved AFL growing up before moving to Sydney. By controlling for this variable, we can explore the relationship between playing AFL Auskick as child and fandom of AFL as an adult.

While the findings here are not necessarily surprising, it is the magnitude of the differences that are particularly insightful. For a sport like AFL that retains an outsider status in Sydney, recruiting a local child to the Auskick program between ages 0-12 sets off a chain of events that many years later downstream, sees that child watch more than twice as many AFL games than someone who did not play Auskick as a child[213]. Given this implication, it is plausible to say that the AFL could pay parents in the northern states $100 per child to play a season of Australian Rules football and they would still see a significant return on their investment in terms of the lifetime value of that child as a future AFL consumer.

For a sport like rugby union, where the differential in television consumption is four-fold if the adult had played rugby union as a child, the folly of not investing in community rugby becomes apparent. Importing talented juniors from the Pacific Islands or providing targeted private school scholarships may provide a cost efficient way of producing elite rugby union athletes, but this process misses the benefit of broad base participation that creates high value consumers downstream.

For soccer, the perennial question has always been why the code's high rates of participation haven't led to strong latent support for a domestic league, which the implication of Figure 21 supports. The answer here, in my interpretation, is that playing soccer DOES lead to greater commercial soccer consumption. However, this consumption migrates to European leagues rather than remaining on Australian shores, as will be discussed in further detail soon.

In light of the data presented in Figure 21, the battle to attract junior participants becomes an even larger commercial issue surrounding fan curation. If rugby league participation erodes to such an extent that it becomes the dominant domain of only 4% of the population, the code will have further ceded a major battlefront of the code wars and face a generational time bomb. In rugby league's favour, the data illustrates that individuals who play/have played either of Touch Football or OzTag, exhibit elevated attitudinal interest and behavioural consumption levels towards rugby league. What is interesting here is that the same is not true of rugby union. In 2019 AusPlay estimates that OzTag had 53,000 junior participants (14 and under) and Touch Football, 82,000. With this in mind, the development of the NRL Touch Premiership appears among the shrewder strategic moves made by the NRL in recent times. Even if it is unlikely to ever yield obvious commercial dividends, the connection between rugby league and touch football is strong enough that playing either sport as a child is associated with stronger support of the NRL into adulthood. The NRL may be better off allocating 100% of their grassroots funding in southern states towards touch football, rather than full-contact rugby league.

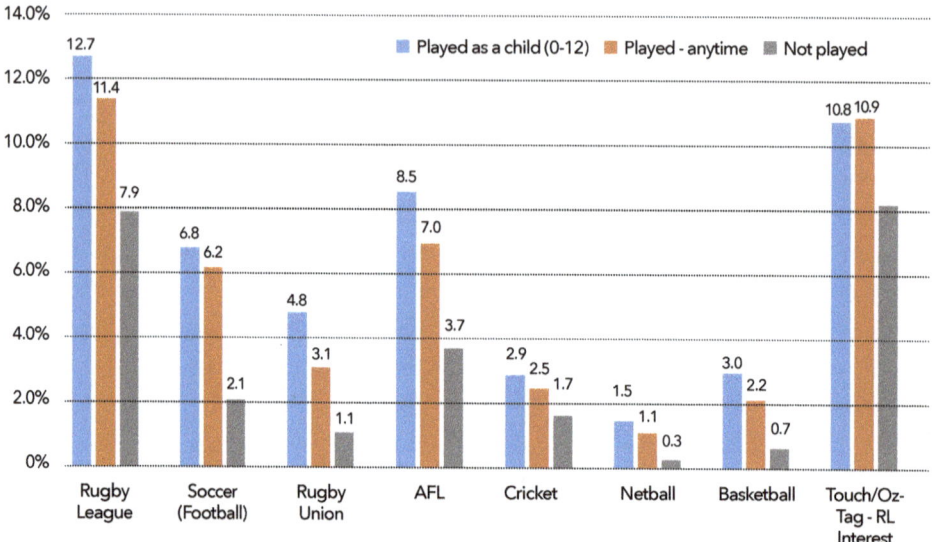

Figure 21: The relationship between having participated in a sport versus the volume of content watched on television (amongst Sydney sport fans who were raised in Sydney)

Safetyism, CTE and the demise of contact football

"In 1905 when 18 [American football] players died, many from head trauma, several university presidents called for the abolition of football. President Teddy Roosevelt famously stepped in to save the sport, convening an emergency summit at the White House. 'Football is on trial' he told representatives of the country's elite college football programs. The summit led to dramatic changes in the way the game was played. The forward pass was legalised and the yardage needed for a 1st down went from 5 yards to 10, increasing the emphasis on speed. Football as we know it was saved" [214]

Of all the trends likely to affect the football landscape of tomorrow, the implications of managing concussion and CTE are perhaps the most profound. As illustrated in the above quote from the acclaimed investigative book *League of Denial: The NFL, Concussions, and*

THE BATTLE FOR FANS, DOLLARS AND SURVIVAL

the Battle for Truth, maintaining perceptions of safety represents one of the most fundamental existential requirements of a sport. Undoubtedly, a contributor to the "white flight" probed in the previous section are perceptions of safety in participating in rugby.

In the case of the American football, the sport faced a genuine threat to its survival in 1905 and responded with changes that radically transformed the game. It is not without its symbolism that American football's transformation intersects rugby league's schism from rugby union in England (1895) and Australia (1908), in which concerns around injury were at least a partial driver of change.

In 2021, with research into concussion and CTE continuing to gain momentum, it is probable that contact sport will soon face another reckoning, once more challenging the existence of contact sport.

No football code is immune from the implications around concussion and safety. The rugby codes have most prominently featured in such discussions as the most similar to NFL, where CTE was first discovered and is most understood. The rugby codes appear most vulnerable to concussion not only as collision is fundamental to their sports, but because the north-south nature of gameplay necessitates more direct frontal collisions. Notably, in approximately 75% of concussion cases in rugby union, it is the tackler, not the ball carrier, who is injured[215]. By contrast, Australian Rules football has been seen as potentially less at risk, due to the 360 degree nature of the game and larger field that leads to fewer and generally less forceful direct collisions. A counterpoint to this view is that the 360 degree nature of AFL gameplay leads to rarer, but potentially more severe concussion instances, where individuals are unaware of an impending collision.

Irrespective of existing views of AFL safety, perceptions of concussion within the sport at least partially shifted in February of 2020 when the late great Graham 'Polly' Farmer became the first official case of CTE within the AFL. Danny Frawley would become the second confirmed case of CTE among former AFL players in September 2020. Undoubtedly, further cases will emerge with time, as has been the trend when sports are first officially linked to CTE.

Even soccer is not immune from the concussion debate. A 2015 study by Purdue University found that the impact of heading a ball was equal to getting a clean jab in a boxing ring or tackled in American football. This was followed by a first ever soccer-specific study of CTE in which the brains of six professional soccer players all showed signs of Alzheimer's and four of the six exhibited signs of the distinctive protein build-up associated with CTE[216]. For a largely non-contact sport, the act of heading may pose some CTE risk, although the evidence thus far is quite limited. FIFA certainly deny any serious concerns around the risk. The day after this study was released in 2017, FIFA respond by saying: "Football does not belong to the high-risk sports for brain and head injuries.... To our very best knowledge, there is currently no true evidence of the negative effect of heading or other sub-concussive blows".

As we sit in 2021 however, it is evident that each football code has some varying risk exposure to concussion and CTE.

While the science of CTE and sport injury rates are vital (and beyond my expertise), it is the *perceptions* of safety which are likely to influence the *management* of football and which intrigue me. For older readers, the importance of the perception of safety can be seen by reflecting upon how the broadcasting of contact sports has changed over time. When a footballer incurred an injury in times past, broadcasters were more far more likely to show frequent replays of the incident and would often retain focus upon the injured player in their agony.

Modern broadcast etiquette dictates typically one or two replays to ascertain the nature of the injury, followed by a respectful avoidance of telecasting the prone player. Should the injury result in an extended break in play, telecasters now lead into either a commercial break or a highlights summary package of the match thus far. In the rugby codes, the emphasis of highlights packages has noticeably shifted over time away from aggressive defence (i.e. 'big hits') towards graceful passing, stepping and try scoring.

Two broader trends, however, appear to be co-conspiring to pose a creeping threat to contact sports. First, interest in the subject and hence the volume of research surrounding concussion continues to grow. Scientific knowledge around concussion has been growing at an incredible rate since 2008 and will undoubtedly continue to do so. The second trend is a social one, being a growing pervasiveness of *safetyism* as a parenting philosophy as first described by Dr Greg Lukianoff and Jonathan Haidt in their acclaimed *The Coddling of the American Mind*.

According to the authors, safetyism: "refers to a culture or belief system in which safety [physical OR emotional] has become a sacred value, which means that people are unwilling to make trade-offs demanded by other practical and moral concerns". A practical example attributed to a safetyism culture has been the rapid rise in child allergies, which resulted in the societal response of banning particular food items from many schools. This would later be shown scientifically to have contributed to the problem by limiting necessary low-dosage exposure to allergens, harming rather than protecting children.

Neither Lukianoff and Haidt's book nor academic studies delve further to consider safetyism in the sport participation context, but it is not difficult to understand how the concept applies. Every parent, in determining whether to let their child play a particular sport, trades off the potential risk of injury against the physical health benefits of exercise and social benefits of group recreation. Social shifts identified by the authors, however, are starting to work against contact sports.

There is the impact of long-term social shifts away from rough and tumble play in outdoor settings towards greater apartment living and electronic game playing. There has also been a parenting shift away from free-play towards supervised play as child safety has become an increasingly anxious issue in the minds of parents. In this context, it is unsurprising that sports previously considered rough may be becoming a tougher sell to safety-conscious parents. Here, the participation trends in American football are certainly stark. Over the past decade or so, participation in full contact American football among youths aged between six and 12 has been reported to have declined in the vicinity of between 20% and 30%. Many parents may prefer their children playing Madden on their X-Box than playing American football in real life.

We have arguably already seen the principles of safetyism embraced within Australian sport. Consider that all our major codes are aligned in not keeping scores, having ladders or finals for their junior participation programs. Auskick (ages 5 to 12) doesn't record the scores, have ladders or finals, nor does soccer's Mini-Roos (4 to 11). Junior rugby union doesn't have scores until age 10, while in early 2020, it was announced that Queensland Rugby League would disallow tackling until late in the Under-7s program and will not have finals until under 13s.

I do not have a strong personal position in either camp, but a safetyism philosophy, rightly or wrongly, is clear: ensuring the psychological safety of all participating children, making sure all kids have maximum fun at all times, takes precedence to exposing children to the emotional highs and lows of competing[217].

The key question as we look forward towards a future football landscape in Australia then, is the degree to which both the informed science of concussion and ensuing societal perceptions of safety will shape how, or if, contact football is played. If it were to be proven that there is no 'safe' frequency in which one can have concussions, and concussions remain an inevitable risk of playing football, do our contact football codes become instantly unviable as recreational activities?

An uncomfortable reality is that if the rugby codes (and to a slightly lesser extent Australian Rules) were new sports being pitched to prospective parents and schools in 2021, it is difficult to imagine getting approval or broad support for them as an appropriate activity for children to participate in. Moreover, if these football codes were new activities, they would probably be uninsurable. Indeed high school rugby union in Nova Scotia, Canada[218] was unilaterally banned mid-season in 2019 by the Nova Scotia School Athletic Federation after the sport reported 149 head injuries to the School Insurance Program. This was more than football, hockey and soccer combined, although rugby was essentially lynched for being the only sport to accurately report, rather than conceal, their true injury rate.

Domestically, there was a 6% risk of sustaining an injury in an NRL game during the 2011 NRL season. In a game that features 17 players a side, this equates to one player on each team getting injured every NRL game. Alternatively, this equates to two of the thirty-four participating players incurring an injury every NRL game. Notably, the study pragmatically defined 'injury' as missing the following week's game. The injury rate thus surely underreports the number of players genuinely injured, who through either toughness, elite physiotherapy or painkilling injections, do not to miss the following game.

Non-sport fans would surely consider it madness that it is permissible for athletes to be injected with pain-killers to play a match, whereas a recreational drug such as marijuana is on WADA's anti-doping list and its use can end a professional sporting career. Over the course of the 2011 NRL season, 76% per cent of NRL players sustained an injury. That is to say, only a quarter of NRL players were able to complete a season without experiencing an injury significant enough to miss a week's play. In any given week an average of six players in each NRL team where unavailable due to injury.

Contact football is undoubtedly a high risk activity when compared with alternative sport activities like tennis or swimming. Moreover, the injury rates reported above largely pre-date the introduction of the modern standard of concussion protocols. In the NRL's case, these were tightened in response to the International Conference on Concussion in Sport held in Berlin in October 2016.

Our football leagues are now increasingly put measures in place to manage concussion, but this does not necessarily mitigate the fundamental risk of a concussion occurring in the first instance. For this reason, our codes are currently transitioning from phase one actions, identifying and managing concussed individuals -towards phase two, mitigating the incidence of concussion itself. This attitude change is summarised by World Rugby's Chief Medical Officer Martin Raftery from 2018:

> "The measure (of success) for us is a reduction in concussion rates. We want to see them start to come down. For the first five years we have spent a lot of time ensuring the players are protected by ensuring they are removed from the field when they should be removed, and are not allowed to go back too early. Now we are about trying to prevent them." [219]

Football codes have started to respond with modifications and proposed modifications. The United States Soccer Federation announced the U.S. Soccer Concussion Initiative 2016, which bans heading for children 10 and under (and limits heading for children aged 11-13 to 30 minutes per week). In February 2020, it was announced that children in England, Scotland and Northern Ireland will no longer be allowed to head soccer balls during training sessions.

World Rugby introduced a trial law change at under-20 competitions in 2018 that lowers the height of tackle to "below the nipple line" to reduce the risk of head injury. The trial was scrapped by 2019, with some reports claiming it actually increased the number of concussions[220], while others suggesting it was too difficult to officiate[221].

The act of tackling is particularly problematic, given its centrality to rugby gameplay. A study commissioned by World Rugby in 2016 reviewed fixtures between 2013 and 2015, identifying and analysing 611 head injury assessments across 1,516 professional matches[222].

THE BATTLE FOR FANS, DOLLARS AND SURVIVAL

The study found that one in every 516 tackles results in a head injury assessment. For context, the top 50 tacklers in the NRL averaged 839 tackles each during the 2019 season. The NRL's leading tackler, Reed Mahoney, completed 1,221 tackles in 2019. Although I am extrapolating rugby union's incidence rate to rugby league, the NRL's top tacklers could be expected to have between one and two head injury assessments per season based on this rate. Whether this is an acceptable level of exposure to potential injury and long term brain degeneration will at some point surely become an existential question for prospective NRL athletes.

How would our football codes respond if health research was to unequivocally conclude that concussion poses an unacceptable risk to human health? The tobacco industry, a basis of much comparison to the NFL within the *League of Denial*, perhaps provides an illustrative case of a product that has shifted from broad public acceptance to health risk, and features some unnerving parallels to sport's response to CTE thus far[223].

The early 1950s saw evidence linking smoking to lung cancer begin to propagate more frequently across popular press and medical journals. The tobacco industry took note of emerging evidence during this time and rather than acknowledge the health risks, hired public relations firms to challenge evidence and defend the industry for the better part of 40 years. Medical doctors and academic scholars were hired to defend the industry's claim that the evidence was "merely statistical" or based only on "animal evidence".

This strategy of obstruction has unfortunate parallels to the behaviour of the NFL during the early research of CTE. Over a period of two decades around the turn of the millennium, the NFL sought to cover up and deny mounting evidence of the connection between football and brain damage. During this period, the league managed to publish 16 academic peer reviewed scientific studies of questionable methodology and findings in an apparent attempt to ingrain and own a positive narrative around concussion. All 16 studies came to the broad conclusion that playing American football was not linked to any negative brain effects. Among the more spurious suppositions made by the research was that NFL players were somehow naturally more immune to concussion than the average human being. Notably, the player class action over concussion which was eventually brought against the NFL not only accused them of negligence, but also fraud, for deliberately hiding the dangers of concussion from them.

The consumer response towards growing evidence of the health risks of smoking in the early 1950s resulted in the decline in cigarette sales in 1953/1954. To allay these health concerns, the tobacco industry introduced and invested in "filtered" cigarettes. Within five years, filtered cigarettes went from a 2% market share (1952) to 40% market share (1957). Unfortunately, filtered cigarettes offered no actual health benefits, a fact known by the tobacco industry as early as the 1930s.

Once more, parallels exist to the NFL case. Helmet manufacturer Riddell, official provider of the NFL since 1989, developed a new helmet in 2000 to address concussion.

Riddell advertised and marketed 'the Revolution' helmet as reducing head injuries and sport concussions by 31%. Yet, a biomechanics firm hired first by the NFL and later by Riddell to test helmets and study head injuries sent the company a report showing that no football helmet, no matter how revolutionary, could prevent concussions.

Given the apparent similarities thus far in the narratives of smoking and contact sport, an alarming hypothetical emerges when considering the future of contact sports.

Like cigarettes, contact sports have moved beyond denying and obstructing their apparent danger. Contact sports appear to now be in the second stage, attempting to mitigate perceived risk through product modifications, albeit ones that are hopefully bona fide (unlike filtered cigarettes). Yet, should future research conclude that the current forms of contact football pose too large a health risk for participants, contact sports may enter cigarettes' third stage: precipitous decline in usage. At its peak 42% of American adults smoked in 1965, down to under 14% in 2020.

If contact sport represents an unmitigatable poor health choice, akin to a cigarette, do football administrators make the minimal changes that maintain the status quo and acknowledge the risks associated with participation? Conversely, will football administrators be willing to make radical changes to protect the wellbeing of athletes and participants?

Such a scenario could see history repeat in a similar vein to Teddy Roosevelt's 1905 Football summit, which saw American football morph from rugby into Grid Iron as we now know it. One perspective is that the risk of litigation and insurance implications will compel contact sports to develop concurrently with our understanding of concussion. The NFL experienced a protracted seven-year legal fight with their insurers, after they refused to cover their portion of the costs associated with the league's more than $1 billion settlement reached with retired players in 2013[224]. Although numerous insurers had provided liability policies for the NFL dating back as far as the 1960s, because the retired players accused the NFL of fraud, the insurers believed that they did not have to cover the league's settlement payments. This risk provides a financial incentive, beyond the moral incentive, to treat concussion protocol seriously.

Sport leagues retain a broad and legally entrenched duty of care toward their athletes, which should necessitate a conservative approach in implementing policies around concussions. This duty of care, for instance, was the core reason the shoulder charge was outlawed from rugby league, having been definitively illustrated to be a dangerous tackle technique.

However, if particularly radical changes are required to the way contact sports are played in future, how much can such a contact sport change before it loses its core identity and appeal? Would people still enjoy playing and watching soccer if heading the ball was no longer allowed? Most probably. Would people's enjoyment of AFL decline drastically if tackling was replaced by two-handed touch? Possibly. Can you imagine watching a rugby league State of Origin played with hip-tags instead of tackling? Is it even logistically possible to remove tackling from rugby union without making it a version of touch rugby league?

Less radically, might we see a strikes policy that sees players automatically retire after a certain concussion threshold? In such a scenario the longevity of athlete careers, which are already comparatively short, may well further fall precipitously. During the period of writing of this book, 700,000 odd television viewers witnessed a rugby league player experience an on-field seizure in response to being concussed from an attempted tackle. Rather than our football heroes retiring in their early to mid-30s as part of pre-planned retirement and transition, it is not difficult to imagine a new norm emerge in which abrupt enforced medical retirements robs athletes and fans of fitting farewells.

Globalisation and the sleeping giant

The English Premier League derives £1.4 billion of broadcast revenue per annum from international markets, 45% of its total broadcast revenue. AUD $60 million of this £1.4 billion comes from Australia. This amount is equal to that which Channel Nine pays Tennis Australia (Australian Open plus lead-in tournaments), double what the FFA are receiving from Fox Sports for A-League season 2020/21, double Netball Australia's total revenue and double what Rugby Australia will receive in cash and contra from Channel Nine in 2021.

It is redundant to detail how globalisation and media technology have been a boon for the average Australian sport fan. Undoubtedly, sport fans have never had greater accessibility to all manner of sport and leagues from across the world.

While this may be great for consumers, it is arguably less ideal for domestic sport leagues. As can be seen from the above comparative broadcast rights and revenue figures, globalisation is translating to increased market power for large leagues in the global context. For some consumers, these international leagues supplement domestic interest and hence grow overall sport consumption. For others, however, such international leagues are substitutes to domestic alternatives. The accessibility of international leagues can therefore be viewed in economic terms as a leakage from the domestic sport system. Given finite time and resources, each additional minute or dollar devoted toward the EPL, NFL or NBA dilutes commitment to domestic sport options[225]

Perhaps the best example of this leakage is the UFC, which is a private commercial enterprise similar to Formula 1 and MotoGP, and is not obliged to operate beyond a profit motive. The UFC is essentially an events company that utilises a tightly controlled non-unionised workforce of independent contractors to maximise the organisation's profits. It would surprise many how little fighters earn, outside the most well-known main event athletes. The UFC then reinvests little to none of their profits into grassroots martial arts within individual host nations[226]. The scale of the organisation's growth and profitability has led to it being described as the biggest non-tech start-up business of the 21st century[227].

In Australia, the UFC 243 in Melbourne, held on October 6th 2019, had attendance of 57,127 and generated a gate taking of $5.5 million for the organisation. The Victorian Government also reportedly paid the UFC AUD$5 million for the privilege of hosting the event[228]. The event was held on the same day as the NRL Grand Final and, although not in the same timeslot or location, can arguably be said to have fragmented leisure alternatives on a day that would otherwise be 'owned' by a domestic football code. This UFC example is not to say that Australia should not bid for international events, as there are valid tourism and branding benefits that governments consider when putting together such bids. However, such examples illustrate how globalisation can result in leakage from the domestic sport system. In this one instance, over $10 million dollars from the Australia sport system migrated offshore, without any meaningful reinvestment in grassroots sport for the betterment of local communities.

The pull of international leagues can be seen by observing Australian search volume towards the NBA and EPL over time, relative to Australian leagues. Figure 22 illustrates AFL search volume as our largest football code, and the A-League as a soccer-specific comparison, relative to global giants NBA and EPL. Remembering that it is the *relative* rather than *absolute* scores that matter, the comparative acceleration of search volume towards the NBA and EPL is stark. In 2004, there was five times more Australian search volume towards the AFL than NBA. By 2019, this ratio had shrunk to 1.7. This trend goes some way to explaining how Australia has become the number one country, outside of the U.S. and China, in terms of both subscribers and revenue to the NBA League Pass. Australia is then followed by Brazil, Canada and the Philippines. Considering Australia ranks 13th in global GDP and 55th in population, it is a telling indictment of Australia's NBA fandom that it is the league's largest subscriber market beyond China.

Similarly, the A-League's comparatively flat growth in Australian search volume represents a sharp contrast to the EPL. The EPL generated 2.5 times the search volume of the embryonic A-League in 2005/06. However, rather than closing this gap as the domestic competition became engrained, the gap continued to grow. By 2019, there was four times as much Australian search volume towards the EPL as there was the A-League. Notice, however, that in the EPL's case, transferring from Foxtel's wider subscriber audience to the smaller and less accessible Optus Sport platform in 2016 resulted in the first decline in search volume for the league between 2016 and 2018. This illustrates that even for mega-leagues, product accessibility matters.

Given that the EPL is able to extract such considerable commercial value and consumer interest from the Australian market, a potentially uncomfortable question is whether Australian soccer is really a sleeping giant of the domestic sport marketplace? Australian soccer's *sleeping giant* status has been predicated upon two factors: a historically and

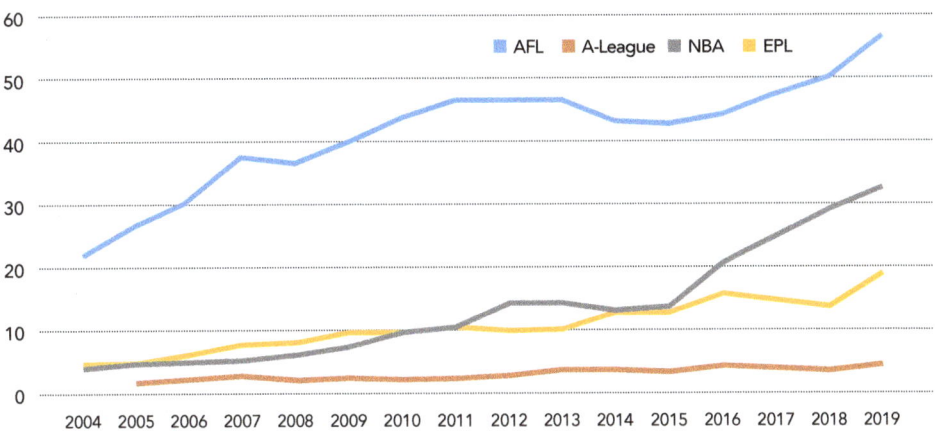

Figure 22: Annualised Australian Google search volume 2004-2019.

consistently large participation rate and sheer popularity of soccer elsewhere in the world. Yet, this has been true of Australian soccer for over half a century with comparatively little progress made.

Australian soccer has no realistic prospects to become a top-tier quality soccer league by world standards. This is a vital and potentially insurmountable limitation for the FFA, as Australian sport consumers are otherwise accustomed to having access to perceived world-class athletes in domestic leagues. Consider that the average sport fan has no heuristic to compare the **absolute** athletic talent of Mitchell Duke (A-League) to Dustin Martin (AFL), James Tedesco (NRL) or Michael Hooper (rugby union). If tested by the Australian Institute of Sport for absolute athletic ability, keeping in mind the obviously distinct needs of their individual sports, their scores would likely be similar. What the average sport fan does know however, is their **relative** athletic ability. The average sport fan knows that Dustin Martin, James Tedesco and Michael Hooper are the best athletes of their sport in the world, whereas A-League players perform in the long shadow of higher-quality international leagues.

This, of course, represents one of the most significant limitations of the A-League, as a competitor to the AFL and NRL domestically. Fans of Australian Rules, rugby league and rugby union (historically at least) have the best their sport has to offer on Australian shores.

A fan of Australian Rules has literally no alternative but to invest 100% of consumption into the sport domestically. Australian rugby league fans are in the same situation with the NRL having firmly accelerated beyond the British game. By contrast, as fans become more passionate and cognitively involved in soccer, they are more likely to shift a significant amount of their attention and consumption towards off-shore leagues. When one further considers that Australia has the privilege of hosting the Australian Open Tennis tournament that provides Australians with an annual dose of the world's best players, as do events like the Formula 1, Australian sport fans are spoilt in respect to their baseline expectations of sport quality. It must be said that, commendably, this perhaps bearish view is not one readily accepted by all soccer purists. When discussing the A-League and FFA's likely future prosperity with Simon Hill, his position was such:

> "I think while maybe I'm an optimist, that any sport that has two million participants in Australia always has a chance. It's about linking the top end of the game to the grassroots. Some people roll their eyes at this, thinking 'we've been hearing this for forty years'. But the reason we've heard it for forty years is because it's as true today as it was then."

Yet empirical evidence from around the world is continuing to illustrate the drawing power of our highest quality global leagues comes at the expense of domestic alternatives. To illustrate that this is a generalizable statement and not necessarily just a soccer-specific issue, I draw on a non-soccer example here.

The impact of sport quality is evident when one observes the experience of Canadians, a nation that is larger both economically (+24% GDP) and in populous (+48%) than Australia. Ice hockey remains the gospel sport of Canada and accordingly, the NHL competition features seven Canadian teams (out of 31) which provides access to the highest quality ice hockey in the world. By contrast, Canada has no NFL teams and instead, a Canadian Football League (CFL), a nine team competition with only slight rule distinctions to American football. Undrafted NFL prospects will sometimes migrate to the CFL as the sports are of sufficient similarity. In doing so, their wage expectations plummet: the CFL salary cap was set at $5.3 million for 2020, compared with NFL's $198.2 million. Similarly, CFL players of sufficient quality have been known to migrate to the NFL. The reason I mention this is to illustrate the impact of having a perceived inferior domestic 'football' product, which is evident when comparing NFL and CFL television ratings in Canada. The 2020 Super Bowl generated an average audience of 9.5 million in Canada, compared with an average audience of 3.9 million viewers for the 2019 Grey Cup (the CFL Grand Final). In a globalising world, sport consumers can no longer be tricked by relative standards of athleticism.

While globalisation and technology have the capacity to, and most certainly are increasing interest towards soccer in Australia generally, this does not automatically strengthen the FFA as the gatekeeper of the code domestically. In this sense, the EPL is a double-edged sword for the FFA.

Given that Optus pays $50 to $60 million per annum for exclusive Australian rights for the EPL, while the FFA's most recent deal with Fox Sports was worth $32 million, Australian soccer essentially receives less than a 33% share of total Australian broadcast dollars spent on soccer content[229]. However, Foxtel's loss of EPL rights was just as much a disaster for the A-League as it was for Foxtel. Undoubtedly, EPL coverage acted as a halo that induced some soccer fans to consume A-League, much more so than A-League being a halo for EPL viewing. As previously mentioned, my data of Sydney sport fans pegged only 6% of Australian soccer fans as exclusively interested in domestic soccer and 34% exclusively in foreign leagues.

A soccer fan can naturally support both a domestic team and a team from an international soccer league (and even multiple), and some might consider this a 'win' scenario for the FFA. Indeed my Sydney-specific data above puts the shared group of domestic and international soccer fans at 60%. But the question then becomes what proportion of such fans' time, money and interest does the domestic team retain relative to international teams? Millennials who support Liverpool or Manchester United and stream EPL matches via Optus Sport provide limited economic value to the FFA, outside of perhaps putting on their Socceroos or Matildas jersey once every four years.

In other contexts, the answer doesn't seem too rosy for the domestic team. Consider that in a study of Scandinavian Liverpool Football Club fan groups, 97% of such fans stated they would support Liverpool against their local team and 78% would support Liverpool against their national side. To see what it looks like to have 97% of fans cheering the visiting foreign team rather than the local team, simply go to YouTube and watch the Liverpool versus Melbourne Victory match of 2013, played in front of 95,000 people at the Melbourne Cricket Ground. As the study author Nash summarises:

"All group interviewees were at best lukewarm about their local football, some totally disregarded or despised it, and all felt that it simply fell so far short of the Anfield experience as to be non-comparable. Seventeen per cent of fans and a minority of interviewees took no interest in it at all. The overwhelming view was, as one fan suggested, 'we have an interest in local football, but we all recognise LFC as the "real thing". Local football is more of a summer pastime.'"

Nash's study focusses on the most attached satellite fans and is therefore perhaps alarmist relative to the overall population of soccer fans. Yet, such figures broadly align to comprehensive studies of the A-League around inauguration, most notably by Dr Daniel Lock. In a study of season one Sydney FC members, only 59% identified Sydney FC as their primary allegiance. When similarly asking Melbourne Victory inaugural season ticket holders, 71% identified as having "closely supported an overseas team" [230]. Remember however that season ticket holders represent a team's most highly identified and passionate fans (besides active fan groups). So within the broader fan base, the proportion of primary allegiance is likely to be far lower as my data suggests.

The NBL also face this limitation, but Australia's premier basketball competition has navigated this limitation well since the league's takeover by Larry Kestelman in 2015. What is interesting in the basketball and soccer comparison is how differently the two national leagues have approached being the comparative minnow of a bigger international league. The NBL has now twice in its history basked in the afterglow of the NBA's shadow in Australia. First, in the 1990s during the Jordan era in which the NBA first grew into an international phenomenon. Second, in the past five years since Larry Kestelman took an equity stake in the competition following a protracted period of decline.

Key to the NBL's rejuvenation has been to position itself as a pathway to the NBA, thus positioning itself as among the best development leagues in the world. Perhaps among the NBL's most successful initiatives has been the introduction of the Next Stars initiative as a genuine alternative pathway to the American College system for aspiring NBA athletes. In the period of Kestelman's stewardship, NBL TV audiences grew 40% between 2014/15 to 2017/18, attendances increased 25% and Facebook followers ballooned from 39,855 to 616,174. Arguably, beyond the NBA and Euroleague, the NBL is now the strongest basketball competition in the world.

Unlike the NBL however, the A-League does not have the luxury of authentically positioning themselves as among the best development leagues in the world. This creates a real chicken and egg problem for the A-League; it struggles to grow into a larger domestic league because it is a comparatively weak soccer league by international standards, but it is a comparatively weak international league because it struggles to grow commercially in Australia. But if the A-League were to magically become Australia's largest football league in terms of commercial revenue, just how big could their player expenditure become and how would this compare with other international leagues?

I estimate that, if making as much revenue as the AFL, the A-League would be the world's 11th most lucrative soccer league (average player salary of USD $463k), although Australia is the world's 13th largest economy. This would see the A-League join the top end of the third-tier pack of developed nations with upper moderate playing salaries, which includes Belgium (USD $403,000), Argentina (USD $379,000), USA/Canada (USD $375,000), and Portugal (USD $358,000). Outside the 'Big 5' leagues, the second tier pack include five leagues (China, Russia, Turkey, Brazil, Saudi Arabia) with less prestige but a significant pay packet, averaging a USD $794,000 player salary in 2018. While this hypothetical would certainly be a vast improvement upon the current quality of the A-League, it would not be a panacea to the leakage of consumer interest towards European soccer leagues.

Accordingly, I am not convinced Australian soccer is a *sleeping giant* of the Australian sport marketplace. Its growth is constrained by an insurmountable inferiority to overseas leagues, and this is a problem which essentially could not be overcome even if the league was as commercially large as the AFL.

As Australian Rules or rugby league fans become more passionate about their sport and a domestic team, the growing value of that fan remains within Australian shores. The AFL and NRL are able to capture all the economic value associated with this fandom: broadcast rights, digital rights, sponsorship, membership. Soccer fans, as they become more interested in soccer, begin to leak the commercial value of their fandom offshore.

The global economics of soccer and the inevitable impact this has on relegating domestic soccer from the Australian mainstream is perhaps best illustrated by developments within the W-League in recent times. In a semi-professional environment, the absence of European riches historically allowed the W-League to remain one of the world's strongest women's soccer competitions. Aided by its alliance with America's NWSL, which in combination provided year-round playing opportunities for women, the W-League has been a globally strong competition for much of its existence since 2008.

Yet season 2019/20 marks the peak and last season in which the W-League was among the world's highest quality leagues. In a report published by the PFA in mid-2020, it was observed that the W-League was now at risk of becoming a fourth choice destination for Matildas players. This happens to coincide with England's FA Women's Super League becoming fully professional in 2018/19 and many other leagues heading down this path, with particularly significant investment in women's soccer among individually large European clubs (e.g. Barcelona, Juventus, Lyon, and Bayern Munich).

In the past couple of years, the exodus of top quality Matildas has gone from a leak to a flood. The most famous name is undoubtedly Sam Kerr, who joined the English competition with Chelsea for three-year, reportedly $4 million contract. In a telling indictment of her local popularity, as a Perth Glory player, Sam Kerr's name and number accounted for 16% of total club sales of numbered men's A-League Perth jerseys[231]. In the past two seasons, the Matildas team has gone from near exclusively playing in the W-League to having almost entirely exited the competition. This list includes Ellie Carpenter (Olympique Lyonnais), Kyah Simon (PSV Eindhoven), Amy Harrison (PSV Eindhoven), Steph Catley (Arsenal), Caitlin Foord (Arsenal), Hayley Raso (Everton), Jacynta Galabadaarachchi (West Ham), Emily Gielnik (Bayern Munich), Lisa De Vanna (Fiorentina) and Alex Chidiac (Atletico Madrid). In the most recent year-on-year comparison, Europe's share of female Australian soccer players grew from 67% to 93% in 2019/2020.

The quality of clubs these women have transferred to and the Matildas' embeddedness amongst the top 10 rankings of women's world football is truly something to be proud of. It also goes some way in explaining why True North research has the Matildas as the national team with which Australians have the strongest emotional connection[232]. One prevailing view is that the Matildas' exodus from the W-League should be viewed as a good thing, as it reflects that women's soccer has finally reached a long over-due level of professionalism. As noted by Samantha Lewis of *The Guardian*:

> "The Matildas' European exodus is no crisis. Instead, it should be viewed as the next step in the evolution of the women's game. Professionalism ought to be the global goal for women's football in the next decade… What we're now seeing is the product

of this next step, where domestic leagues – not just national teams – are becoming the key driver of growth" [233]

That female athletes are increasingly able to earn a full-time living from professional sport is something to celebrate. That this can't be done in Australian women's soccer is something to commiserate. But it speaks to inevitable limitations to soccer's growth in Australia: economics dictate there will never be world-class athletes playing in a domestic Australian soccer competition.

In a nation in which soccer has two to three football competitors that can be positioned as world-best, and with technology that makes the EPL as accessible as the A-League, the *sleeping giant* may have missed its best and final moment to awaken in the mid 1970s.

Rugby league: a century of bad business

Although it is easy to criticise Australian soccer for blowing its golden opportunity for future prosperity, undoubtedly, rugby league retains the football crown for historical mismanagement and poor commercial acumen. A lot of the finger pointing regarding why the NRL has such a weak balance sheet as of 2021 has been directed at central headquarters, in particular a perception of excessive spending. ARLC Chairman V'landys has supported this narrative, confirmed by intentions to strip $80 million of operating costs from the NRL's $180 million operation. Undoubtedly NRL headquarters owns considerable responsibility for the game's perils, yet criticisms of excessive spending have been naïve, driven by populist media reporting.

In reality, the root cause of the NRL's financial problems historically, currently and into the future, is that is has many commercially weak clubs that manage to spend much more than they earn. Most fundamentally, rugby league clubs are much more proficient at spending money than making money. Perhaps most evident of this is that, despite combined annual losses in the tens of millions per year, spending on NRL football departments continued to grow at an annual rate of 35% between 2013 and 2017. The formation of the AFL's independent commission in the mid 1980s, with few assets and half a competition of near-bankrupt clubs, saw the game change and develop its business models. Rugby league never experienced its puberty moment, because its poker machine reliance transitioned into broadcast money reliance without a singular crunch point to drive institutional change.

Rugby league has historically never been a particularly profitable business, and in this respect the poker machine revenue that has sustained rugby league over time has perhaps been more of a curse than blessing. On the one hand, it has historically underpinned the financing of the game, yet the very reliance on leagues clubs to underwrite football club losses has been what has institutionalised a commercial laziness amongst Sydney rugby league clubs that has yet to see them become self-sufficient after 100 years of trying. The combined losses across clubs totalled $45 million in 2015 and $56 million in 2016, offset by Leagues Club grants of $25 million and $39 million in these two years.

In one hundred years of trying, Sydney rugby league clubs have made impressively little progress in detaching themselves from a reliance on leagues clubs, and hence poker machine revenue that derives from society's least affluent. The South Sydney Rabbitohs are the only Sydney-based team able to regularly make profits without gaming revenue. In 2018, the eight remaining Sydney NRL teams made a collective loss of $27 million between them before leagues club contributions[234]. When you consider the NRL gave each club a bonus $2.82 million in central grant money over and above the salary cap in 2018, the difference between the eight Sydney clubs real income and expenses was $49.5 million. As a matter of comparison, the AFL's ten Melbourne clubs posted a collective **profit** of about $34.5 million in 2019.

In June 2020, Peter V'Landys noted that "the clubs have got to make smart decisions and be responsible. They are autonomous and they make those decisions as they see fit. But they have to act for the benefit of the game as a whole".

A long view on history would suggest making smart decisions hasn't been a strength of rugby league clubs, and neither has acting for the benefit of the game as a whole. Consider the case of NRL's finals match between St George Illawarra and the Parramatta Eels in 2009, where St George elected to keep the match at their suburban ground rather than risk losing home ground advantage in a major stadium befitting the occasion. Parramatta CEO Paul Osborne's appraisal of his counterpart: "In all honesty, his decision is madness. Instead of having 42,000 fans at the Sydney Football Stadium we'll have 17,000 in seats and a few poor buggers squashed on the hill… God help us if it rains". Lightning struck again in 2020 when, despite being starved of attendees all season, the Penrith Panthers elected to play their finals match against the Sydney Roosters at their suburban venue. With a COVID-19 capacity of 10,000 odd at Penrith Stadium, the league forewent the very real prospect of a 40,000 crowd at ANZ Stadium.

In a game starved of the regularly large crowds needed to build an attendance culture, the last thing the NRL needs to do is voluntarily lock-out fans. Yet, once the NRL changed the structure of the finals venues to ensure games were played at appropriately large stadiums befitting a finals fixture, the response from commercially weak Sydney NRL clubs was unsurprising. Rather than strive to fill large stadiums with their seemingly invisible fan bases, they once more started to complain about the new system and the stripping of home ground advantage and atmosphere. Finances aside, the frequency of salary cap cheating in the NRL is not a glowing endorsement of NRL clubs' ability to act to the benefit of the game as a whole.

In terms of making smart decisions, journalist Phil Rothfield notes: "NRL clubs have squandered almost $400 million in a decade [2010–2020] of financial mismanagement that has led to an astonishing turnover of 116 different chief executives and chairmen at the 16 clubs"[235].

Perhaps amongst the most bizarre appointments was that of ex-player Corey Payne, recruited as Penrith Panthers CEO in 2016, a tenure which lasted five months. At commencement, he was 32 years old and younger than many active NRL players at the time. Considering as a random example that Collingwood's CEO Mr Mark Anderson had banked 10 cumulative years' experience as a CEO of both Swimming and Hockey Australia and prior football experience as a Chief Commercial Officer before obtaining his role, and the comparison in executive expertise is stark.

Coincidently, the Penrith Panthers football club made a loss of $8.3 million before licensed club contributions in 2018, nearly double the next largest loss (Bulldogs $4.9million)[236]. In 2019, the Penrith Panthers were simultaneously paying the wage bill of three head coaches as part of negotiated financial settlements to secure the coach they desired. The coach they desired so desperately (Ivan Cleary) had himself been previously fired from the Penrith Panthers in 2015, with a year to run on his contract. Without a tinge of irony then, former general manager of football for the Penrith Panthers Phil Gould noted that he has been "saying for years" [237] that NRL head office needs to significantly cut its spending. The polarising Gould typifies an outdated 'insider' philosophy that still strongly pervades rugby league. As Gould says himself:

> "There's no doubt as our game brought in more revenue we needed business people, which is why we moved to a commission... We felt that these people, having been successes in their own life in the business world, could guide our game... But the system just hasn't worked like that, unfortunately... It hasn't produced the results... we've tried to make it too difficult... It's football, it's not BHP. This is not the NAB, this is a football competition" [238]

The above sentiment, an almost anti-intellectualism, anti-outsiderism characterises rugby league much more than any of its counterparts, except perhaps soccer. Barely a media article would be written involving former NRL CEO David Smith (2012-2015) without explicit mention to his banking background and implicit reference to non-rugby league background.

Yet 'rugby league people' have seemingly done an abjectly terrible job of running rugby league, evidenced by the sheer number of NRL clubs that are so unprofitable despite the code's allegedly wide popularity. The vapid commercial underperformance of NRL clubs is particularly stark when you consider the conversion of NRL 'fans' into active customers, compared to the AFL. Perhaps the best dataset to evaluate fandom over time belongs to Roy Morgan Research, who have been tracking football fan bases since before the turn of the millennium.

THE BATTLE FOR FANS, DOLLARS AND SURVIVAL

A curious trend emerges from their longitudinal dataset. Roy Morgan suggests that there are in fact fewer AFL and NRL fans today than there were in 1999. The cumulative total of AFL club fans was 7,931,000 in 1999, declining to 7,871,019 in 2019 despite the addition of two new teams. The NRL's drop off has been far more significant, from 6,738,000 in 1999 to 5,963,000 in 2019. The 1999 figure however, does not include the expelled South Sydney Rabbitohs (or Norths), who upon readmission had 334,000 fans in 2001. When you consider population growth and include dormant Souths fans, Roy Morgan estimates the NRL fanbase to have declined by 16% over two decades during which the population has grown 35%.

That both the AFL and NRL have fewer fans at the broadest level in 2019, compared with 1999, should be surprising[239], given these codes has never been more accessible. What is perhaps more interesting however is that, if the figures are to be believed, the gap in fan base size between the AFL and NRL is not particularly large. If you include Souths' 2001 tally in 1999 aggregates (as dormant fans), the AFL had only 12% more fans than the NRL in 1999. Fast-forward 20 years and for all the AFL's game development in Northern states, the gap has grown to only 32%. This illustrates once more that while the AFL's development has been decisive, the league it is by no means unequivocally more popular than the NRL.

What is more equivocal is the AFL's ability to convert fans into revenue. The AFL ecosystem created around $1.5 billion in revenue in 2019[240], to the NRL ecosystem of around $850 million. Accordingly, from 32% more 'fans', the AFL generates 80% more revenue.

If you looked purely at the sponsorship of AFL and NRL team jerseys to assess how popular each code must be, the neutral observer would surely predict a greater gap than 32%. Indeed observing each code's suite of sponsors gives us a good indication as to why NRL clubs generate comparatively weak revenue compared with AFL clubs, before even considering membership and attendance rates. Four of the five largest automotive brands in Australia (by sales volume) sponsor AFL teams. While AFL clubs are heavy on automotive brands, finance and insurance and large consumer-facing brands, NRL teams have often gone extended periods without a major sponsor at all. For instance, the Canterbury Bulldogs remained without a major sponsor for much of 2020.

When one considers that Richmond (453,000 fans; 103,358 members) and South Sydney (426,000 fans; 29,626 members) have comparable fan base sizes, share similar historical prestige and have both experienced recent success, the divergence in their major sponsors is telling: Jeep/NIB (Richmond) and Aqualand/Alcatel (South Sydney).

While AFL teams are sponsored by large and often international brands; Jaguar, Zurich, QBE, Ford, Hungry Jacks, and Emirates, NRL teams are associated with smaller and often regionalised companies; Durakote Roofing, Brydens Lawyers, Aqualand and URM. Given AFL and NRL television audiences are largely similar, and the leagues have largely similar aggregate fan bases, what does the discrepancy in sponsorship say about corporate perceptions of the NRL?

Perhaps an even greater struggle for NRL clubs than attracting premium partners has been converting 'fans' into active consumers via membership or attendance. The closest rugby league came to matching the Australian Rules attendance penetration was in 1994, where rugby league achieved an attendance penetration rate 78% the size of Australian Rules. By 2009-2010, nearly half as many people (55%) had attended a rugby league match compared with Australian Rules, a 30% decline from 1994.

Analysis of membership growth is even starker. The AFL had more cumulative club members in 1999 (441,711) than the NRL has 20 years later in 2019 (319,375). Of more concern for NRL clubs is that, having recognised the importance of membership a decade or so ago, NRL membership growth has now completely plateaued. From 142,859 members in 2010, there were 301,809 in 2016 for an annualised growth rate of 14%. From 2016 to 2019 however, NRL club membership grew to only 319,375, an annualised growth rate of just 1.4%. Between 2015 (267,465) and 2016 (301,809) NRL clubs hit a membership growth threshold.

The most logical explanation for this is that between 2010 and 2016, clubs signed up most of the 'low hanging fruit' of avid fans who were easy to entice into membership. Forced to then try grow memberships beyond an easily obtained baseline from 2017, NRL clubs have collectively failed to grow further since. While this might seem like a reasonable challenge to expect, consider that the AFL was still able to achieve 6.5% annual growth rate in memberships from 2016 to 2019 (1,057,572 members), seemingly immune to a NRL style plateau. In response to the COVID-19 affected season, cumulative AFL membership in 2020 declined only 6.1% compared with 9.5% among NRL clubs.

That the AFL operates on a completely different fan commercialisation level to its football rivals is evident in Figure 23. This diagram plots the 2019 fan base size (X-Axis) against membership base (Y-axis) of all 42 Australian-based AFL (red), NRL (blue) and A-League clubs (green). The insight is simple: AFL clubs are able to convert 13.4% of 'fans' (7,869,000) into club members (1,057,572) compared with 5.4% in the NRL and 4.2% in the A-League. In real terms, this means that AFL clubs are converting 1 in 7 fans into members, the NRL 1 in every 18 and the A-League 1 in every 24. The trend lines of Figure 23 clearly illustrates that from a consumer perspective, NRL clubs perform more like A-League clubs than AFL clubs.

The diagram is also able to reveal relative over and under performance of individual clubs in converting fans to members. Dots above the line of the same colour are overperforming (higher ratio of members to fan) and dots below its line are underperforming (lower ratio of members to fans).

There are some anomalies here worth noting. First, the Sydney Swans, Melbourne Storm, Brisbane Broncos and Brisbane Lions naturally underperform due to their large fan base sizes, being their city's sole representatives. The Gold Coast Suns (furthest bottom left)

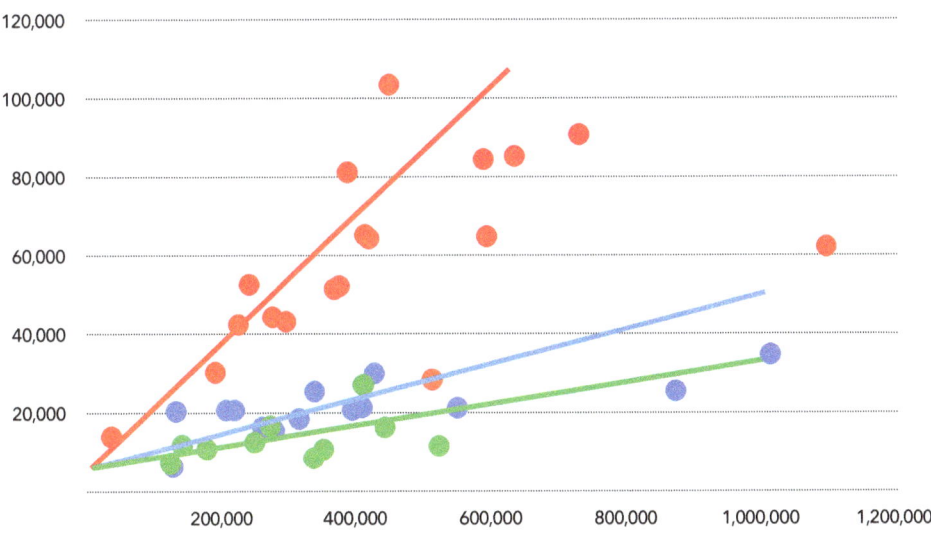

Figure 23: X-Axis- 2019 club membership tally, Y-Axis- 2019 fanbase (Roy Morgan). AFL (red), NRL (blue), A-League (green).

overperform because they allegedly had so few fans (35,000) at the time of sampling. Disregarding such outliers, the worst performing NRL clubs are the North Queensland Cowboys (3.8% conversion) and Manly Sea Eagles (5.0%) while the best are the Canberra Raiders (15.2%) and Penrith Panthers (10.0%). The AFL's best are the Richmond Tigers (22.8%) and the worst Adelaide Crows (10.8%). The Melbourne Demons are a quintessential niche sport brand: a very small base of supporters (242,000 fans) with seemingly very high loyalty (52,421 members). The A-League's best fan converter is the Newcastle Jets (8.2%) and worst Brisbane Roar (2.2%), who achieved near identical membership tallies despite the latter having nearly four times as many 'fans'. If you order the 42 clubs based on the conversion rate from fans to members (including outliers), AFL clubs make up 16 of the top 17 spots.

Where do NRL clubs go to from here? Much like Australian soccer missing the boat to build a strong domestic league prior to globalisation, rugby league appears to have missed the boat in building an attendance and membership culture before the rise of broadcast technology. Therefore while the NRL can gloat about recording the highest rating in annual television events, only 5% of fans appear passionate enough to actively support their team through a membership. Sydney NRL clubs in particular have remained amazingly devoid of criticism, given they appear to have barely grown in local popularity over 50 years.

The Manly Sea Eagles recorded an average Brookvale attendance of 10,493 between 2016-2019, less than their average for <u>every season</u> between 1967 and 1984. Cronulla Sutherland began consistently recording five figure average crowds from 1994 (11,848), after which the 14,000 barrier has only been broken twice in the 26 years since. The Penrith Panthers entered the five-figure crowd club in 1990 (10,025) and thirty years later, their eleven suburban games averaged 12,619 in 2019. The Sydney Roosters (Easts) averaged 12,197 at the SCG/Sydney Sports Ground in 1957. In 2018, a year they won the premiership in, they averaged 13,274 home game attendees.

If Sydney NRL clubs were being assessed by a social psychologist, they would likely be diagnosed with having a fixed mindset and an external locus of control, two traits never seen in most successful individuals or activities. That is to say, Sydney NRL clubs have been quick to point to external factors that explain their poor commercial performance, deflecting rather than embracing criticism.

More broadly, Sydney NRL clubs have perennially complained about being disadvantaged against bigger interstate teams in one-team markets. Yet, no Sydney club has ever accepted the significant financial inducement historically offered to them by the NRL to relocate. This mindset was most recently on show in 2020 when NRL clubs circled headquarters to criticise their financial management, ignoring that most Sydney NRL clubs would become instantly insolvent without the sugar hit of their leagues' club funding and the NRL's broadcast rights grants.

Because AFL and NRL clubs have been around for so long, they have become cultural institutions that protect them somewhat from criticism through a purely commercial lens. An unfortunate by-product of this in the case of Sydney NRL teams appears to have been complacency, or perhaps a sense of entitlement, to remain in the competition irrespective of contribution or performance.

Compare this to the FFA establishing performance parameters for the Wellington Phoenix as part of their licence extension agreement to remain in the A-League in 2015. Then FFA CEO David Gallop was quoted as saying: "We're ambitious for the growth of the A-League. You can't expect to squat on a licence in our competition...If you want longevity in the competition you need to produce results"[241]. The club did not meet these benchmarks in 2018/19 and hence the FFA invoiced the club $942,889.20 for their underperformance against agreed benchmark targets[242].

Arguably, too many teams in the NRL are squatting on their licences. In 2019 the Cronulla Sharks made $8.5 million from match revenue, member subscriptions and sponsorship combined, while receiving $13.6 million in grant funding from the NRL. The AFL's Western Bulldogs, who according to Roy Morgan have a mere 1,000 more fans (279,000) than the Cronulla Sharks, derived $22.5 million from match returns, partnerships and membership, against AFL grant income of $16.5 million. Meanwhile, the Brisbane Broncos derived $31.4 million in revenues from membership, game day and sponsorship in 2019.

How the Cronulla Sharks and other geographically niche Sydney NRL clubs grow is a tricky challenge, one that they've been grappling with largely unsuccessfully for 50 plus years. If there is a solution, it must surely start with keeping NRL clubs (and indeed all of the games stakeholders) far more accountable for their performance (and under performance) than has historically been the case.

Rugby union: the game now mostly played in heaven

If one were to follow the happenings of the football codes only in the Australian context, you would likely have formed quite a negative outlook upon rugby union's prospects. Yet, it is interesting to note that Australia happens to be just about the only country in the world where rugby union is in a period of prolonged decline. The introduction of Rugby 7s to the Olympic program has otherwise been a great catalyst for the game's global development, with many positive stories to be told from the rest of the world that provide a sharp contrast to Australia.

The inclusion of Rugby 7s into the Olympics was a huge strategic victory for World Rugby in several respects. As an Olympic event, it mandated representation from both genders. This acted as a coercive pressure upon domestic governing bodies to invest greater resources and attention towards developing female rugby athletes. The game's inclusion also opened opportunities for many local governing bodies to obtain funding from their respective government agencies, which often use Olympic inclusion/qualification as a resourcing criteria. Supported by the legitimacy of the Olympic halo, the truncated format of Sevens is a perfect pathway tool in establishing rugby into new markets compared with the full form of the game. Coupled with the annual HSBC Sevens Series world tour and its corresponding lower-division events, World Rugby has perhaps the perfect tool for global game development.

Rugby union's tangible internationalisation progress can be seen across many developing rugby markets around the world. The Japanese Sunwolves of the Super Rugby competition were generating larger attendances than any of the Australia sides, despite not having a winning season percentage at any point in their existence prior to their dissolution. Their national team also performed admirably at the 2019 Rugby World Cup, which they successfully hosted (typhoons aside). Argentina's Jaguares made the final of the 2019 Super Rugby competition, by far the best non-New Zealand team as evidenced by their semi-final thrashing of the ACT Brumbies 39-7. Argentina famously beat the All Blacks for the first time in 2020, despite having gone 402 days without an international fixture. From coming last (=18th) and without a point in their inaugural Sevens series appearance in 1999/2000, the United States finished second in the 2018–19 series, ahead of traditional powerhouses New Zealand, South Africa and England.

Rugby union is now well established in the North American university system, and a professional Major League Rugby competition has recently commenced the difficult process of mainstreaming the sport on the continent. In the UK, rugby league and union have gone in opposite directions to that in Australia, as was detailed earlier. The sport in England has now somewhat begun to sneak out of the shadow of the mighty EPL. Even Russia announced an intention to bid for the hosting rights of the 2027 Rugby World Cup, despite being banned by WADA from doing so.

For all this progress, Australia stands alone as quite a notable outlier. However, it is important to note that there aren't many particularly comparable sport landscapes to Rugby union's status in Australia, neither as the dominant code (New Zealand, South Africa), nor an emergent code (America, Canada, Japan, Argentina). However if we ignore considerable nuance to compare rugby's progress in Australia to that of the UK and France, where the code turned professional as an established but non-dominant sport, then Australian rugby has undoubtedly underperformed compared with its peers. The reasons for this underperformance have been discussed at length, so what does the future hold for rugby union in Australia?

Of greatest concern is that, even prior to COVID-19, Rugby Australia were already exhibiting financial stress, such that it could not properly fund the commercial and community levels of the game simultaneously. Of the football codes, Australian Rugby's prospects are perhaps the most challenging of the four. As Roy Masters wrote in February 2020, rugby union and soccer "are competing with each other to see who reaches the bottom of the Australian football barrel the quickest"[243]. After arguably being Australia's number two code following the 2003 Rugby World Cup, a year in which the code's revenue exceeded the AFL's by $100 million, rugby union and soccer have since been neck-and-neck commercially. In the 13 years between 2007 and 2019, the cumulative central revenue between the two organisations has been near identical, with the FFA ($1.38b) earning 3% more than Rugby Australia ($1.34b).

Yet key structural differences between the organisation of rugby union and soccer place the former in a far worse position to confront the impending challenges of a post pandemic environment. The most pressing challenge is the structure and funding of the domestic elite competition.

The FFA have been able to let the A-League run at a loss because the participating clubs are privately owned. Accordingly, A-League club owners have lost a combined $350 million over a 12 year period, with Tony Sage reportedly having personally lost $35 million over his 14 year period as Perth Glory owner. The financial short-fall in operating the A-League therefore comes from funds outside of the game. With the A-League having gained independence from the FFA in 2020, any financial challenges of the competition will be somewhat disentangled from the governing body.

By contrast, Australia's Super Rugby clubs are owned by their respective state unions, which means their losses are funded from inside the game. This means that should the NSW Waratahs' on-field performance diminish to the extent that the club was unprofitable, the shortfall in revenue would be picked up by the NSWRU, which would have to offset this by carving out costs from other parts of the organisation or draw upon available equity. The implications of balancing the books can be seen in the reporting on the NSWRU's 2017 annual report: "Drops in sponsorship, gate takings and a reduced Rugby AU contribution, were some of the major factors in a reduced revenue for NSW in 2017… On the flipside, the organisation almost halved its marketing spend in 2017, helping to avoid a net loss"[244].

Heading into restarted tendering of Rugby Australia's broadcast rights in late 2020, there was considerable bearishness surrounding the code's likely financial outcome for 2021 and beyond. Some estimates placed the value of their rights as low as $20 million, $15 million less than the original renewal offer put forward by Foxtel[245]. Roy Masters pointed to a Super Rugby ratings decline from 180,000 in 2004 to the low 30,000s by 2019 as reflecting Foxtel boss Patrick Delany's explicit omission of rugby union (and soccer) from the list of sports he considers 'tier one' (AFL, NRL, cricket and motorsport) going forward.

A further challenge for Rugby Australia was not just 'how many' people are watching, but 'who'. Rugby Australia is sitting on a demographic time bomb, with a fan base far older than its rivals. While 42% of soccer fans are under 40 and Future Sports research puts 44% of A-League audiences as under 34[246], only 29% of rugby union fans are under 40. Given the comparative youthfulness of the soccer audience, the FFA and A-League can at least contemplate a digital future where they develop their own streaming app if there are no better offers from traditional broadcasters.

Indeed for the FFA/A-League, there is some strategic logic in trying to acquire the best value soccer content they can afford from around the world (most likely starting from the lower end of the 'Big 5' plus MLS and working downwards), along with state-league content, to package into a soccer-specific streaming app for Australian consumers. This very idea has been put forward by 'The Golden Generation' group, led by former Socceroos Craig Moore, Lucas Neill and Mark Viduka, to create a 'FFA TV'[247]. In Rugby Australia's case however, their fan base trends toward an older demographic. From a technological adoption perspective then, a digital streaming platform exclusively for rugby union could be predicted to be far less successful.

Given the negativity that has enshrouded rugby union over the past decade or so, it likely came as a surprise to some that Rugby Australia's broadcast arrangement with Channel Nine did not appear as catastrophic for the code as foreshadowed. With a three year deal worth $100 million that finally achieves the necessary FTA coverage for Super Rugby to grow, Rugby Australia CEO Rob Clarke described the outcome as "The fantasy has become a reality for the Australian rugby community".

Rugby Australia have perhaps been the beneficiary of good timing here. In the past couple years, Channel Nine's streaming platform Stan, upon which most rugby union will now be telecast, has been a net-loser of international content due to shifts in the global media and streaming landscape. This has increasingly required Stan to reposition itself according to its Australian content offering. From Nine's perspective then, the deal provides its streaming platform content that fits its positioning, distinguishes it from larger international rivals and provides well-rating Wallabies test matches for the FTA channel, for a cost that makes experimentation into sport streaming viable.

The deal however is not without risks for both parties. For Chanel Nine, it is difficult to envisage Super Rugby matches on Channel Nine achieving commercially viable ratings remotely akin to an AFL or NRL fixture. The solution here has been to predominantly scheduled large-market teams, the NSW Waratahs and Queensland Reds, into the majority of these FTA timeslots. Yet, in 2020 with Rugby Australia and New Zealand Rugby running individual tournaments, there was evidence that Australian audiences are almost equally interested in foreign fixtures as domestic ones. In evidence, the round three NSW Waratahs vs ACT Brumbies match generated a Fox Sports audience of 53,000 people, compared with 49,000 for New Zealand's Hurricanes vs Blues match in the typically lower-rating preceding timeslot.

For Rugby Australia, the code will benefit from its weekly primary fixture on FTA, but how many subscribers will be willing to incur a further expense for a secondary pay-wall within Stan to access the vast majority of rugby content? Stan's primary platform reached 2.2 million in June 2020, a highly respectable tally from which to start. However, it is difficult to predict how many fans will be willing to purchase a supplemental subscription for rugby. The people who can make the most accurate prediction here are the data analysts at Kayo Sport, who now have access to immense behavioural data regarding sport viewership behaviour, which they do not generally share with their sport content partners.

With average audiences between 30,000 and 60,000 for Super Rugby on Fox Sports in recent seasons however, it is not inconceivable that the total subscriber base for a rugby-based Stan Sport will initially sit near 100,000. There is a good chance that the average audiences for Super Rugby games on Stan Sport will be too low to warrant publicising, but this will not be of high importance to Stan or RA, who are now just as much in the business of subscribers as ratings. If there is some hope to be found here, it is that there are an estimated 568,000 New Zealanders residing in Australia, forming 2.3 per cent of the population and representing our fourth-largest migrant community[248]. Accordingly, the inclusion of New Zealand Super Rugby content into the Nine/Stan deal has been a potentially underplayed component of value for in the brave new world Rugby Australia have ventured.

A seemingly good domestic deal with Nine however, conceals that Rugby Australia are still likely to end up with less broadcast revenue than their previous cycle. This is because previously, competitive tension between pay television broadcasters in the northern hemisphere resulted in broadcast uplifts that comprised a large proportion of Rugby

THE BATTLE FOR FANS, DOLLARS AND SURVIVAL

Australia's $57 million in annual revenue. With this competitive tension now dissipated, coupled with a yet to confirmed component of non-cash within the Nine deal, the code is highly likely to receive less broadcast income in aggregate from 2021, placing pressure to achieve cost savings in other others.

One such area will be in regards to the remuneration of players. Rugby Australia currently pays players 29% of the revenue generated by the professional game, yet already faces mounting challenges in retaining elite players from offshore leagues. Hence, from a previous broadcast deal worth $57 million per annum, even a possible reduction in aggregate rights to $40 million per annum would see the player payment pool reduce by $5 million. This would further weaken the code's capacity to retain both top talent and those at the precipice of becoming top talent. A weakening domestic talent pool further erodes the capacity for a high-quality domestic competition, further diminishing the game's commercial value in what could become a vicious downward spiral. Already, it has been announced that Michael Hooper will take a sabbatical year playing in Japan's Top League, which coincides with the domestic rugby calendar. While such sabbaticals may be a necessary compromise to keep the code's draw-card athletes tied to Rugby Australia, it further complicates and diminishes the value proposition of a domestic competition to prospective media partners.

The game in Australia undoubtedly sits at a knife-edge, with the most alarmist voices suggesting the game is on a regressive path to semi-professionalism, even with the announcement of their new broadcast deal[249]. Certainly, there appear to be no obvious quick fixes for the code and there appear to be more holes in the ship than available bandaids to patch them. I consider the code's biggest issues to reside predominantly off the field. Specifically, rugby union's fan base is now comparatively small and old, a by-product of limited mass-media exposure, cripplingly little investment into community rugby to cultivate younger generations of fans and poor on-field performances.

Ben Darwin, whose company *GAIN LINE Analytics* is gaining prominence within the sport industry, takes a different perspective and is unequivocal in his belief of the root cause of Australian rugby's problems. When I asked him what he thought represented best the path forward was for Rugby Australia, he stated:

"Australian rugby needs to understand what it's there for. The NRL doesn't care about the Australian national team, nor the AFL about International Rules. You can't serve two masters. Introducing new domestic teams reduces national team cohesion. The biggest driver of people playing and watching rugby is the Wallabies winning. We've spent $75 million domestically on the Force and Rebels to produce four Wallabies"

Unlike the FFA and their 2 million participants, I don't not believe it the case that Rugby Australia simply needs to re-engage with an existing, latent fan base by winning a Bledisloe or two. Rugby union's challenge is more difficult as they need to create both new fans and reenergise the loyalty/passion of the fans that remain. At a national level, out of 37% of Australians who are exclusively interested in one football code, only 2% are exclusively interested in rugby union.

Like a house destroyed in a storm, Rugby Australia need to build a new house that is fit for purpose for 2021 and beyond, rather than try rebuild what was destroyed. Getting Super Rugby fixtures on FTA television would appear to be a good start and long overdue. However, if these fixtures are of poor match quality or contain players with limited familiarity to prospective audiences, there will be little achieved from being on FTA television. Whereas Rugby Australia has throughout its professional history had a sufficient stable of marketable Wallabies stars, 2021 will see Rugby Australia launch its domestic competition on FTA television when it has precisely the weakest stable of established stars in its domestic ranks.

Culture war and the unassailable rise of Victorian rules football

It has been well-documented that, compared to counterparts, the AFL is a historically well-run, future-focussed, strategically efficient organisation. The code's significant financial clout is actually a modern circumstance. Remembering that when the AFL's independent commission was established in the mid-1980s, the AFL had total net assets of only $3 million and many of its clubs were teetering upon financial collapse. By contrast, consider that between 2012 and 2019, the AFL centrally derived about as much revenue as the NRL, FFA and RA combined.

The financial dominance of the AFL among its football competitors in modern times is stark. Excluding AFL distributions to clubs to avoid double-counting revenue, Collingwood Magpies' revenue in 2019 surpassed $70m, more than half that of Rugby Australia ($112m) or the FFA ($132m) as a single AFL club. If AFL clubs signed individual broadcast deals, the Magpies would already be a commercially larger operation than RA or the FFA in 2020. By mid-decade, when these two codes will have replaced their existing lucrative broadcast rights with potentially less lucrative new deals, there is every possibility that the commercially larger AFL clubs will be deriving more revenue than RA or the FFA.

The key question posed by the financial dominance of the AFL is therefore, is the code upon an unassailable trajectory toward complete market dominance?

In addressing this critical question, it is notable that the AFL is not only financially larger than its rivals, but that the gap between the AFL and its counterparts appears to be

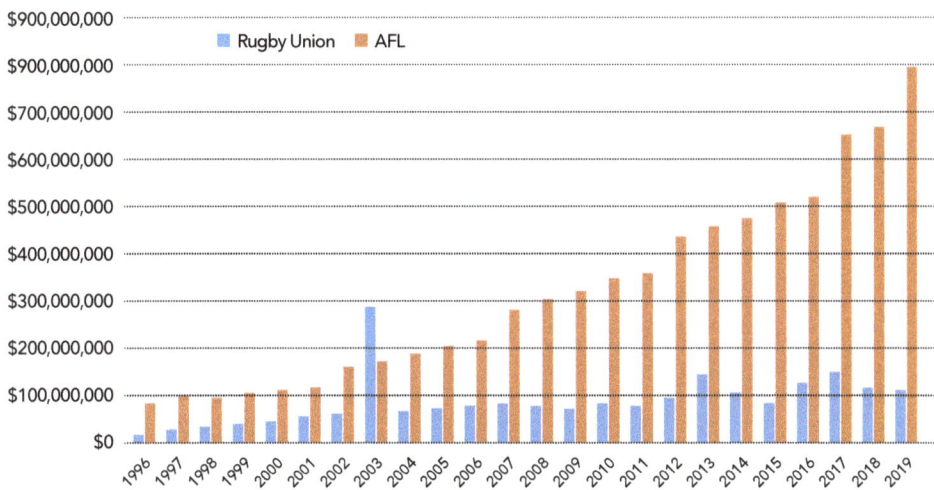

Figure 24: AFL versus Rugby Australia central revenue 1996-2019.

continually growing (see Figure 24 above). In rugby union's second year of professionalism, their revenue ($21m) was a quarter to that of the AFL's ($85m). By 2019, Rugby Australia's revenue ($112m) was only 14% that of the AFL's ($794m). Over this 24 year period then, Rugby Australia revenue has grown 544% to the AFL's 936%.

Yet, Australian Rules' overwhelming financial strength can also be viewed as by-product of its accumulated historical successes and as a dividend derived from superior governance. From strong foundations, the game has grown robustly. While AFL histories such as Blainey's provide detailed recounts of these great successes, with some 'inadvertent deception' thrown in as detailed earlier, many such successes can be aggregated to be described as victories in the battle of culture warfare. As was previously noted by Ian Syson: "The development of Victorian Rules around Australia in this time (1880) is not so much an inevitable development 'out of the soil' but is a product of patterns of politicised advocacy, evangelism and imposition". This section explores how advocacy and evangelism has perhaps been Victorian rules greatest weapon in becoming Australia's most dominant football code, and the value of this advantage into the future.

Australian Rules has been propagated upon a base of perceived cultural superiority. Syson described this in historical terms as evangelism, but undoubtedly perceptions of superiority are supported by tangible evidence in the form of superior crowds and generally positive word of mouth that has surrounded Victorian rules almost from inception. Such large crowds have been favourably compared with rugby and soccer crowds for over a century since. As historian June Senyard described, Australian Rules spectatorship became a sport in of itself; "Reporters found the size of the crowds watching the game almost as significant as the outcome of play"[250].

Like major wars of both the military and cultural variety, Australian Rules have historically been an effective propagator of code war propaganda. The formation of the Australian Football Council in 1906 to advocate for Australian Rules saw the explicit establishment of a 'propaganda' fund. In modern times, this would be called 'marketing' or 'New Market development' as the AFL did in their financial accounts between 2007 and 2015, but in 1906 the ANFC were evidently less sensitive to the optics of being at war with their fellow codes. From the ANFC meeting of 1906:

> "a tax of 5 per cent on the net income of clubs affiliated with the controlling body of each State… to be used in propaganda work in New South Wales, Queensland, Western Australian and Tasmania" [251]

For those in the soccer tribe, the great success of Australian Rules and its advocates has been cultural, to position itself at the centre of the Australian sporting culture and where possible, position soccer as foreign and wicked. This has been part of Australian rules agenda for over a century, as evidenced from the inception of the ANFC in 1906. Their inaugural creed left no doubt over the code's willingness to cohabitate with other football codes: 'One flag, one destiny, one football game'. Eddy McGuire brought this juxtaposition to life in August 2020 when describing the worst features of Australian Rules football as being derived from soccer: "So everything we hated about soccer, we're bringing into the game. We've got blokes diving, we've got little cheap shots – that's not what our game's about".

For the rugby tribes, the great success of Australian Rules has been to become so much more nationally influential, despite the northern states historically holding the balance of power in terms of Australia's national population and economic output. Australian Rules' great success has been to position itself as 'Australia's Game', long before every becoming truly national sport as objectively measured. To achieve this success, the AFL's greatest weapon has been, and will continue to be, the influence and advocacy of the code's agents in the broader cultural war.

The AFL's dominance in modern culture war perhaps most strongly manifests in perceived double-standards in the media reporting of Australian Rules compared with other football codes. First we consider the reporting of crowd behaviour between AFL and soccer. Noteworthy is crowd violence in Adelaide only four months apart for an A-League match in December of 2017 and an AFL match in April of 2018. The A-League was widely criticised, including a public condemning by former AFL players Kane Cornes and Warren Tredrea, while the AFL violence was given comparatively little prominence. Speaking of this difference at the time, journalist Andrew Maher on SEN Breakfast:

> "There's definitely a double standard, there's no question about that… I have got no doubt in my mind that there is a willingness and there is a hunger for mainstream

media, particularly the News Limited press, to highlight anything that goes wrong in a game of soccer. There was not only the brawl at Adelaide Oval [AFL], but there are allegations that two players were racially abused in that game on Saturday night which is an absolute disgrace that in 2017 that is still happening... I hate bringing racism into this but if you go right back to the barest of bones, I feel like there is still somewhere in the Australian psyche that it's 'wog ball'. It's their game, it's not our game. They dive, their crowds are no good, there's ethnicity involved, you can't control the wild people from Eastern Europe, they bring their problems from over there to here... I think it is dangerous, I think it is unfair. If I'm a soccer fan and see it highlighted in our game but not in theirs, if you want to break it down like that, I can feel the frustration" [252]

Perhaps the best of New Limited's reporting was from the *Herald Sun* in early 2014 with an article titled '*Secret files reveal violent A-League antics in our sports capital*'. The article reports on 'secret dossiers' compiled by police that describe soccer fans as **"totally different to AFL and cricket"**. Quoting a Victorian Police Inspector: "They're not true fans of the sport. They're using A-League football as a vehicle for violence"[253].

By 2014 however, the targeting of soccer fan behaviour would begin to appear misaligned with reality, given the AFL's commencement of a horror run of behavioural incidents between 2013 and 2019. The *Herald Sun*'s article was of course six months after Adam Goodes was first called an ape, after which crowd booing soon followed which for a long period was justified by many as game rather than race related. Perhaps the next worst incident in this time period was in 2019, when a disabled Hawks fan was assaulted by a Demons supporter at the MCG. Many crowd skirmishes at AFL matches would occur in-between.

It is perhaps unfair, on a statistical basis, to expect AFL games to be free of crowd troubles. With AFL crowds on average two to three times larger than its football counterparts, while also playing more aggregate fixtures, an analysis of spectator incidents per capita would be intriguing. Yet, as much damage as the above identified incidents have done to the AFL's moral high ground around fan behaviour, if they had instead occurred at an A-League match, the media reporting and ensuing brand damage would have been magnitudes larger for the FFA.

The power of controlling the media narrative cannot be understated, and the AFL have undoubtedly been net beneficiaries of media agendas. Yet, some consider the FFA to have contributed to the problem by playing poor defence, disenfranchising their own fans in the process. As Simon Hill notes on the matter:

"Sydney derbies worked because there was tribalism. There was a rivalry. East versus west, rich versus poor. It was the same with Sydney versus Melbourne. They resonated because of the fans and the atmosphere they created. But we killed that because the *Sunday Telegraph* published an article [in 2015] saying we were hooligans. Football fans were outraged and demanded a response, but instead of defending the game, David Gallop defended the article. Those disenfranchised fans never came back. We shot ourselves in the foot with a double-barrelled shotgun. You go to games now and the atmosphere is sterile. We tried to play the mainstream game because we didn't have enough belief in ourselves and it has failed"

The AFL's dominant control of media reporting extends beyond suppressing soccer and represents a broader strategic advantage in the football culture war: when it does something well it will be well publicised, when it does something poorly it can (to a degree) be obfuscated, downplayed or justified. This advantage comes straight out of the Sun Tzu Art of War playbook.

Whether if out of fear or loyalty, southern media outlets show a loyalty to the AFL unrivalled by other codes. As Geoff Parkes notes: "The majority of the AFL media, are dismissive, indifferent or, at best, curious. Mostly, they struggle to distinguish between rugby union and rugby league, and headlines like 'This sport (rugby union) is in serious trouble' merely reinforce their prejudices"[254].

It is apparent that the rugby codes are provided considerably less protection in the northern markets, and it is here that the difference to the AFL is particularly stark. Consider for instance the NRL club Canterbury Bulldogs 2018 'Mad Monday' antics at the Harbour View Hotel in Sydney, which resulted in an initial record fine of $250,000 for poor player behaviour. Despite having exclusively booked the venue as a private function, media were able to place themselves at opportune vantage points and use long-range photographic lenses to capture the team's wild behaviour within the confines of the venue.

Only five years earlier in 2013, the St Kilda Football Club held their 'Mad Monday' at South Melbourne pub, also upon the more wild side of private functions. Unlike the Bulldogs antics, whose behaviour was limited to each other, the St Kilda Mad Monday resulted in a player (Clinton Jones) setting a dwarf entertainer on fire, after other players had been critical that he was not being entertaining enough[255]. The player was fined a grand sum of $3,000 for the incident.

AFL CEO Andrew Demetriou thought the incident so outlandish that he initially laughed when questioned about it live on air, presuming it to have been a joke. Notably, in the 2021 environment even laughing at such a joke would no longer be considered appropriate. When the performer emailed Leigh Montagna (the event organiser and St Kilda player) to request his burnt cloths be replaced, Montagna was alleged to have replied:

"If you actually followed your job description and said you would entertain us, I would be happy to... But to sit on a seat and drink water for two hours and still want your money does not constitute work in my book... I am sorry if you felt your clothes were affected, but I also feel ripped off that I paid you money to entertain and you did not make any effort to try and entertain" [256]

The purpose of the above is not to compare atrocities across codes, nor consider the relative morals of the Canterbury Bulldogs' team behaviour. Rather it is to illustrate that northern news outlets thrive on the opportunity to report on off-field behaviour of the NRL, perhaps more than any other form of content and more so than southern media on AFL. This creates a strange conflict of interest: on the one hand News Limited and Fairfax/Nine pay hundreds of millions of dollars to be associated with rugby league, yet simultaneously monetise tearing it down in a way that the AFL does not experience amongst its own stakeholders.

This is not to say that rugby league is a victim of media, although how much more scandal prone the NRL are compared with their AFL, union or soccer counterparts is a tricky empirical question to measure. Upon having to defend their new 'no fault stand down' policy in Federal Court in 2019 however, the NRL cited an average rate of one scandal every 22 days between 2015 and 2018. This strike rate undoubtedly stifles rugby league's ability to grow support amongst particular key target groups such as women, white collar workers and southerners. Yet, the NRL does not hold a monopoly on misbehaviour to the degree that is perpetuated by media or perceived in popular culture. The particularly high profile COVID-19 breach by Sydney Stack and Coleman-Jones, as well as the surfacing of serious criminal allegations against several AFL players in 2020, illustrate that the AFL and NRL may not be as far apart on the transgression spectrum, despite being polls apart in the court of popular opinion. This public perception then feeds into sponsorship valuation, media rights and rates of fandom.

Headlines such as '*Female fans are AFL's secret weapon in drawing crowds*', '*Secret files reveal violent A-League antics in our sports capital*' or '*Rugby Union is in serious trouble*' each contribute to shaping consumer perceptions of our respective codes. These perceptions eventually lead to preferences formed in the conscious or subconscious mind, which eventually lead to behavioural outcomes. For established fans of each code, such headlines may not particularly matter. In fact, threats to our social identity can often act as a rear-guard that leads to stronger identification (for instance being admonished as a member of the Western Sydney Wanderers active fan group RBB). But for those who do not strongly identify with any one code (the great majority of people), such headlines can shape future behaviours.

Consider the Melbourne resident with little previous direct exposure to rugby union who sees the headline '*Rugby Union is in serious trouble*' in their local newspaper. This will likely be the only rugby union article in the paper that day, which will likely be five pages deep following AFL related commentary. In two months' time when an opportunity presents itself to attend a Melbourne Rebels fixture through a spare ticket or promotion, the brand association will have been formed that rugby union is an inferior sport because of the game's broader troubles. Similarly, the parent with a soccer-playing child who reads to the headline *'violent A-League antics in our sports capital'* becomes reticent to encourage their child make the leap from playing soccer, to attending Melbourne Victory games.

The broader potential journalistic implications associated with the AFL becoming too powerful perhaps came to full fruition in 2020. A good way to control what the media say about you, as China has illustrated, is to either own or control the media outlets themselves. And so it was in 2020 that AFL Media 'journalist' Mitch Cleary was stood down for reporting (accurately) that the wife of AFL player Trent Cotchin had breached COVID-19 protocols. The incident caused considerable furore around the purpose and positioning of AFL Media, which had long attempted to position itself as a 'credible news source'[257]. Several commentators are worth citing here. First, Eddie McGuire:

"They have no problem telling us they're independent when they're shredding players, clubs and officials… But don't say you've got an independent website if you stand down the journalist for printing the name of the person who went on Instagram, a public page itself" [258]

Respected journalist Gerard Whateley too was succinct in thoughts on AFL Media as an independent, credible news source:

"The AFL standing down Mitch Cleary is a betrayal of journalism and it is an exposing moment and I would think it's an unnerving moment if you worked at AFL Media and you believed that you were working as a journalist rather than as an employee of the AFL." [259]

Common among the sources reporting on the topic cited that a key reason Cleary was stood down was because AFL Media employees are reportedly required to put their obligations to the league ahead of any motives as journalists. Such prioritisation exposes *AFL Media* to questions of legitimacy, of whether it is a genuine journalistic operation or simply a modern day propaganda tool for the league. If one subscribes to this latter hypothesis, then AFL Media is indeed an incredibly powerful tool. It allows the league to propagate good news stories under the guise of credible news, but underpinned by public relations objectives, utilising 'journalists' that are alleged to be required to put their leagues' obligations ahead of journalistic integrity.

Beyond the influence of media however, Australian Rules appears culturally unassailable due to the customs and rituals that have uniquely developed in south-west Australia that are unmatched in the north-east. Sydney does not have a dominant rugby league culture like

THE BATTLE FOR FANS, DOLLARS AND SURVIVAL

Melbourne has Australian Rules, leaving Australia's largest city ripe for slow fragmentation in football preferences. Sydney's relationship to rugby league and union is incredibly region-variant: where you travel to in the city will dictate how popular the codes are. By comparison, Australian Rules is geographically ubiquitous across all of Melbourne, Adelaide and Perth (and corresponding regional areas).

The impenetrable cultural ubiquity of Australian Rules in Melbourne, Adelaide, Perth and Tasmania establishes social norms. As Parkes notes: "Many rugby [Union] people living in Melbourne support the Melbourne Storm in rugby league, and adopt an AFL team to support because that's the done thing... Yet this is rarely reciprocated". This cultural pressure to assume an AFL team upon migrating to Melbourne represents a norm not replicated in New South Wales or Queensland in respect to rugby teams. Such a custom is but part of a larger suite of norms that indoctrinates Australian Rules football into Melbourne culture. In the study of the 'Anti-Football League' discussed previously that attempted to create a counter-culture to AFL, the experiences of moving to Melbourne as a non-AFL fan was vividly described as such:

> '[Melbourne] society was full of fervent, foaming-at-the-mouth Australian Rules football fans... It was an unpleasant surprise, and even worse was the assumption that everyone had a football team they were devoted to. '"Who do you follow?" was the standard follow-up to "pleased to meet you". To fail to declare a team invited consternation, and the occasional curled lip' [260]

When you live in a city in which 56% people express an interest in AFL and has ten local teams that had 665,000 members[261] between them in 2019, it is unsurprising that 'which team do you follow' is a natural starting point of conversation. However this cultural ubiquity translates to other notable rituals too. For instance, one can anecdotally observe that nationally dispersed companies are considerably more likely to run workplace tipping competitions of the AFL variety than offer AFL and NRL simultaneously, let alone Super Rugby or A-League tipping.

The AFL grand final parade is able to attract 100,000 attendees as part of a highly successful broader week of festivities. Another such festivity is the longest kick competition upon Melbourne's Yarra River, in the process successfully integrating the iconography of Melbourne into Australian Rules coverage. By comparison, this is how rugby league journalist Phil Rothfield described Sydney's NRL grand final week festivities in 2018:

> "If you go to Melbourne in AFL grand final week it's one big party... This week Sydney hosted its own major event — Sunday night's NRL grand final. The build-up to the game was the lamest ever. The city was like a ghost town...The NRL did absolutely nothing. They had no presence and no atmosphere...If you weren't a

rugby league fan you wouldn't have known there was a game on… This state, this city and the NRL need to get their act together" [262]

Aside from the AFL's considerable financial dominance, I contend it is in fact cultural dominance that has allowed the league to develop such a stranglehold upon the modern Australian football landscape.

The FFA arouses the national psyche once every four years with the Socceroos and increasingly the Matildas. Rugby Australia too can lean into the Rugby World Cups and Bledisloe matches. Rugby league takes the national centre stage three times annually via State of Origin. Yet, these are relatively limited artillery shells when it comes to breaking the AFL's cultural stranglehold in southern markets. Such events might provide momentary peaks of attention toward these codes, but they pale as change agents to the social norms that surround the AFL and their fans. Therefore whereas intermittent events across league, union and soccer capture the national spotlight, social norms that surround the AFL are embedded in many people's everyday life.

With the AFL needing to devote few resources to playing defence in its heartland markets, the code has been able to spend much of the past century and a half in offence. There are few signs within the future landscape to suggest this pattern will change any time soon.

Conclusion

Australia's sport marketplace is truly like no other in the world, blessed with an unusually large supply of elite sport content. There are two peculiar features of the Australian sport system that distinguishes us from other nations, being the inspirations to write this book and my PhD thesis. The first is the presence of four commercially viable football codes, despite having the 55th largest population in the world. Here, perhaps only Ireland is similar. The second is that our two commercially largest sports have, for over a century and half, divided Australia into near-perfect halves with a cultural ferocity akin to America's modern red/blue state political partisanship. While sport preference variation is certainly common elsewhere, such as baseball (rural) versus basketball (urban) in America, rarely do such differences transcend into battles over national culture as 'football' does in Australia.

While the beginnings of the accelerated commercialisation of sport can be traced to Kerry Packer's World Series Cricket in the 1970s, the football codes have been at war for well over a century. From their respective inceptions, each code's administrators and advocates have appeared acutely aware of the finite volume of infrastructure, media attention, players and supporters available to them. Hence, the off-field competition between the codes is long and storied, providing the basis for this book.

Of the codes, it is undoubtedly Australian Rules that has historically most embraced a war and conquer mindset, diverting Victorian profits to northern markets for 'propaganda' funding before rugby league had even been created. A century later, the AFL continues to divert Victorian profits into these northern states via the GWS Giants and Gold Coast Suns. It is telling that in comparison, by 2019, neither rugby code featured a domestic team in their competitions beyond the east-coast of Australia.

The AFL is undoubtedly winning the code war, although it doesn't take an entire book realise this. Thanks to the code's cultural dominance across the south-west of the continent, one in five Australians are interested exclusively in AFL and no other football code. The AFL generated more central revenue than its three competitors combined in 2019, and the gap is only likely to grow. Furthermore, AFL clubs are largely profitable, a feature which is not true of the remaining codes.

A long view on history however, shows that while the AFL has been comprehensively winning the code war for much of it, the remaining codes have each squandered golden opportunities to become stronger than they are in 2021. While a confluence of strong governance, leadership acuity and some good fortune has resulted in the modern AFL being among the strongest incarnations of itself that history could produce, the remaining codes are each much weaker versions than what alternative historical paths could have produced.

The onset of COVID-19 in 2020 provides a firm marker to reflect upon the development of Australia's sport and football marketplace and revaluate what the future may hold. The AFL and NRL, perhaps guilty of creeping organisational inefficiencies that arise from opulence, have both identified a need to streamline their operations. The NRL and its clubs, having historically lived hand-to-mouth from poker machine and then broadcast revenue, may now be fully appreciating the game's financial vulnerability. Meanwhile, Rugby Australia and the FFA are both in a period of larger reorganisation, with the previous fortunes of Super Rugby and the A-League built upon broadcast revenue and consumer interest that now appear exhausted. While the four football codes have managed to maintain their own patch in the sport market, as largely $100+ million operations in the last decade, significant change in the comparative strength of the codes looks more probable than maintenance of the status quo.

Attempts to commercialise Australian soccer in some ways has parallels to the stock market rally during the onset of the COVID-19 pandemic. Economic analysts were shocked by the decoupling of the surging Wall Street from the sinking 'Main Street', as the stock market was thought to be an indicator of the health of the real economy. So too has it been considered that Australian soccer would inevitably prosper, because the game's strong international appeal and domestic participation rate would eventually translate to commercial success. Yet the decoupled nature of Australian soccer's commercial success from its grassroots success is yet to change under the FFA banner. This banner is once again being rebadged in 2021 to Football Australia, perhaps reflecting an organisational impatience to stick with one path for any extended period of time.

Australian soccer's commercial struggles was perhaps no more so evident than on 17 July 2020, when the A-League's table topping fixture between Sydney FC and Wellington Phoenix drew a pay television audience of 12,000, in comparison to the NRL (804,000), AFL (978,000) and even Super Rugby AU (53,000) and the Hungarian F1 Grand Prix (83,000). Although these audiences undoubtedly overlap, if we treat them as discrete, the A-League achieved a 0.62% share of the Friday night sport audience on that evening. Almost poetically, the same day as the A-League's meek relaunched ratings were reported, Robbie Slater, an employee of Fox Sports, wrote in his column:

> "Next season is critical, for the A-League, for FFA, for the clubs and for everyone in the game to show Fox why they should continue — or show anyone why it should be a viable product…Everyone is bored of hearing how football is the biggest sport and

that more kids play it than any other. That's not good enough…Instead, we fall into traps comparing our game to the major European leagues…What the FFA, club owners and the game need to do is convince the football people in this country that the A-League is a good league, it's our league and it's one to be proud… Comparing our competition to the English Premier League? That is dumb and stupid, and will get us nowhere" [263]

Undoubtedly, the game faces a critical juncture, with the only progress to seemingly show in the past 15 years found in the women's game. From this perspective, winning the right to host the 2023 Women's World Cup appears a welcome stimulus for the game. Yet it is difficult to see how the A-League remerges from the pandemic as a mainstream commercial league. The most likely exception would be from an injection of private capital from white-knight foreign ownership of clubs, or perhaps a private equity buyout of the entire league. While the game's administrators should certainly avoid the traps of comparing the domestic game to Europe, it is unavoidable that football savvy consumers will. Convincing consumers to support the A-League when the 'Big 5' leagues are just a stream away is perhaps Australian sport marketing's single most difficult challenge.

Rugby league also faces existential challenges. It has been commonly expressed, in some variation, that rugby league thrives despite itself. Undoubtedly, the code has missed opportunities to be Australia's most popular football code for reasons entirely self-inflicted. Controversially then, one line of reasoning is that that rugby league is in fact Australian football's sleeping giant. Since at least the beginnings of professionalisation and commercialisation, rugby league has not been run smart enough for long enough to take advantage of the code's latent popularity. The AFL started investing in northern expansion in 1906, and have now invested hundreds of millions of dollars over decades strategically propagating the game, yet progress in some respects has been slower than many would expect.

Meanwhile, rugby league has dithered strategically and still disregards a large chunk of Australia's population. That in 2020, Peter V'landys describes the vision for rugby league as: "We've got the left arm in New South Wales and the right arm in Queensland," appears incredibly insular. Yet, rare moments provide insight to the code's potential. The Melbourne Storm's second Grand Final appearance in 2006 generated a Melbourne viewing audience (871,000) that was larger than Sydney (817,000) or Brisbane (806,000). State of Origin fixtures are able to generate commendable audiences in the southern states. Despite the code's challenges and limited strategic orientation, the AFL and NRL generate similar broadcast audience sizes, while Roy Morgan suggests the AFL, with two more teams, had only about 30% more fans than the NRL in 2019.

On the other hand, another line of reasoning might suggest that rugby league has never been more vulnerable, seeming to suffer from fair-weather fans and a game that may not stand the test of time in respect to scientific research around concussion. In relation to the former issue, Roy Morgan believes 5.96 million people support NRL teams. OzTAM measured the cumulative 2019 State of Origin audience to be 8.87 million across three games. More than double the amount of people follow the NRL (2.25m) on Facebook than the AFL (1.02m)[264]. Yet, where are these fans in the physical world? How is it that the Cronulla Sharks have as many 'fans' (Roy Morgan) and more Facebook followers than the Western Bulldogs, yet have only one-third as many members and generate one-third as much club revenue?[265]

The challenge here is that while AFL fans have been loud and proud advocates of their code for 150 years, as are the soccer tribe, rugby league fandom carries both a lethargy and a social stigma distinct from its competitors. While members of A-League active fan groups will chant and march to their team's stadium, Manly Sea Eagles' fans won't leave the northern beaches to attend away matches, unless it's a grand final. Rugby league is a code consumed from lounge chairs and engaged with via a screen, but with comparatively fewer people wearing merchandise, buying memberships or attending games.

Defeatist administrators and media advocates call rugby league a 'television game'. This obfuscates an uncomfortable reality that rugby league is less popular in a tangible sense in 2021 than it was in 1990 and prior, obstructed by the use of digital consumption metrics to suggest the game is widely popular. Rugby league indeed achieves very strong digital fandom metrics, but this simply is not comparable to traditional measures of popularity, such as memberships and attendances. Rugby league would do well to invest their efforts into improving the culture of their fandom, but is handicapped by poorly run NRL clubs whose responsibility this would largely be to execute. The NRL must soon seriously consider the degree to which its clubs are squatting on their licences, and determine how many are adequately contributing to the overall health of the league and broader game.

It is, however, Rugby Australia who may need to perform the most introspection to determine the sport's purpose, vision and strategy moving ahead. Although the code has appeared to salvage a reasonable broadcast deal, particularly in the COVID-19 environment, much longer term uncertainty still remains. A five team, 12 week competition in season 2021, plus a New Zealand cross over competition, appears a stock-gap solution for a COVID-19 environment, and is simply not enough premium rugby union content to remain a mainstream product. Normalisation post COVID-19 will require Rugby Australia to either expand its domestic competition, or more likely, reintegrate with the New Zealand counterparts.

More broadly, the code is perhaps the most appropriately placed to consider the benefits and risks of introducing private equity partners into the sport, as has already been the case in European rugby. If the organisation lacks the capacity to properly invest in community rugby and an elite competition simultaneously, then a logical path forward would be the sale or part-sale of Australia's domestic competition. This would leave Rugby Australia to focus on grassroots development and national teams instead.

Many might recoil at the idea of 'selling' the commercial game to private equity, yet the idea is not completely foreign. Basketball Australia is focussed on community basketball and the national team, having previously unsuccessfully attempted to run the NBL and realising the league was better off in the hands of private capital. With the NBL now flourishing under the ownership and management of Larry Kestelman, Basketball Australia now benefit from a stronger player pathway to their men's national team than had they retained control of a languishing domestic league.

As all of this transpires, the weakening of the overall Australian sport marketplace provides the AFL with a great opportunity to further entrench itself in the centre of Australian football culture. As the league noted within internal correspondence surrounding operational changes in response to COVID-19: "We want to rebound from this unprecedented time on the offence."[266] Economic downturns see a 'flight to quality', which sees investment shift in concentration from riskier to safer assets. We can interpret Foxtel's 2019 announcement of cuts to 'non-marquee' sporting content as signalling a flight to quality that will likely benefit the AFL and potentially the NRL. While the AFL has the largest cost-base, they have developed a club membership culture that has resulted in far more financially sustainable clubs and overall business model. It is therefore difficult to envisage a scenario other than the continued advancement of the Australian Rules. Although the AFL's gain does not have to equate with equally sized losses to the other codes, undoubtedly the AFL's advancement comes at some expense to the balance of the football hierarchy.

Although the most passionate of fans within each football tribe cheer for the uprising of their code and the subjugation of the others, the unique diversity of our Australian football landscape is something to cherish. Each code no doubt desires to be larger and stronger, yet the four codes have largely managed to begrudgingly co-exist in an equilibrium that has benefitted Australian sport fans immensely. The erosion of one or more codes from the mainstream would undoubtedly leave the sport landscape poorer, certainly not something to be celebrated. Consumers never do well in monopolised industries, and so it is that we should hope that the code wars rage on for a further hundred years, with each code able to find a place in our sporting hearts and minds.

Appendix

Appendix 1:
Proposed rules of Universal Football per 1915

Administrative components

- The game would be played on a rectangular field 140 yards long and 100 yards wide, plus 10 yard in-goal areas at each end. This equates to a field similar in size to an Australian Rules football field, but with the rectangular shape of a rugby league field.
- The game would be played fifteen players per side – compared with thirteen per side in rugby league and eighteen per side in Australian Rules football.
- There would be a set of rugby-style goal posts on each goal line, with two uprights 18 feet apart and a crossbar 10 feet high. There are no behinds goals posts.
- The game would be played with an oval shaped ball, which was common to both sports.
- The time keeping of the game was not originally identified, but when finally trialled in 1933, was played under Australian Rules quarters.

Game play components

- Scoring:
    - 3 points: scoring a Rugby try.
    - 1 point: conversion attempt on to a Rugby try. The try scorer must take this kick.
    - 2 points: goal scored from general play
    - 1 point: goal scored from a mark or free kick
    - -1 point: grounding the ball within your own defensive in-goal area. Equivalent to a 'safety' play in American football
- Passing and tackling:
    - Rugby league passing permitted (i.e. no need to hand-ball)
    - Forward passes and knock-ons would not be permitted, akin to rugby league rules

THE BATTLE FOR FANS, DOLLARS AND SURVIVAL

- ○ Rugby league style tacking between the hips (but not below) and shoulders would be permitted.
- Game play:
  - ○ The rugby league scrum would be abolished,
  - ○ Play restarts by Australian Rules a ball-up, both in terms of within the field of play or a boundary throw-in.
  - ○ The middle 70 yards of the field would be governed by AFL rules (no offside). The nearest 35 yards to the tryline would be governed by modified rugby league rules (with offside).

Proposed Universal Football pitch structure [267]

Appendix 2:
ABS Attendance rates 1994-2009/10

Total number of people attending each code in the last 12 months

	1994	1999	2002	2005	2009/10
AFL	1,874.00	2,509.00	2,486.00	2,527.00	2,832.00
Rugby League	1,462.00	1,501.00	1,465.00	1,486.00	1,564.00
Soccer	559.00	621.00	802.00	561.00	939.00
Rugby Union	358.00	446.00	674.00	682.00	576.00

Women attending each code in the last 12 months

	1994	1999	2002	2005	2009/10
AFL	700.00	1,012.00	982.00	1,011.00	1,171.00
Rugby League	486.00	531.00	513.00	543.00	595.00
Soccer	184.00	221.00	283.00	212.00	355.00
Rugby Union	120.00	146.00	204.00	232.00	209.00

Men attending each code in the last 12 months

	1994	1999	2002	2005	2009/10
AFL	1,174.00	1,497.00	1,504.00	1,515.00	1,661.00
Rugby League	976.00	970.00	951.00	944.00	969.00
Soccer	374.00	400.00	519.00	349.00	584.00
Rugby Union	239.00	300.00	470.00	450.00	366.00

Proportion of population attending each code in the last 12 months

	1994	1999	2002	2005	2009/10
AFL	13.3%	16.8%	17.1%	15.6%	16.2%
Rugby League	10.4%	10.1%	10.1%	9.0%	8.9%
Soccer	4.0%	4.2%	5.5%	3.4%	5.4%
Rugby Union	2.5%	3.0%	4.6%	4.3%	3.3%

Total number of people attending 6+ games in each code in the last 12 months

	1994	1999	2002	2005	2009/10
AFL	816.00	963.00	842.00	868.00	882.00
Rugby League	465.00	421.00	354.00	405.00	425.00
Soccer	245.00	256.00	356.00	188.00	307.00
Rugby Union	98.00	128.00	261.00	125.00	115.00

Proportion of attendance base attending 6+ games in each code in last 12 months

	1994	1999	2002	2005	2009/10
AFL	43.6%	38.4%	33.9%	34.4%	31.2%
Rugby League	31.8%	28.1%	24.1%	27.3%	27.2%
Soccer	43.9%	41.3%	44.4%	33.5%	32.7%
Rugby Union	27.4%	28.6%	38.7%	18.4%	20.0%

Appendix 3:
Attitudinal interest in sport relative to having participated in that sport (Sydney sport fans)

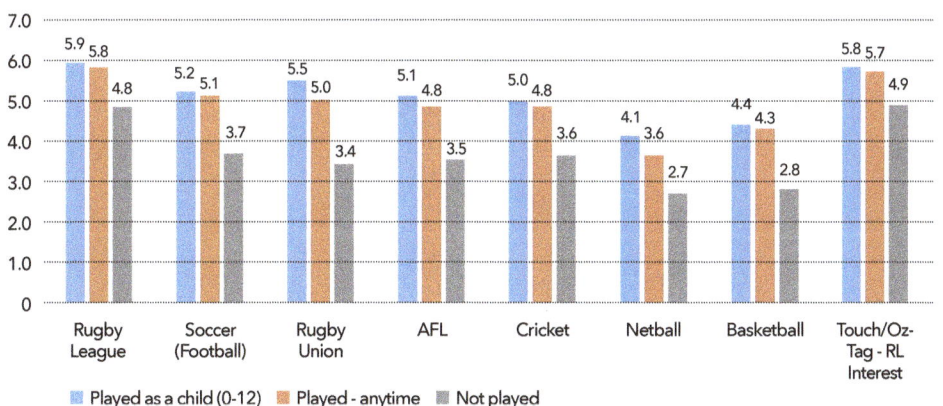

Glossary of Terms

ABS	Australian Bureau of Statistics
ACCC	Australian Competition and Consumer Competition
AFL	Australian Football League
AIS	Australian Institute of Sport
ARLC	Australian Rugby League Commission
ARU	Australian Rugby Union, now Rugby Australia
BBC	British Broadcast Corporation
BBL	Big Bash League
BRIC	Brazil, Russia, India, China
CA	Cricket Australia
CFL	Canadian Football League
COMPPS	Coalition of Major Professional and Participation Sports
CRL	Country Rugby League
CTE	Chronic traumatic encephalopathy
EPL	English Premier League
FFA	Football Federation Australia which changed its name to Football Australia (FA) in December 2020
FTA	Free to Air
GAA	Gaelic Athletic Association
GDP	Gross domestic product
IMF	International Monetary Fund
MCG	Melbourne Cricket Ground
MLB	Major League Baseball
MLS	Major League Soccer
MMA	Mixed Martial Arts
MoU	Memorandum of Understanding
NBA	National Basketball Association
NBL	National Basketball League
NCAA	National Collegiate Athletic Association
NFL	National Football League
NHL	National Hockey League
NRL	National Rugby League
NSL	National Soccer League
NSWRL	New South Wales Rugby League
NWSL	National Women's Soccer League
RA	Rugby Australia

RBB	Red and Black Block
RWC	Rugby World Cup
SANZAAR	South Africa New Zealand Australia Argentina Rugby
SANZAR	South Africa New Zealand Australia Rugby
SCG	Sydney Cricket Ground
UFC	Ultimate Fighting Championship

Footnotes

1. The closest has been an excellent academic book edited by Dr Bob Stewart, although this is a collection of individual chapters about football by various authors: Stewart, Bob. Games Are Not the Same: The Political Economy of Football in Australia, Carlton, Vic.: Melbourne University Press, 2007. Carlton, Vic.: Melbourne University Press, 2007. ISBN 9780522853667.
2. The Australian football wars: fan narratives of inter-code and intra-code conflict.
3. All depending on how and who we include in counting. This figure includes 2019 AFL central and team revenue, excluding gaming revenue but including grant revenue.
4. https://www.aihw.gov.au/getmedia/384eafec-fa90-412d-8c98-b279fddc7911/ah16-4-4-overweight-obesity.pdf.aspx
5. https://theconversation.com/sport-is-more-than-just-a-fringe-player-in-australias-economy-71212
6. The Australian football wars: fan narratives of inter-code and intra-code conflict.
7. https://www.news.com.au/sport/nrl/origin-afl-not-nrls-biggest-threat/news story de9bbb70c03804f5a2ae2942c6da3af5
8. https://www.smh.com.au/sport/racing/the-cult-of-racing-nsw-boss-peter-v-landys-20181013-p509fe.html
9. VFL report: 'The Sydney Solution: VFL at the Crossroads'.
10. Our wicked foreign game.
11. Chasing Leather and Choosing a Code: How Western Australia Opted for Australian Rules Football.
12. My proof-reader, colleague and good friend Dr Greg Joachim astutely notes that the saying "Australia is a lucky country" has been incredibly misattributed. It has been co-opted to refer to objectively good things in the years since, but with the true implication being that Australia is successful despite itself.
13. My conceptualisation of a 'mainstream' sport league is one that receives above-incidental revenue from a commercial broadcaster for telecast rights. Note this excludes the WNBL in this example, who only in late 2020 reached a broadcast deal with Fox Sports. It would have therefore only started including netball upon moving from the ABC as the Commonwealth Bank Cup to Channel Nine as the ANZ Championship.
14. Paradise of Sport, p192.
15. Sport and Society: A Student Introduction, by Barrie Houlihan
16. Bernard, A. B., & Busse, M. R. (2004). Who wins the Olympic Games: Economic resources and medal totals. Review of economics and statistics, 86(1), p413-417.
17. Forrest, D., Sanz, I., & Tena, J. D. D. (2010). Forecasting national team medal totals at the Summer Olympic Games. International Journal of Forecasting, 26(3), p576-588.
18. http://www.medalspercapita.com/#medals-per-capita:2000
19. https://www.sportaus.gov.au/__data/assets/pdf_file/0005/677894/Sport_2030_-_National_Sport_Plan_-_2018.pdf
20. http://www.afl.com.au/news/2018-04-26/nba-or-afl-aussie-star-reveals-tough-choice
21. https://www.smh.com.au/sport/nrl/tepai-moeroa-has-eyes-set-on-olympic-gold-and-blue-and-golds-20150307-13xxj0.html
22. http://www.greatestsportingnation.com/global-cup-2018/results
23. https://www.pri.org/stories/2011-06-17/why-australians-are-obsessed-sports
24. Although there is no perfect method to compare league search volume popularity given season lengths can vary so greatly.
25. Although Pro Kabbadi was only created in 2014, and has made strong commercial inroads since.
26. Mahony, D. F., & Howard, D. R. (2001). Sport business in the next decade: A general overview of expected trends. Journal of sport management, 15(4), p275-296.

27 This number is subjective, but my calculation is based on team sports within leagues that are of at least a semi-professional scale that are predominantly broadcast as commercial products on commercial networks. This excludes WNBL and predecessors of W-League and WBBL, and excludes the new Hockey1 competition and other smaller sports which are beginning to receive greater streaming coverage.
28 https://sports.usatoday.com/ncaa/finances/
29 https://www.theaustralian.com.au/sport/australias-sporting-obsession-is-waning/news-story/603cf59adc9ba72010e10489e1efa5f1
30 I have included the following for each. New York (state)- MLB 3, NFL 2, NBA 2, NHL 3, Lacrosse 4, MLR 1, MLS 2. London- EPL 5, Lower division soccer 7, RU 3, RL 1, Cricket 2.
31 (or buy a ticket off an existing holder)
32 https://www.buzzanglemusic.com/wp-content/uploads/BuzzAngle-Music-2018-US-Report-Industry.pdf
33 https://news.gallup.com/poll/224864/football-americans-favorite-sport-watch.aspx
34 Kerr, A. K., & Emery, P. R. (2011). Foreign fandom and the Liverpool FC: a cyber-mediated romance. Soccer & Society, 12(6), p880-896.
35 Foreign fandom and the Liverpool FC: a cyber-mediated romance.
36 I am mixing datasets here. The NBA figure comes from a survey of fans interest towards teams, whereas the figure is at a sport level of interest.
37 http://www.roymorgan.com/findings/8422-nrl-return-to-boost-tv-viewership-may-2020-202006010637
38 Cashman, R., & Hickie, T. (1990). The divergent sporting cultures of Sydney and Melbourne. Sporting Traditions, 7(1), 26-46.
39 The divergent sporting cultures of Sydney and Melbourne, p27.
40 Alistair John, Bob Stewart, and Brent McDonald (2013). Mixed doubles: Political hegemony, urban entrepreneurialism and the Australian Open Tennis Championships, The International Journal of the History of Sport, 30(2), p.162-178.
41 O'Hanlon, S. (2009). The events city: sport, culture, and the transformation of inner Melbourne, 1977–2006. Urban History Review/Revue d'histoire urbaine, 37(2), p30-39. Quote from p32.
42 Alistair John, 'Sports city: A critical analysis of Melbourne's sportscape', Doctoral dissertation, Victoria University, 2015.
43 Mixed doubles: Political hegemony, urban entrepreneurialism and the Australian Open Tennis Championships.
44 The events city: sport, culture, and the transformation of inner Melbourne, 1977–2006.
45 Senyard, 'Marvellous Melbourne, consumerism and the rise of sports spectating'.
46 Thomas Keneally, Good Weekend, 19 May 1990, p. 46
47 Sports city: A critical analysis of Melbourne's sportscape.
48 Sport in Victoria: a history' edited by Dave Nadel and Graeme Ryan
49 https://sydney.edu.au/news-opinion/news/2016/07/26/which-is-australia-s-most-successful-olympic-town-.html
50 Lidor, R., Côté, J., Arnon, M., Zeev, A., & Cohen-Maoz, S. (2010). Relative age and birthplace effects in division 1 players–Do they exist in a small country. Talent Development & Excellence, 2(2), 181-192.
51 Abernethy, B: From theory to practice. In: Farrow D, editor. Proceedings of the Applied Sport Expertise and Learning Workshop 2005 [CD1]; Canberra (ACT): Australian Institute of Sport, 2005
52 Phillips, E., Davids, K., Renshaw, I., & Portus, M. (2010). Expert performance in sport and the dynamics of talent development. Sports medicine, 40(4), p271-283.
53 The book 'Range' by David Epstein provides a reader friendly guide to the broader topic of specialisation vs generalists.
54 Based on my anecdotal estimates as a 12 year old.
55 https://www.fairplaypublishing.com.au/product-page/encyclopedia-of-matildas

56 https://www.abs.gov.au/statistics/people/population/national-state-and-territory-population/mar-2020
57 * = statistical significant difference ** = those who serf-identify as 1-3 on the sport fandom scale.
*** = those who serf-identify as 8-10 on the sport fandom scale.
Early in the book, I refer to 80% of people being interested in sport. This comes from a more segmentation analysis of this dataset to more rigorously identify sport 'rejecters'.
58 Hickie, T (1993). They ran with the ball: how rugby football began in Australia. Longman Cheshire Pty Ltd.
59 This is a tongue-in-cheek comment.
60 It should be noted, as pointed out by Ian Syson later in this book, that the first game of soccer appears to have actually been in Tasmania, but soccer football adminstrators have appeared to be lax with the integriy of the games historical narrative.
61 Horton, P. (2009). Rugby union football in Australian society: An unintended consequence of intended actions. Sport in Society, 12(7), 967-985.
62 Although, with the two sports approaching a combined 250 years of history, I am sure there are many more sociological and historical events that have shaped divergences between the codes/cities not discussed here.
63 Carlton were the last team to centralize, playing their last season at Princes Park in 2004.
64 Depending on how you categorise Parramatta's Bankwest Stadium.
65 https://www.theage.com.au/sport/afl/from-the-archives-1996-rival-factions-clash-over-demons-hawks-merger-20190913-p52r1o.html
66 Brawley, S. (2012). 'Can You Imagine the Shire Without the Sharks!?': Building the Community Capital of the Cronulla-Sutherland Rugby League Club–From 1967 to the Eve of Super League in 1996. The International Journal of the History of Sport, 29(3), p492-508. Brawley, S. (2009). 'Your Shire, Your Sharks': The Cronulla-Sutherland Sharks and Delocalization v. Glocalization in Australian Rugby League. The International Journal of the History of Sport, 26(11), p1697-1715.
67 The Central Coast would not be considered part of Sydney by most locals, but included as such here (and in my academic studies) because it is considered a sub-region of Sydney by both the Australia Bureau of Statistics and more importantly, OzTAM, who measure television audiences. As the Central Coast is part of Northern Sydney in OzTAM's measurement of Sydney television audiences, the region is materially significant to the value of NRL broadcast rights.
68 Of course, the Bears still exist and play in the lower divisions, but without a top flight presence are essentially lost to the game.
69 Moore, A. (2008). Interpreting 100 years of rugby league. Centenary Reflections: 100 Years of Rugby League in Australia, p4
70 'The Convert' by Peter Lewis, p8.
71 It is worth noting however, that according to Paul Gallen, the North Brisbane pub would have 94 heads in it.
72 Sharp, P. (1987). Australian football in Sydney before 1914. Sporting Traditions, 4(1), p27-45.
73 Although the methodologies of measurement are very different and perhaps incomparable.
74 Stewart, B., Nicholson, M., & Dickson, G. (2005). The Australian Football League's recent progress: A study in cartel conduct and monopoly power. Sport Management Review, 8(2), p95-117.
75 Linnell, G. (1995). Football Ltd: The inside story of the AFL. Pan Macmillan Australia. p323
76 https://www.smh.com.au/sport/nrl/rollcall-of-shame-20100422-tfyj.html
77 As quoted in The Rugby League Digest: "The Super League War: Prelude"
78 https://www.smh.com.au/sport/nrl/perth-nines-a-precursor-to-perth-team-no-chance-says-v-landys-20200213-p540c0.html
79 Adding up to 100% is a coincidence.
80 Daily Telegraph, May 31 2012. "Galloping in a little late".
81 Thank you to Darren of Birdsville Hotel for his time.

THE BATTLE FOR FANS, DOLLARS AND SURVIVAL

82 https://www.afl.com.au/news/494986/afl-statement-on-grand-final-date-and-venue#:~:text=The%20AFL%20on%20Wednesday%20announced,confirmed%20in%20the%20coming%20weeks.
83 http://www.roymorgan.com/findings/7707-afl-premierships-boost-support-for-tigers-dogs-hawks-201808170433, http://www.roymorgan.com/findings/7725-nrl-supporter-ladder-june-2018 201809141006. 14+ population = 19,037,278 based on 2016 census.
84 Syson, I. (2013). The 'chimera'of origins: Association football in Australia before 1880. The International Journal of the History of Sport, 30(5), 453-468.
85 Hay, 'How footy kicked off: Origins of our great game unclear', Geelong Advertiser, 6 November 2004, 37
86 https://www.abc.net.au/news/2019-06-14/afl-latest-stance-proves-history-of-aussie-rules-is-in-debate/11202802
87 https://www.theguardian.com/world/2019/jan/27/one-in-20-britons-does-not-believe-holocaust-happened; https://www.theguardian.com/world/2020/jan/22/holocaust-survey-americans-pew-research-center
88 Cashman, Paradise of Sport, p18.
89 Paradise of sport, p31.
90 The 'chimera'of origins: Association football in Australia before 1880
91 Note that Fremantle and Perth were distinct colonies, but amalgamated here for narrative purposes.
92 Errington, S. (2007). Chasing Leather and Choosing a Code: How Western Australia Opted for Australian Rules Football. Early Days: Journal of the Royal Western Australian Historical Society, 13(1), p68-83. Errington suggests the combatants likely used the Victorian rules because the regiment had played under those rules in Melbourne during 1867.
93 Population of Victoria: https://trove.nla.gov.au/newspaper/article/196482695
94 Population of New South Wales: https://trove.nla.gov.au/newspaper/article/13203963
95 Cowan, S. (2015). Cracking the code: Why Western Australia abandoned rugby for Australian Rules football in 1885 (Doctoral dissertation, Murdoch University).
96 Richard Kreider's 'Paddocks to Pitches' is the most comprehensive book on Soccer in Perth.
97 Cowan, S. (2015). Cracking the code: Why Western Australia abandoned rugby for Australian Rules football in 1885 (Doctoral dissertation, Murdoch University). p17.
98 There appears to be differing accounts of what happened in Fremantle. Errington's account has Fremantle playing Rugby in 1883, with the Fremantle Union club choosing Victorian Rules. Another prominent historian has Fremantle swapping codes from Rugby to Victorian Rules in 1883, although he may be likely to conflating the two distinct clubs.
99 The Inquirer and Commercial News. Perth, WA. "Football Gossip". 24 June 1885, p. 6.
100 The West Australian. Perth, WA. "Football Match". 5 May 1885, p3.
101 https://saintsandheathens.wordpress.com/states/western-force/
102 Excluding ACT and NT
103 https://saintsandheathens.wordpress.com/states/rugby-sth-aust/
104 The Advertiser. Adelaide, SA. "Football Notes". 8 July 1893, p7.
105 Tasmanian Telegraph, 16 March 1859, p5.
106 AFL Licence Taskforce Business Plan 2019. http://www.premier.tas.gov.au/documents/AFL_Taskforce_Report_Tasmania.pdf
107 https://saintsandheathens.wordpress.com/states/qld-reds/
108 https://saintsandheathens.wordpress.com/states/qld-reds/
109 There is disagreement around whether NSWs tally was 26 or 28. What is known is that they scored four goals and four tries to Queensland's one goal.
110 The Week. Brisbane, QLD. "Football". 10 November, 1883, p6.
111 https://www.newshub.co.nz/home/new-zealand/2017/12/revealed-the-real-reason-new-zealand-didn-t-become-part-of-australia.html

112. https://www.afr.com/companies/sport/state-of-origin-could-be-worth-100m-a-year-20190531-p51t4n
113. The rules, formed in consultation with Rugby World Cup winning coaches Bob Dwyer (rugby union) and Bob Fulton (rugby league), dictated that rugby league rules were to be applied in the defensive end of the field and rugby union in the offensive part of the field, with a shot clock of 60 seconds per possession. As Master's noted; "At first glance, this is not designed to showcase rugby league skills".
114. Westralian Worker. Perth, WA. "Football – New game explained". 12 February 1915, p8.
115. The council had several name changes throughout its history, but I stick with the ANFC acronym throughout for consistency
116. Westralian Worker. Perth, WA. "Football – New game explained". 12 February 1915, p8.
117. The Register. Adelaide, SA. "Carnival Football". 17 August 1914, p7.
118. Referee. Sydney, NSW. "Football Utopia- A Universal Code for Australia". 23 September 1914, p10.
119. Naturally however, this $101 million includes game development officers who facilitate junior participation, of which there would still be a need to fund irrespective of an amalgamation of the codes.
120. Observer. Adelaide, SA. 13 February 1915, p22.
121. Across the first three days, for fair comparison
122. 1914 Queensland Rugby League annual report.
123. The Australasian. Melbourne, VIC. 17 April 1915, p26.
124. Leader. Melbourne, Vic. 5 September 1914, p20.
125. Winner. Melbourne, VIC. 9 December 1914, p5.
126. Referee. Sydney, NSW. 25 November 1914, p16.
127. Westralian Worker. Perth, WA. 12 February 1915, p.8.
128. Leader. Melbourne, VIC. 28 November 1917, p21.
129. The Register. Adelaide, SA. 23 January 1915, p.7.
130. Westralian Worker. Perth, WA. 5 March 1915, p7.
131. The Mercury. Hobart, TAS. 30 March 1915, p8.
132. The Sun. Sydney, NSW. 18 April 1915, p5.
133. The Mail. Adelaide , SA. 12 August 1933, p9.
134. Referee. Sydney, NSW. 20 July 1933, p1.
135. Sydney Morning Herald. Sydney, Australia. "Football Codes. Lively Debate". 8 August 1933 p9.
136. Among Australia rules fans, only 35% are rugby league fans, which is low compared with cricket (58%), tennis (48%), swimming (34%).

    Among rugby league fans, only 44% are Australian Rules fans, low compared with cricket (59%), tennis (45%), swimming (46%) and rugby union (41%).
137. https://www.smh.com.au/culture/tv-and-radio/nine-network-tops-2019-ratings-ending-seven-s-12-year-winning-streak-20191129-p53fd3.html
138. https://variety.com/2019/tv/news/top-rated-shows-2019-game-of-thrones-big-bang-theory-oscars-super-bowl-1203451363/
139. https://www.fifa.com/u17worldcup/news/sleeping-giant-slowly-awakening-75009
140. Hay, R. (2006). 'Our wicked foreign game': why has association football (soccer) not become the main code of football in Australia?. Soccer & Society, 7(2-3), p165-186.
141. Majumdar, B & Bandyopadhyay, K (2005). Looking beyond the sleeping giant syndrome: Indian football at crossroads. Soccer and society, 6(2/3).
142. https://www.theage.com.au/sport/afl/sleeping-giant-looms-over-footys-fragile-web-20140628-zspbk.html
143. Our wicked foreign game
144. In December 2020, FFA rebranded itself to 'Football Australia' or FA
145. Rosenberg, B. C. (2009). The Australian football wars: fan narratives of inter-code and intra-code conflict. Soccer & Society, 10(2), p245-260.

146. I use the acronym NSL instead, to create consistency throughout the manuscript. Phillips were only the league sponsor during for the establishing years of the National Soccer League.
147. http://www.ozfootball.net/ark/NSL/1978/Round14.html; https://www.rugbyleagueproject.org/matches/kiwis-tour-1978/game-1/newcastle--au--vs-new-zealand.html
148. Quote from 'Death and life of Australian Football' by Joe Gorman (p,17), perhaps the best and most reader-friendly book written about Australian soccer.
149. Sourced from John Maynard's 'The Aboriginal Soccer Tribe', p19.
150. Suarez, F. F., & Lanzolla, G. (2007). The role of environmental dynamics in building a first mover advantage theory. Academy of Management Review, 32(2), p377-392.
151. Klugman, M. (2011). 'Football is a Fever Disease Like Recurrent Malaria and Evidently Incurable': Passion, Place and the Emergence of an Australian Anti-Football League. The International Journal of the History of Sport, 28(10), p1426-1446.
152. Nash, R. (2000). Globalised football fandom: Scandinavian Liverpool FC supporters. Football Studies, 3(2), p5-23.
153. The Jordan era commenced in 1984, but the Championship period of note is 1990-1998.
154. Dabscheck, B. (2010). Australian Rugby union: Lessons from other codes. Sporting Traditions, 27(1), p37.
155. Dabscheck, B. (2003). Paying for professionalism: industrial relations in Australian rugby union. Sport Management Review, 6(2), p105-125.
156. https://www.westmeathexaminer.ie/2019/10/03/gaa-must-make-tough-choices-or-let-amateur-status-fade-away/
157. https://www.limerickleader.ie/news/sport/354003/research-shows-gaa-overtakes-soccer-as-country-s-most-popular-sport.html
158. https://www.canberratimes.com.au/story/6181641/where-are-the-fans-brumbies-feel-financial-pinch-of-record-low-crowd/#gsc.tab=0
159. https://www.theaustralian.com.au/leadership-not-brawling-is-key-to-solving-crisisextended-headline-goes-here/news-story/d4a265ee73c6af57eb7f6aed20a13484
160. A world in conflict
161. https://www.abc.net.au/news/2020-06-01/rugby-australia-axes-forty-percent-of-staff/12302232
162. It is worth qualifying that administration and marketing expenses inevitably increase as commercial revenue does, because there are unavoidable costs derived from 'servicing' such revenue.
163. The Economics of Sports Broadcasting by Chris Gratton and Harry Arne Solberg
164. https://www.ipsos.com/ipsos-mori/en-uk/public-interest-sport-decline
165. https://www.foxsports.com.au/nrl/super-league/nrl-2020-super-league-news-papa-johns-pizza-sponsorship-deal/news-story/ca53cf568fa03c93aee5425a420b35e3
166. 'How Brands Grow' by Byron Sharp.
167. Australian Bureau of Statistics. "Census of Population and Housing: Socio-Economic Indexes for Areas (SEIFA). http://www.abs.gov.au/AUSSTATS/abs@.nsf/DetailsPage/2033.0.55.0012011?OpenDocument.
168. These figures are based on individual Google Trends data, rather than relative data as presented in the figure.
169. That is to say, that KPMG believed the business was in a position to keep operating into the future.
170. Fainaru-Wada, M., & Fainaru, S. (2014). League of denial: The NFL, concussions, and the battle for truth. Three Rivers Press (CA).
171. Healy, M. (2002). Hard sell: Australian football in Sydney (Doctoral dissertation, Victoria University of Technology).
172. For this, please refer to The Rugby League Digest podcast with Andy Paskin, who have put together an incredibly comprehensive series on the topic, from which I obtain some of the information found in this section.
173. The first of which can be found here: https://www.ausstats.abs.gov.au/ausstats/free.nsf/0/A9929603A092FECBCA2572250004957D/$File/41740_1994.pdf
174. http://www.roymorgan.com/findings/7344-nrl-supporters-ladder-2017-201709221418

[175] It should be noted that NRL controls marketing for finals fixtures, not NRL clubs. This however, has not seemed to stop AFL finals from selling out.
[176] https://www.sportingnews.com/au/league/news/nrl-crowd-size-gus-gould-priority-melbourne-brisbane-scheduling-drama/p0ri4to0bymk1ne79upjaonu5
[177] Although interpretation of the 2005 figure must be done with caution as sampling occurred between June 2005 and July 2006, complicating the interpretation of soccer attendance data for this period.
[178] Half being Wollongong
[179] The document actually says five seasons, but excludes 1997.
[180] http://www8.austlii.edu.au/cgi-bin/viewdoc/au/cases/cth/FCA/2000/1541.html
[181] Including Illawarra.
[182] https://www.couriermail.com.au/sport/nrl/super-league-20-years-on-former-ceo-john-ribot-opens-up-on-the-deals-the-money-the-mistakes/news-story/482f5ea94cd85d0e8aa0b2efda2bc6af
[183] https://www.theaustralian.com.au/sport/australian-sporting-market-has-hit-saturation-point/news-story/b72e9647ea0caf76d9955381e1daefad
[184] https://mumbrella.com.au/the-current-sports-right-model-is-broken-nine-and-seven-weigh-in-on-the-future-of-sports-broadcasting-588013
[185] https://www.nrl.com/siteassets/documents/nrl-annual-report-2017.pdf
[186] https://www.heraldsun.com.au/sport/afl/more-news/how-a-bloated-afl-plans-to-streamline-itself-and-shed-hundreds-of-staff/news-story/9c923a835f7520b547f21e400eb6d8eb
[187] https://www.smh.com.au/sport/nrl/nrl-goes-offshore-to-secure-250-million-loan-20200415-p54jya.html
[188] https://www.theage.com.au/sport/afl/ex-afl-and-nrl-powerbroker-why-the-afl-is-so-much-better-off-20200404-p54h3k.html
[189] Roy Morgan: 7539-Sports-Participation-Battle-Football-Codes-December-2017
[190] https://www.abc.net.au/news/2017-02-03/nrl-wants-compulsory-education-training-for-players/8236712
[191] https://www.theage.com.au/sport/afl/ex-afl-and-nrl-powerbroker-why-the-afl-is-so-much-better-off-20200404-p54h3k.html
[192] https://www.smh.com.au/sport/nrl/the-nrl-had-its-books-open-but-clubs-and-players-didn-t-want-to-read-them-20200330-p54fdr.html
[193] https://www.smh.com.au/sport/rugby-union/our-priority-has-been-to-survive-more-than-a-quarter-of-staff-let-go-at-nsw-rugby-20200629-p557cr.html
[194] https://www.theage.com.au/sport/afl/swans-chairman-fearful-of-v-landys-nrl-20200630-p557nd.html
[195] https://www.smh.com.au/sport/soccer/a-league-set-for-winter-switch-after-securing-new-fox-sports-deal-20200619-p554dx.html
[196] AFL, NRL, A-League, Super Rugby, Big Bash, Australian Open; https://www.smh.com.au/sport/soccer/the-numbers-that-underline-the-danger-of-a-league-s-winter-switch-20200819-p55n8c.html
[197] IBIS WORLD. INDUSTRY REPORT C1211A Soft Drink Manufacturing in Australia
[198] Ogden, D. C., & Hilt, M. L. (2003). Collective identity and basketball: An explanation for the decreasing number of African-Americans on America's baseball diamonds. Journal of Leisure Research, 35(2), p213-227.
[199] Appiah, K. A. (2000). Racial identity and racial identification. In L. Black & J. Solomos (Eds.), Theories of race and racism (pp. 607-615).
[200] https://www.theatlantic.com/business/archive/2014/02/which-sports-have-the-whitest-richest-oldest-fans/283626/
[201] Côté, J., Macdonald, D. J., Baker, J., & Abernethy, B. (2006). When "where" is more important than "when": Birthplace and birthdate effects on the achievement of sporting expertise. Journal of sports sciences, 24(10), p1065-1073.
[202] 3222.0 - Population Projections, Australia, 2017 (base) - 2066

203 https://www.smh.com.au/sport/w-league-at-risk-of-becoming-fourth-choice-competition-for-matildas-20200715-p55c5w.html?fbclid=IwAR1IDDC_2aAzLRcKZWFkp7tbXBucM0nJ6NKXszNxNWUi7DqpHw669-ZKJ8A
204 This observation should not be construed as a scientific evaluation of tennis champions, but rather a top-line observation.
205 https://www.finder.com.au/where-to-buy-a-property-if-you-want-your-kid-to-play-in-state-of-origin?utm_source=redditorigin
206 These of course aren't mutually exclusive groups, as Pasifika athletes can come from major cities
207 Lakisa, D., Teaiwa, K., Adair, D., & Taylor, T. (2019). Empowering voices from the past: The playing experiences of retired Pasifika Rugby League athletes in Australia. The International Journal of the History of Sport, 36(12), p1096-1114.
208 Although this is somewhat imprecise, given some Pasifika players come directly from their home nation to play in the NRL.
209 https://www.nzherald.co.nz/sport/news/article.cfm?c_id=4&objectid=12179139
210 https://www.nzherald.co.nz/sport/news/article.cfm?c_id=4&objectid=12179139
211 Roy Morgan article number 7539
212 AusPlay survey results January 2019 - December 2019. https://www.clearinghouseforsport.gov.au/research/ausplay/results
213 The finding here needs to be diluted somewhat as it is entirely plausible that internal migration from an AFL state to Sydney reduces the power of this effect somewhat.
214 League of denial: The NFL, concussions, and the battle for truth, chapter 8.
215 https://www.rugby.com.au/news/2018/09/26/high-tackle-world-rugby
216 Ling, H., Morris, H. R., Neal, J. W., Lees, A. J., Hardy, J., Holton, J. L., ... & Williams, D. D. (2017). Mixed pathologies including chronic traumatic encephalopathy account for dementia in retired association football (soccer) players. Acta neuropathologica, 133(3), 337-352.
217 https://www.theaustralian.com.au/inquirer/scoreless-kids-sport-contests-breeding-out-resilience/news-story/1e8a8dd085c29a5c480453cc92bb99ed
218 Greetings to my two favourite Nova Scotians Katherine and Katrina!
219 https://www.rugby.com.au/news/2018/09/26/high-tackle-world-rugby
220 https://www.independent.co.uk/sport/rugby/rugby-union/news-comment/rfu-tackle-height-trial-armpit-nipple-line-ended-scrapped-concussion-risk-increase-a8745776.html
221 https://www.nzherald.co.nz/sport/news/article.cfm?c_id=4&objectid=12132572
222 https://sportsscientists.com/2019/08/protecting-the-rugby-players-head-the-paradox-of-tackler-height-and-head-injury/
223 Cummings, K. M., & Proctor, R. N. (2014). The changing public image of smoking in the United States: 1964–2014. Cancer Epidemiology and Prevention Biomarkers, 23(1), 32-36.
224 https://www.nytimes.com/2019/09/12/sports/football/nfl-concussion-settlement.html
225 This should not be considered a zero-sum game however. An additional hour spent watching the EPL does not necessitate a lost hour of consumption towards A-League.
226 https://www.theringer.com/2019/1/23/18193121/ufc-unionization-efforts-project-spearhead-leslie-smith
227 https://www.afr.com/companies/sport/how-the-ufc-cage-fighting-became-the-biggest-nontech-trade-of-the-century-20170704-gx4fp5
228 https://www.dailytelegraph.com.au/sport/the-victorian-government-paid-5-million-to-land-rober-whittakers-ufc-243-blockbuster/news-story/215e8c6b3ae0b60a4aa6b06dba196394
229 Before even considering other international leagues.
230 Ratten, V., Tsiotsou, R., McDonald, H., Karg, A. J., & Lock, D. (2010). Leveraging fans' global football allegiances to build domestic league support. Asia Pacific Journal of Marketing and Logistics.

231 https://www.smh.com.au/sport/soccer/kerr-ching-why-sam-kerr-is-worth-400-000-a-year-as-a-marquee-20190215-p50y5l.html
232 https://www.smh.com.au/sport/soccer/matildas-have-strongest-bond-with-fans-in-australian-sport-20191126-p53ec8.html
233 https://www.theguardian.com/football/2020/jan/21/matildas-european-migration-exciting-but-fanning-w-league-anxiety
234 https://www.theaustralian.com.au/sport/nrl/nrl-club-finances-big-dollar-broncos-nrls-richest-team/news-story/d123ee3a016c3695227593b0faae838a#:~:text=The%20Rabbitohs%20were%20also%20among,of%20more%20than%20%242%20million.
235 https://www.dailytelegraph.com.au/sport/nrl/how-116-club-bosses-burned-through-396-million-in-10-years/news-story/1142d5422b012b02ec42c01bcfefd56c
236 https://www.theaustralian.com.au/sport/nrl/nrl-club-finances-big-dollar-broncos-nrls-richest-team/news-story/d123ee3a016c3695227593b0faae838a#:~:text=The%20Rabbitohs%20were%20also%20among,of%20more%20than%20%242%20million.
237 https://www.smh.com.au/sport/nrl/league-was-lucky-to-survive-here-is-how-it-can-thrive-once-again-20200620-p554i3.html
238 https://www.foxsports.com.au/nrl/nrl-premiership/nrl-2020-phil-gould-vs-nrl-power-to-clubs-rugby-league-todd-greenberg-ceo/news-story/b75f46b74ec64b70da2cc8f7c7bb9dd6
239 It also speaks to the necessary caution needed when measuring 'fandom' through a simple attititudinal research question of 'are you a fan of these teams'
240 Excluding gaming income but including grants and removing the double-counting of AFL central revenue distributions.
241 https://www.stuff.co.nz/sport/football/a-league/73477629/david-gallop-delivers-wellington-phoenix-ultimatum
242 https://www.smh.com.au/sport/soccer/phoenix-to-pay-1-million-to-ffa-after-missing-off-field-goals-20190529-p51sgd.html
243 https://www.smh.com.au/sport/rugby-union/how-rugby-was-drawn-into-race-to-the-bottom-of-australian-sport-20200207-p53ypm

html?fbclid=IwAR2wk_2mGJ9KwJsHO7LUi8ikPbf9L3dPL35hh5PZzkBn7M8LJACahPWI8Rs
244 https://www.rugby.com.au/news/2018/04/27/super-rugby-nsw-rugby-waratahs-board
245 https://www.theaustralian.com.au/sport/rugby-union/rugby-broadcast-deal-worth-only-10-a-year/news-story/7992dd4aaf1cac6259ceeda58156bdcb
246 https://www.theaustralian.com.au/sport/football/research-offers-hope-for-aleague-with-digitallyengaged-audience/news-story/670670b8b626179091c54a8989ac4f9d
247 https://www.thegoldengeneration.org.au/ffa-tv
248 https://www.aph.gov.au/About_Parliament/Parliamentary_Departments/Parliamentary_Library/pubs/rp/rp1920/Quick_Guides/NewZealandersInAustralia#:~:text=As%20at%2030%20June%202018,our%20fourth%2Dlargest%20migrant%20community.
249 https://www.smh.com.au/sport/rugby-union/fantasy-league-rugby-must-be-careful-not-to-become-nrl-s-poor-cousin-20201113-p56ed3.html
250 Senyard, 'Marvellous Melbourne, consumerism and the rise of sports spectating'.
251 Chronicle. Adelaide, SA. "Football – the Australasian council". 17 November 1906, p18.
252 https://www.sen.com.au/news/2017/04/11/maher-slams-double-standard-in-crowd-violence-reporting/
253 https://www.heraldsun.com.au/news/law-order/secret-files-reveal-violent-aleague-antics-in-our-sports-capital/news-story/9eb8b208e77309d4808e040662608200
254 'A World in Conflict: The Global Battle for Rugby Supremacy' by Geoff Parks.

255 https://www.heraldsun.com.au/sport/afl/dwarf-entertainer-set-on-fire-criticised-for-not-entertaining-players-during-st-kildas-mad-monday-celebrations/news-story/3522d6a83b94cbf146b2f6c3d483db6c
256 https://www.theage.com.au/sport/afl/dwarf-entertainer-draws-montagna-into-saints-fiasco-20130904-2t5j5.html
257 https://www.abc.net.au/mediawatch/episodes/paying-for-news/9974074
258 https://www.foxsports.com.au/afl/afl-2020-mitch-cleary-stood-down-afl-media-journalist-brooke-cotchin-richmond-spa-trip-independence-of-media/news-story/bee7fad6ca8e255f376f7bdc60461d70
259 https://7news.com.au/sport/afl/layers-to-this-theory-emerges-on-why-afl-journo-was-really-sacked-c-1212014
260 Football is a Fever Disease Like Recurrent Malaria and Evidently Incurable': Passion, Place and the Emergence of an Australian Anti-Football League.
261 Noting of course that not all members of Melbourne teams likely reside in Melbourne.
262 https://www.dailytelegraph.com.au/sport/nrl/the-nrl-has-to-turn-grand-final-week-into-a-party-for-sydney/news-story/4973ed44224f83a7f94ee163410c3a55
263 https://www.dailytelegraph.com.au/sport/football/aleague-ffa-must-connect-grassroots-with-the-main-game-to-win-over-broadcasters/news-story/1a734a334acd293f20f731a8114a7052
264 11 August 2020
265 2019 membership tally- 15,826 (Cronulla) vs 44,373 (Western Bulldogs)
266 https://www.heraldsun.com.au/sport/afl/more-news/how-a-bloated-afl-plans-to-streamline-itself-and-shed-hundreds-of-staff/news-story/9c923a835f7520b547f21e400eb6d8eb
267 Westralian Worker. Perth, WA. "Football – New game explained". 12 February 1915, p8.

Index

Note: Page locators in *italics* denote figures and/or tables

1994 World Series, 110
2019 Grey Cup, 144
2020 Super Bowl, 144

A

Aboriginal People and Australian Football in the Nineteenth Century (Hay), 53
ABS attendance data, 113, 114, 117, 175
ABS Socio-Economic Indexes for Areas, 107
ACT Brumbies, 88, 109, 155
    match attendance, 97–8, 114
    v NSW Waratahs, 158
Adelaide
    average television viewership for AFL, 14
    first Victorian Rules club, 59
    football interest by regions, *39*, 40
    NRL rationalisation of club, 117
    own form of football, 60
Adelaide Crows, 69, 117, 153
The Advertiser, 60
AFL Auskick, 133, 137
AFL Commission, 42
AFL Grand Finals 2019, 81
AFL Grand Finals 2020, 48
AFL Licence Taskforce, 62–3
AFL Media, 166

AFLW, 13, 127
The Age, 42
A-League, 13
    clubs' combined losses, 156
    COVID-19 impact on broadcast deals, 126
    cumulative fan base 2019, 49
    digital streaming possibilities, 157
    fanbase conversion into club membership, 153
    financial and performance accountability, 154
    games played at Campbelltown stadium, 36
    internet search volume 2004–2019, *108*, 109
    internet search volume compared to EPL, 142
    lack of iconography and cultural currency, 93
    launch, 87, 95, 100, 114
    pay television audience numbers, 170
    proposed shift to winter competition, 126, 127
    revenue from Fox Sports, 22
    salary caps, 127–8
    satellite fandom impact on domestic teams, 145

share of media coverage, 127
as sole code of interest, 50
south-west team, 36, 38–9
struggle to grow a domestic market, 146–7
Allianz Stadium, 112
Amazon, 125
American football
   decline in junior participation, 137
   growth in popularity, 20
   safety issues, 135
Anderson, Mark, 150
Anti-Football League, 91–2, 167
ANZ Championship, 13
ANZ Stadium, 107
Argentina Super Rugby, 155
Art of War (Sun Tzu), 4
Ashfield Town Hall, 31
Auckland Blues
   v Hurricanes (2020), 158
   v NSW Waratahs (2020), 97
AusPlay participation data, 132, 133
Australia
   average sport interest score by region, *29*
   beginnings of modern sport, 55–6
   colonial relationship to sport, 54–5
   as host to major sporting events, 6, 171
   impact of urbanisation, 130–1
   international performance 2018, *8*
   international performances, 7–9
   Olympics medals performance, 7
   sport market in, 6–7, 169, 173
   standardised football interest by city sub-regions, *39*
   Women's World Cup 2023 host, 171
The Australian, 98
Australian Football Council, 41, 162
Australian Football League (AFL), 160–8
   attempts to reframe history with indigenous culture, 52–3

attendance rate, 111–12, 113
average age of fans, 21
behavioural incidents, 163
calibre of sponsorship, 151
centralised inner-city stadiums, 32
compared with Rugby Australia central revenue (1996–2019), *161*
contributing factors for dominance, 161–2, 169–70
control of media narrative, 163–4, 166
counter-culture movement, 91–2, 167
COVID-19 impact on 2020 season, 48–9
cultural dominance, 161–3, 168, 169
cumulative club membership, 152
cumulative fan base 2019, 49, 151
expansion, relocations and proposed mergers, 32–3
expenditure cap during COVID-19, 122–3
expenditure on FTA networks, 42
expenditure on games development, 73, 103, 126
fanbase conversion into club membership, 152–*3*
financial success, 160
frames soccer as 'other,' 162–3
FTA broadcast strategies for exposure, 106, 108
funding distribution to northern clubs, 73
governance, 124
grand final parade, 167
independent commission, 123, 148, 160
internet search volume, 18, *108*
investment in Riverina region, 46
marketing campaigns 1990s, 41–2
Melbourne clubs' profits, 149
players' off-field transgressions, 165
racism towards players, 53–4
revenue, 151
revenue 2018/2019, 120

191

revised COVID-19 broadcast deal, 122
as sole code of interest, 50–1
sponsorhips, 151
website fan commentaries on soccer, 86–7
See also Australian Rules; Victorian Football League (VFL)
Australian Institute of Sport, 27, 143
Australian Kangaroos, 69
Australian National Football Council (ANFC), 67, 70, 162
   conferences, 72
   Universal Football talks with NSWRL, 76–80
Australian Open tennis tournament, 6, 25, 143–4
   accessibility and affordability, 13
Australian Rugby League (ARL)
   Bradley Report 1992, 117
   merger with Super League, 115–19
Australian Rugby League Commission (ARLC), strategic plan 2012–2017, 124–5
Australian Rugby Union (ARU)
   corporate rival takes on, 96
   impact of alliance with SANZAAR, 98–9
Australian Rules
   bias in sport history, 52–3
   blocks infrastructure access for soccer, 85–6, 91
   cross-over fans, 80
   CTE cases, 135
   female spectatorship, 26
   first game played, 31
   formal codification, 55
   'propaganda' funding for northern markets, 4, 162, 169
   rate of interest, 80
   as sole code of interest, 18, 20
Australian Rules interstate carnival, 72, 73
Australian Schoolboys Union, 5

Australian Soccer Association, 86 *See also* Australian Soccer Federation Australia (ASF)
Australian Soccer Federation (ASF), 91, 95 *See also* Football Federation Australia (FFA)

B

Ball, SG, 80
Balmain Tigers, 33, 118
Bandyopadhyay, K, 83–4
Barassi, Ron, 14
Barassi Line, 4, 14, 15, 18, 88
   in 2021, 43
   Birdsville and Outback Queensland football interests, 47–8
   Broken Hill and the Far West football interests, 47
   heat map of AFL and rugby interest by region, *44*
   Murray region football interests, 44–6
   plaque celebrating, 45–6
   reality and hypothetical, *68*
   Riverina region football interests, 46–7
baseball
   declining popularity in US, 20, 129–30
   effect of players' industrial strike, 110–11
   sport market in US, 10
   Taiwanese market, 12
basketball
   dominance of African American players, 131–2
   reasons for popularity, 129–30
   sport market in US, 10
   Taiwanese market, 12
Basketball Australia, 173
BBC, 104
   v BSkyB audience for rugby league, *105*
Bedourie Rugby League Nines, 47
Big Bash Leagues (BBL), 13, 127
'Big five,' collective central revenue, 13–14

Birchgrove Oval, 31
Birdsville and Outback Queensland, 47–8
Black Lives Matter movement, 130
Blainey, Geoffrey, 53, 62
Bontempelli, Marcus, 8
boxing, average age of fans, *22*
Bradley Report 1992, 117
Brawley, Sean, 34, 35
Brisbane, 63–5
    first football club, 63
    Fitzroy Football Club relocation, 32
    football interest, 48–9
    own form of football 'Brisbane rules,' 63, 69
Brisbane Broncos, 48, 125, 152
    average sport interest score, 28
    average television audience, 14
    revenue, 154
The Brisbane Courier, 63
Brisbane Line, 4
Brisbane Lions, 14, 48, 152
Brisbane Roar, 153
'Brisbane rules' form of football, 63, 69
British Lions, 72
Brogan, Dean, 8
Broken Hill and the Far West, 47
Brown, Ash, 28
Brownlow, Charles, 73
Bruce Stadium, 88
BSkyB, 104, *105*
Bundesliga, 9
Butler, Mr, 71

C

Cain, John, 24
Campbelltown stadium, 32, 36
Campese, David, 92
Canada
    audience for domestic and American football, 144
    bans high school rugby union, 137
    Commonwealth Games hosting, 6
    major league franchises, 12
Canadian Football League (CFL) salary cap, 144
Canberra City NSL, 88
Canberra Raiders, 42, 88, 153
Canterbury Bulldogs, 36, 151, 164, 165
Canterbury-Bankstown Club, 118
Carey, Wayne, 27, 43
Carlton club v Waratah club (1977), 41
Carpenter, Ellie, 147
Cashman, Richard, 23, 55
Castle, Ray, 92
Catley, Steph, 28, 147
Channel Nine, 120–1
    broadcast deal with Rugby Australia, 122, 126, 157–8
    live VFL telecast audience numbers, 41
    sports broadcast rights, 141
    streaming platform, 157–8
    See also Stan Sport
Channel Seven, 106, 120–1
    broadcast deals with AFL, 42, 122
Chelsea Football Club, 147
children in sport
    AFL Auskick, 133
    attitudinal interest in sport relative to participation, 176
    generalist skills development, 27
    participation rates, 132
    rugby league participation, 133–4
    safetyism culture, 136–7
Chinese Professional Baseball League, 12
Clarke, Rob, 157
class
    associated with football codes, 31, 85
    inaccessibility of pay TV, 107–8

Cleary, Ivan, 150
Cleary, Mitch, 166
Coalition of Major Professional and Participation Sports (COMPPS), 120
The Coddling of the American Mind (Lukianoff & Haidt), 136
Coleman-Jones, Callum, 165
Collingwood Football Club, 32, 150, 160
Commonwealth Games, 6
Commonwealth Games 2006, 25
community rugby, expenditure allocated to, 99, *102–3*
concussion and safety, 135
    Canadian school program, 137
    football codes' safety measures, 138–9
    NFL's obstructionist strategies, 139–40
    See also safetyism culture
Condon, Andrew, 12, 120
Cornes, Graham, 86
Cornes, Kane, 162
Cotchin, Trent, 166
COVID-19, 170
    AFL players' breaches, 165, 166
    impact on AFL, 48–9, 122–3, 152
    impact on crowd numbers, 97–8, 149
    impact on NRL, 124, 152
    impact on rugby union's broadcast deal, 104, 125–6
    impact on sport broadcasting, 121–2
Cowan, Sean, 57, 59
Crawford Report (2003), 100
cricket
    first inter-colonial game, 24
    popularity in regional areas, 130
    revenue 2018/2019, 120
    Sheffield Shield 1892–1893, 73–4
    value to Foxtel, 127
Cricket Victoria, 28
Cronulla-Sutherland Sharks, 33, 34, 118, 153–4

CTE (chronic traumatic encephalopathy) cases, 135, 139
culture wars, 1, 3, 169 *See also* football wars
Cundy, WH, 61, 62

D

Dabscheck, Dr Braham, 96
Daily News, 57
Daniher, Neale, 43
Darwin, Ben, 159
Davey, Brianna, 28
de Moore, Greg, 53
De Vanna, Lisa, 147
Deakin University, 1–2
Delaney, Patrick, 157
Demetriou, Andrew, 164
Dettre, Andrew, 89–90
digital technology
    impact on satellite fandom, 21
    NBA League Pass streaming platform, 21–2, 142
    streaming behaviours, 16
    streaming future for A-League, 157
    streaming future for rugby union, 158
Dixson, Hugh, 58
Docklands stadium, 32
Domain, first inter-colonial cricket game, 55
Doorn, Paul, 126
Drennan, Angus, 28
Duke, Mitchell, 143
Dunstan, Keith, 92

E

Eagle Farm Racecourse, 64
Ella, Mark, 92, 98
Encyclopedia of Matildas (Werner), 28
English Premier League (EPL)
    accessibility on pay TV, 142
    fan base demographic, 20–1

impact on domestic soccer leagues, 93–4
impact on soccer fandom, 93–4, 145
international broadcast revenue, 141
Liverpool Football Club fandom, 145
revenue from Optus Sport, 22
satellite fandom, 145–6
Errington, S., 56, 59
'Establishing the Basis for Future Success' (1984), 41
Ethnic Television Review Panel 1979, 90
European promotion and relegation league system, 11

F

Fagan, Sean, 59, 60, 64–5
Fairfax/Nine, 165
Farmer, Graham 'Polly,' 135
FFA TV, 157
FIFA, 83, 84, 135
FIFA World Cup 2022, 5, 85
Fireflies Club, 64
Fitzroy Football Club relocation, 32 *See also* Brisbane Lions
Flemington Racecourse, 23, 25
Flinders Park sport precinct, 25
Folau, Israel, 109
Foord, Caitlin, 147
football, confusion around word, 3
Football Australia (FA), 170
football codes
    attendance standardised against AFL, *114*
    central revenue generated, 2
    class divisions and, 31, 85
    competition among, 2–3, 5
    concussion safety measures, 135–6, 138–9
    growing gap between AFL and rugby union, 54
    interest across capital cities, *19*
    internet search volume by state 2014–2018, *15*
    internet search volume 2004–2019, *108–9*
    marketing iconography, 92–3
    proportion of adults attending games, *112*
    relationship between participation and television consumption, *134*
    rivalry between rugby league and Australian Rules, 4
    salary cap breaches, 42–3
    socio-geographic divisions, 14–22, 43
    See also Barassi Line
Football Federation Australia (FFA), 3, 86, 95
    annual revenue, 100
    broadcast deal with Fox Sports, 144
    convincing fans to support A-League, 99
    cumulative central revenue, 156
    FIFA World Cup 2022 bid, 5, 85
    introduction of south-west A-League team, 38–9
    junior participation, 11
    A-League financial and performance accountability, 154
    reorganisation phase, 170
    revised COVID-19 broadcast deal, 122
    See also Football Australia (FA)
football wars, 169
    contributing factors, 128–9
    as popular culture wars, 1, 3
    war metaphor, 4
Formula 1, 6, 25
Fox Sports, 108, 127
    deal with FFA, 144
    rugby union audience numbers, 158
    value of A-League final season, 22
Foxtel, 11, 107, 108
    cuts to sports content, 120, 125, 126, 157, 173
    loss of EPL rights, 144–5

Super Rugby broadcast, 128
value of cricket content, 127
France, hosts Rugby League World Cup 1954, 66
Franks, Phil, 69
Fraser, Malcolm, 90
Frawley, Danny, 135
Freemantle Football Club, 57, 58
free-to-air (FTA) television, 159
   AFL strategies for game exposure, 106
   AFL's expenditure 2015, 42
   BBC cumulative rugby league audience, 104–5
   COVID-19 revised deals, 122
   declining interest in sports broadcast, 120–1
   importance of sport to, 83
   inability to get Super Rugby on, 103
   Rugby Australia's deal with Channel Nine, 122, 126, 157–9
   See also individual channels
Fremantle Dockers, 57
Fremantle Temperance Society v Town on the Green, 56
Fremantle Unions, 58
Future Sports research, 157

G

Gaelic Athletic Association (GAA), 96–7
Gaelic football, 2, 97
GAIN LINE Analytics, 159
Galabadaarachchi, Jacynta, 147
Gallop, David, 46, 83, 154, 164
Gallup Poll, 110
Galvin, Kieran, 97
A Game of Our Own (Blainey), 62
Geelong Cats fan base demographic, 21
Gemba, 12, 120
Germany, internet search query behaviours, 9

Gielnik, Emily, 147
Gill, WH, 70, 77
Giltinan, JJ, 70, 71, 74
Gladwell, Malcom, 131
globalisation
   EPL's international broadcast revenue, 141
   impact of EPL on domestic leagues, 93–4
   sustainability of local and national sports culture, 1
Gold Coast Suns, 48, 73, 152–3, 169
Goldfields Football Association, 77
Goodes, Adam, 54, 163
Google Trends data, 9, 14
   football codes search volume 2004–2019, *108*
   trends by country and league, *10*
   See also internet search queries
Gorman, Joe, 88, 89
Gould, Phil, 112–13, 150
Gratton, Chris, 104–5
Greater Western Sydney Giants, 46, 73, 169
Greatest Sporting Nation, 8
Greenberg, Todd, 3
Gregson, G, 61
Grow, Robin, 53
The Guardian, 147–8

H

Haidt, Jonathan, 136
Hale School, 57
Harrison, Amy, 147
Hawthorn Football Club, 32–3
Hay, Roy, 53, 83, 85
Herald Sun, 16, 123
Hess, Rob, 53
Hibbins, Gillian, 53
Hickey, Con, 70, 72, 74, 78, 79, 80
Hickson, Mr, 64
Hill, Simon, 144, 163–4
Hilt, Dr Michael, 129

Hooper, Michael, 143, 159
Horton, Peter, 31
Hosch, Tanya, 53
Hougoumont (ship), 56
HSBC Sevens Series world tour, 155
hybrid football games *See* International Rules; Universal Rules
Hybrid Rugby trial games, 69

I

Illawarra Steelers, 33, 35, 88
India, internet search query behaviours, 9
Indian Premier League, 9
Indian Soccer League, 9
Indigenous ball game *See* Marngrook
Indigenous population, obesity, 1
International Conference on Concussion in Sport 2016, 138
International Rugby Board (IRB), 96
International Rules, 69
internet search queries, 9–10
    domestic and international sport, 142, *143*
    football codes search volume by state 2014–2018, *15*
    football codes search volume 2004–2019, *108*
    NFL, 16–18
Ireland
    GAA 'professionalisation creep,' 96–7
    sport culture, 2, 169

J

Japan Super Rugby, 155, 159
John, HW, 75
Johnson, James, 126, 128
Jones, Clinton, 164

K

Kafer, Rod, 98–9
Kelly, Paul, 27, 43
Kennett, Jeff, 25
Kensington Club, 60
Kerr, Sam, 147
Kestelman, Larry, 145, 146, 173
Klugman, Dr Matthew, 91
KPMG, 109

L

La Liga, 12
La Liga2, 12
'The Last Dance' (documentary), 94
Launceston Rugby Club, 62
Lea, FO, 64
Leader, 76
League of Denial: The NFL, Concussions, and the Battle for Truth (Fainaru & Fainaru-Wada), 134–5, 139
Levy, Geoff, 96
Lewis, Peter, 37
Lewis, Samantha, 147–8
Lewis, Wally, 5
Lidcombe Oval, 31–2
Linnell, Gary, 42
Liverpool Football Club fandom, 145
Liverpool Supporters' Club, 94
Liverpool v Melbourne Victory (2013), 145
Lock, Dr Daniel, 145
Lockett, Tony, 38
Louis-Schmeling paradox, 66–7
Lowy, Frank, 95
Lukianoff, Dr Greg, 136

M

Macarthur Football Club, 36
Maher, Andrew, 162–3
Mahoney, Reed, 139
Major League Baseball (MLB)
    African American players in, 129
    industrial dispute 1994, 110–11

Major League Baseball Players Association, 110
Major League Rugby, 156
Majumdar, B, 83–4
Malone, Tom, 121
Mandle, Bill, 53
Manly Sea Eagles, 38, 112, 153
   unsuccessful merger, 36
Manly-Warringah Sea Eagles, attendance at matches, 118
marketing theory, 32
Marngrook, 53
Martin, Dustin, 143
Marvel Stadium, 123
Masters, Roy, 69, 156, 157
Matildas, 28, 168
   players' exodus to European clubs, 147
Matthews, Dave, 46
McGuire, Eddy, 162, 166
McKellar, Dan, 98
McLachlan, Gill, 48
McLelland, Dr, 78
media
   AFL control over types of reporting, 163–4
   A-League share of coverage, 127
   bias in reporting on football codes, 162–5
   contributing factor in sport industry growth, 1–2
   coverage of women's AFL, 16
   digital behaviours around, 16
   hostility towards rise of soccer, 86–7
   hypothetical implications of Universal Football on, 82–3
   reaction to proposed Universal Rules, 75–6
   WA newspapers push for Victorian Rules, 57
Melbourne
   average sport interest score, 28
   average television viewership for AFL, 14
   competition between Sydney market and, 12–13
   fan base demographic of NBA and EPL, 20–1
Melbourne as sport capital, 23–30
   economic decline 1970s/1980s, 24–5
   geographic advantage for infrastructure, 23, 26, 30
   hosts Commonwealth Games 2006, 25
   investment in sports infrastructure, 25
   secures Australian Open tennis tournament, 25
   strong female involvement, 29
Melbourne Cricket Club, 23
Melbourne Cricket Ground (MCG), 23
   first inter-colonial cricket game, 24, 55
   Liverpool v Melbourne Victory (2013), 145
   NSW Firsts v British Lions, 72
   Sheffield Shield cricket crowd numbers, 74
Melbourne Demons, 32, 153
Melbourne Football Club, 31, 55
Melbourne Hawks, 32
Melbourne Park, 25
Melbourne Rebels, 103, 166
Melbourne rules, 60, 63, 64
Melbourne Storm, 152, 167, 171
   salary cap breach, 42
Melbourne Victory v Liverpool (2013), 145
Miller, Harold, 78, 79, 80
Mini-Roos, 137
Mixed Martial Arts (MMA), average age of fans, 22
Moeroa, Tepai, 8
Moloughney, Pat, 121
Montagna, Leigh, 164–5
Mooney, Cameron, 43
Moore, Andrew, 36–7
Moore, Craig, 157
Moore Park, 31, 35

Mortimer, Steve, 43
Mortimer brothers, 27
MotoGP, 6
Mumbrella, 121
Murdoch, Rupert, 121–2
Murray region and football interests, 44–6

N

Nash, R, 145
National Basketball Association (NBA), 146
   African American viewers, 130
   average age of fans, 21
   Chicago Bulls popularity, 94
   fan base demographic, 20–1
   streaming platform, 21–2
National Basketball League (NBL), 87–8
   Next Stars initiative, 146
   under private equity management, 145–6, 173
National Collegiate Athletic Association (NCAA), 11
National Football League (NFL), 71
   obstructionist strategies regarding concussion, 139–40
   salary cap, 144
   US internet search volume, 16–18
National Rugby League (NRL)
   annual report 2017, 121, 125
   broadcast revenue, 122
   calibre of sponsorship, 151–2
   clubs' lack of financial accountability, 154–5
   clubs' self interests and mismanagement, 149–50
   COVID-19 impact, 124
   cumulative club membership, 152
   cumulative fan base 2019, 49, 151
   declining grand final audience, 49
   expenditure on games development, 73, 103, 126

   fanbase conversion into club membership, 152, *153*
   financial vulnerabilities, 170
   Grand Final 2019, 81–2, 142
   grand final week, 167–8
   grant funding to clubs, 154
   internet search volume 2004–2019, *108*
   Memorandum of Understanding 1997, 116
   'no fault stand down' policy, 165
   Pasifika and Indigenous players, 131
   poker machine revenue, 148, 170
   poor club merger strategies, 118–19
   Queensland Grand Final 2020, 48
   rationalisation process of clubs, 116–19
   reliance on broadcast revenue, 125
   revised COVID-19 broadcast deal, 122
   salary cap breaches, 149–50
   social media followers, 172
   state of finances, 123–4
   television ratings on Foxtel, 11
National Soccer League (NSL), 38, 87
   disbands, 100
   financial resources, 91
   Newcastle v Western Suburbs match (1978), 88
NBA League Pass streaming platform, 21–2, 142
Neill, Lucas, 157
netball, 120
Netflix, 94
New South Wales
   attendance of AFL matches, 113
   birthplace of Victorian rules football, 31
   Broken Hill and the Far West football interests, 47
   first season of rugby league, 70
   inaugural rugby league season 1908, 31–2
   Murray region football interests, 44–6
   'National Day' round 1952 matches, 43

Queensland's rugby tour 1886, 64
Riverina region football interests, 46–7
rugby tour to NZ (1882), 65
early rugby union dominance, 5
sport participation rates, 26
supply of national cricket players, 28
New South Wales English Football Association, 31
New Zealand
   Commonwealth Games hosting, 6
   dominance in international rugby union, 66
   Hurricanes v Blues match, 158
   lack of interest in Australian Rules, 67
   NSW rugby tour (1882), 65
   as part of prospective Australian state, 65–6
   Pasifika players, 131
   QLD rugby tour (1896), 65
   Rugby World Cup host, 6
   sport culture, 2
   voting power over football merger, 77
New Zealand All Blacks, 69, 155
   dominance in international rugby union, 66
New Zealand Rugby, 158
New Zealand Rugby League, 74
New Zealand Super Rugby, 158
Newcastle International Sport Centre, 88
Newcastle Jets, 153
Newcastle KB United, 88
Newcastle Knights, 88
Newcastle v Western Suburbs soccer match (1978), 88
News Corporation, 95–6, 100, 103–4, 123
News Limited, 115, 116, 117, 163, 165
Newtown Rugby League Club, 33
North Melbourne Football Club, 33
North Melbourne v South Melbourne (1952), 43
North Queensland Cowboys, 115, 153
North Sydney Bears, 33, 36–7

Northern Rugby Union (NRU), 64 *See also* Queensland Rugby Union (QRU)
Northern Territory, football codes, 15
Nova Scotia School Athletic Federation, 137
NRL Touch Premiership, 133–4
NSW Rugby League (NSWRL), 70, 72, 74
   board kills off Universal Football, 80
   Universal Football adoption talks with ANFC, 76–80
NSW Waratahs, 157
   match attendance, 114
   Super Rugby fixtures played 2018, 107
   v ACT Brumbies, 158
   v Auckland Blues (2020), 97
   v Queensland Reds (1882), 64
NSWFA, 64
NSWRU, 62, 126
   annual report 2017, 121, 125, 157
   strategic intervention into QLD, 64, 68
NWSL, 147

O

obese population, 1
Observer, 73
Ogden, Dr David, 129
O'Hanlon, Seamus, 24–5
Olympics
   Australia as host, 6
   Australian athletes study, 26–8
   inclusion of Rugby 7s program, 155
   medal estimation study, 7
   Melbourne's unsuccessful bid (1996), 25
Olympics Melbourne 1956, 24
O'Neill, Kristy, 26–8
Optus, 125
Optus Sport, 142
   EPL value, 22, 144
   streaming service for EPL, 145
Osborne, Paul, 149

OzTag, 133
OzTAM, 49, 172

P

Packer, Kerry, 1, 96, 169
Papa John's, 106
Papworth, Brett, 99, 102
Paradise of Sport (Cashman), 6
Parkes, Geoff, 97, 98, 164, 167
Parramatta Eels, 8, 118, 149
pay television
    A-League audience numbers, 170
    cuts to broadcast sports, 120, 125, 126, 157, 173
    EPL broadcast, 142
    impact of exclusive rights on British rugby league, 104–6
    inaccessibility to low-socioeconomic, 108
Payne, Corey, 150
Pendlebury, Scott, 8
Penrith Local Government Area (LGA), 34–5
Penrith Panthers, 33, 34, 153
    attendance rate, 154
    CEO appointment and anti-outsider sentiments, 150
    fan base, 112, 149
Penrith Stadium, 149
Perth
    average sport interest score, 28
    average television viewership for AFL, 14
    football interest by regions, *39*, 40
    formalisation of football clubs, 57
    NRL rationalisation of club, 117
Perth Collegiate School, 56
Perth Glory, 147, 156
Perth High School, 57, 58 *See also* Hale School
Philips Soccer League, 87, 90 *See also* National Soccer League (NSL)

poker machine revenue, 148, 170
population demographic, impact on sport market, 20–1
Port Adelaide, 69, 117
Pridham, Andrew, 126
Pro Kabaddi League, 9
Proven-Summons Trophy, 92
Purdue University study 2015, 135

Q

Queensland
    AFL's Grand Final in Brisbane 2020, 48–9
    Birdsville and Outback Queensland football interests, 47–8
    dual-code football association, 63
    first dedicated rugby clubs, 64
    first inter-colonial rugby match (1882), 64
    rugby tour into NSW (1886), 64
    rugby tour to NZ (1896), 65
Queensland Australian Rules team, 79
Queensland Football Association (QFA), 63
Queensland Reds, 109, 158
Queensland Reds v NSW Waratahs (1882), 64
Queensland Rugby League (QRL), 72, 74
    Under-7s program, 137
Queensland Rugby Union (QRU), 5, 64–5
Quirk, Alicia, 27

R

racism
    Colour Barrier 1947, 129
    racist incidents in AFL, 53–4, 163
    See also white flight in sport
Raftery, Martin, 138
Randwick Racecourse, 23
Raso, Hayley, 147
Referee, 75, 78, *81*
The Register, 76–7
Ribot, John, 117

Richmond Tigers, 151, 153
Riddell, 139–40
rink hockey, 11, 12
Rio Olympics 2016, 7
Riverina region and football interests, 46–7
   rugby league fundraising trial match, 46
Robinson, Jackie, 129
Robinson, Mark, 16
Roosevelt, Teddy, 134, 140
Rosenberg, Buck, 3, 86
Rothfield, Phil, 149–50, 167–8
Rovers Football Club, 58
Rowe, David, 9
Roy Morgan Research, 112, 124–5, 150–1, 154
   2019 survey of AFL and NRL, 49, 50, 171, 172
   junior rugby union participation rates, 132
Rugby World Cup, Australia as host, 6
Rugby 7s, 155
Rugby Australia
   analysis of revenue 1980–2019, 99–100
   broadcast deal with Channel Nine, 122, 126, 157–9
   broadcast revenue, 100, 158–9
   broadcast rights deals, 95–6, 157
   broadcast strategies during COVID-19, 125–6, 172
   commercial mistakes, 97, 98
   community rugby expenditures, 99, *102*–3, 126
   compared with AFL central revenue (1996–2019), *161*
   cumulative central revenue, 156
   embryonic professionalism phase 1986–1994, 100
   financial difficulty, 109–10
   financial distributions to state unions, 102
   governance complexities, 98–9
   growth phase 1995–2007, 100
   hosts World Cup 1987, 100
   hosts World Cup 2003, 11, 100
   inability of Super Rugby to get on FTA, 103
   operating losses, 101
   player remuneration, 159
   'purely amateur era' phase 1980–1985, 99–100
   reorganisation phase, 170
   revenue, 161
   revenue and expenditure 1980–2019, *101*
   similarity between British broadcast deal and, 104–6
   staff redundancies, 126
   'volatility' phase 2008–2019, 101–2
rugby league, 148–55
   anti-outsider sentiments, 150
   attendance rate, 112, 113, 152
   average age of fans, 21
   average attendance at Sydney games, 35–6, 38
   Bradley Report 1992, 117
   breakaway from rugby union, 31, 41
   challenges ahead, 171–2
   club mergers, 33, 36–7, 115–19
   clubs' annual rate of expenditures, 148
   combined financial losses, 149
   concussion and safety, 141
   cross-over fans, 80
   crowd attendance and television ratings, 111
   defending heartland from soccer, 36
   digital fandom nature, 172
   fan base changes between 1994 and 2010, 111–14
   first season in NSW, 70
   flow of talent between union and, 5–6
   foundation teams 1908, 88

growth in popularity during war, 78
impact of exclusive pay TV rights for British, 104–6
inhibitive factors for growth, 165
marketing iconography, 92
media's reporting of players' behaviours, 164
poker machine revenue, 148, 170
rate of interest, 80
rationalisation process of clubs, 114–19
relocation and rationalisation period, 32, 33–8
revenue 2018/2019, 120
risk of sustaining injury, 137–8
as sole code of interest, 18
sponsorships, 151
sprawl of Sydney suburban clubs, 32
Sydney heartland, 34
television ratings 2019/2020, 48–9
Tri-series 1997, 67
women's attendance, 113
See also Super League; Universal Rules
rugby league hybrid games *See* International Rules
Rugby League World Cup, 66
Rugby Pass, 125
rugby union, 95–110, 155–60
   3 year rolling average revenue, *101*
   amateurism concept, 31
   average age of fans, 21
   broadcast deals criticisms, 103, 104, 109
   broadcast rights deals, 95–6, 100, 103–4
   in colonial South Australia, 60
   in colonial West Australia, 56–7
   competition between soccer and, 156
   concussion rates, 135
   consequences of exclusive pay TV broadcast, 107–8
   contributing factors for decline, 159–60
   dispersion of interest across Sydney regions, 34
   early history, 54
   fan base, 159
   first inter-colonial game (NSW v QLD), 64
   first inter-colonial game (NSW v VIC), 41
   flow of talent between league and, 5–6
   future post-COVID-19, 172–3
   inclusion in Olympics program, 155
   junior safety programs, 137
   Louis-Schmeling paradox, 66–7
   marketing iconography, 92
   need for broad base participation, 133
   New Zealand dominance, 66
   Pasifika players, 131, 133
   pay television ratings decline, 157
   'professionalisation creep' in Ireland, 96–7
   professionalisation of code, 5, 49–50, 96, 97
   revenue in 2nd professionalisation year, 161
   as sole code of interest, 160
   sponsorship revenue, 100
   unique qualities, 95
   WA switches code to Victorian Rules, 58–9
   See also Super Rugby
Rugby Union Football Club (SA), 60
rugby union hybrid games *See* International Rules
rugby union (junior) participation rates, 132
Rugby World Cup 1987, 100
Rugby World Cup 2003, 11, 38, 109, 156
Rugby World Cup 2019, 155
Rugby World Cup 2027, 156

S

safetyism culture, 136–7
Sage, Tony, 156
salary caps

AFL clubs' breaches, 42–3
Canadian Football League (CFL), 144
A-League, 127–8
Samuel, Graeme, 124, 125
SANZAAR (South Africa, New Zealand, Australia and Argentina Rugby), 97, 98–9
SANZAR (South Africa, New Zealand and Australia Rugby), 95–6
satellite fandom, 21
SBS, 90
Scandinavia's EPL fandom, 93, 94, 145
School Insurance Program (Canada), 137
Senyard, June, 161
Sharp, Peter, 43
Sharpe, Nathan, 27
Sheffield Shield cricket, 73–4
Shipard, Sally, 27
Simmons, Ben, 7–8
Simon, Kyah, 147
Slater, Michael, 27, 28
Slater, Robbie, 93, 170–1
Smith, David, 150
Smith, Sir Joynton, 78
soccer, 83–95
   3 year rolling average revenue, *101*
   attendance at Newcastle games 1970s, 88
   attendance rate, *114*
   competition between rugby union and, 156
   concussion safety measures for children, 138
   Crawford Report (2003), 100
   ethnicised nature of clubs, 89, 90
   failure to convert first-mover advantage, 87, 94
   first commercial franchise, 88
   first recorded game, 31
   future post-COVID-19, 170–1
   head trauma risks, 135
   impact of EPL on domestic leagues, 93–4
   impact of negative media reporting, 163–4
   lack of access to sport infrastructure, 5, 85–6, 91
   marketing iconography, 92–3
   media hostility towards, 86–7
   Mini-Roos, 137
   participation and consumption rates, 133
   perceived as 'outsider' sport, 84–5, 87, 89, 162–3
   perceived quality of domestic players, 143–4
   sleeping giant metaphor, 83–5, 87
   sponsorship deals, 106
   television broadcast strategies, 90
   W-League players' exodus to European clubs, 147
   See also A-League
Soccer Australia, 3 *See also* Football Federation Australia (FFA)
Soccer World Cup 1974, 87, 89
Soccer World Cup 2006, 92
Socceroos, 87, 89, 168
   qualification for 2006 World Cup, 92–3
   Victoria's under contribution of players, 28
social identity, 168
   soccer perceived as 'outsider'sport, 84–5, 87, 89, 162–3
   sport teams as source of, 2, 86, 130
Solberg, Harry, 104–5
South African Springbok team, 96
South Australia
   Sheffield Shield tripartite series 1892–1893, 74
   sports participation rates, 26
   Universal Football approval, 76, 77
South Australian League, 78
South Melbourne Football Club, 32 *See also* Sydney Swans
South Rugby Football Union (SRFU), 41

South Sydney Rabbitohs, 125
  cumulative fan base 2001, 151
  fan base demographic, 21
  profitability, 149
  protest rally supporting, 115
  sponsorships, 151
  two-year sabbatical, 33
Spain's sport market, 11, 12
sport, negative aspects associated with, 54–5
Sport 2030 national sport plan (2018), 7
Sport Australia
  AusPlay participation data, 132
  Sport 2030 national sport plan (2018), 7
  sport participation 2015–2019, 26
  Winning Edge strategy (2012), 7
sport consumption, correlation with sport participation, 132–3, *134*
sport culture
  accessibility and affordability, 6–7, 25–6
  counter-culture movement, 91–2
  unique Australian, 2
sport industry
  'big five' collective central revenue, 13–14
  commercialisation and financial growth 1970s, 1, 3, 169
  reframing importance of broadcast rights, 128
  saturation point speculations, 11
sport management, growth industry, 1–2
sport market, 6–14
  Australian compared with US, 9–12
  average age of fans, *22*
  average revenue, 120
  European, 11, 12
  globalisation effects, 93–4
  Google search trends by country and league, *10*
  population demographic impact on, 20–1
  soccer player salaries, 146
  stretching playing seasons, 13
  summer season competition, 127
  United States tier one level, 9–10
sport teams
  satellite fandom of overseas teams, 21
  social identity, 2, 86, 130
The Sporting Globe, 89
Spotify, 16
St George Dragons, 33, 35, 118
St George Illawarra, 21, 118, 149
St Kilda Football Club, 164
St Kilda Saints fan base demographic, 21
Stack, Sydney, 165
Stan Sport, 157–8
State of Origin game, 168
  audience, 81, 171, 172
  state of origin of players, 131
Sterling, Peter, 27
Stockell, John, 61
Streem, 127
subscription television *See* pay television
Sun Tzu, 4
Sunday Age, 84
Sunday Telegraph, 164
Sunshine United, 28
Super League, 104, 110–19
  British league's sponsorship deal, 106
  contributing factors, 111
  fans switch allegiance to AFL, 37
  impact of merger on clubs, 114–19
Super League war, 32, 96
  impact on fans, 111
  impact on rugby league interest in Sydney, 36–8, 49
Super Netball, 13
Super Rugby, 49–50, 106–7, 155
  balance of popularity and revenue, 128
  creation, 37, 114
  declining attendance, 97–8

expansion of teams, 97, 98
inability to get on FTA, 103
international expansion, 155–6
internet search volume 2004–2019, *108*, 109
pay television audience numbers, 158
structure and funding of domestic competition, 156–7
Sutherland Local Government Area (LGA), 34
Swan Football Club, 58
Sydney
  attitudinal interest in sport relative to participation, 176
  average sport interest score, 28
  average television viewership for AFL and NRL, 14
  competition between Melbourne market and, 12–13
  establishment of rugby union code, 31
  fan base demographic of NBA and EPL, 20–1
  first inter-colonial Victorian rules game, 41
  Fitzroy v Collingwood match (1903), 41
  football interest by regions, *39*
  gains economic advantage over Melbourne, 24–5
  geographic challenges for sport infrastructure, 23
  population size and rugby league interest across regions, *33–5*
  region-centric football codes, 30, 31–2
  relationship between participation and television consumption, *134*
  rugby league clubs' access to stadiums, 35
  rugby league heartland, 34, 36
  rugby league wastelands, 36, 38
  rugby union dispersion of interest, 34
  south-west A-League team, 36, 38–9
Sydney Australian National Football Carnival, 79

Sydney Cricket Ground (SCG), 24, 35, 154
  Australia v New Zealand rugby match 1907, 31
  British Lions matches, 72
  Hawthorn v Melbourne, 41
  Sheffield Shield cricket crowd numbers, 74
Sydney Football Club, 145, 170
Sydney Football Stadium, 35, 107
Sydney Roosters, 34, 35, 149, 154
Sydney Swans, 49, 113, 152
  average television audience, 14
  premiership 2005, 38
  salary cap breach, 42
Sydney University Club, 31
Symons, Mr, 70–1
Syson, Ian, 52, 54, 56, 60–1, 161

T

Taiwan sport market and football premier league, 12
Tajfel, Henry, 86
Tasmania, 60–3
  AFL focussed viewership, 15–16
  football preference ballot, 62, 68
  forms of football played in colonial, 61, 69
  internet search volume for AFL, 18
  voting deferment in Universal Football merger, 77
Tasmania Football League, 77
Taylor, Mark, 27–8
Tedesco, James, 143
television broadcast
  2017 International Rules series, 69
  changing etiquette towards sport injuries, 136
  dominant sports in US, 20
  relationship between participation and consumption, *134*
  replay of VFL games in Sydney 1960s, 41

See also free-to-air (FTA) television; pay television
television ratings
  AFL and NRL audience numbers, 14
  American Football, 82
  high-rated programs, 82
  NBL, 146
  rugby league, 125
tennis, popularity in major cities, 130
Tennis Australia, 25, 120
The Tipping Point (Gladwell), 131
tobacco industry and denial of smoking health risk, 139, 140
Tomlinson, Mr, 71
Touch Football, 133
Touch Football Australia, 125
Town on the Green v Freemantle, 56
Tredrea, Warren, 162
True North research, 147
Turnbull, Ross, 96
Turner, Ian, 14, 43, 88

U

UFC 243, 142
Ultimate Fighting Championship (UFC), 141–2
United Kingdom
  BBC cumulative rugby league audience, 104–5
  British Lions tour in Sydney (1914), 72
  Commonwealth Games hosting, 6
  FA Women's Super League, 147
  impact of pay TV rights on rugby league, 104–6
  internet search query behaviours, 9
  price of attending sports, 13
  sport culture, 2
  Super League's sponsorship deal, 106
United States
  amateur college teams, 11

  American football overtakes baseball in popularity, 110
  average soccer player salary, 146
  Colour Barrier 1947, 129
  comparative search volume of major leagues 2014–2018, *17*
  concussion and safety issues in football, 134–5
  concussion safety measures for children, 138
  declining popularity of baseball, 20
  dominant sports on television, 20
  establishment of rugby union competitions, 155–6
  franchise model of league structure, 11
  internet search volume for major league sports, 16–18
  major league franchises, 12
  MLB's industrial dispute and consequences, 110–11
  price of attending sports, 13, 83
  smoking trends, 139, 140
  sport culture, 2
  sport market, 9–11
  urbanisation impact on type of sport played, 129–30
  white flight in sport, 131–2
United States Soccer Federation, 138
Universal Rules, 69–83, 91
  hypothetical current-day audience, 81–2
  hypothetical implications on infrastructure and media, 82–3
  key features of proposed rules, 75–6
  last attempt to redevelop, 78–80
  merger stumbling block, 71–2
  primary motivation for merger, 73, 75
  private trial match (1933), 79–80
  prominent critics, 74
  proposed rules, 174–5

Sydney–Melbourne rivalry, 74
World War I disruption, 70, 78
University of Sydney Football Club, 55
University of Western Australia, 27
urbanisation, impact on popularity of sport, 129–30
U.S. Soccer Concussion Initiative 2016, 138

V

Victoria
  new form of football, 1
  sport participation rates, 26
  under supply of cricket and soccer players, 28
Victorian Football Association (VFA), 40–1
Victorian Football Club (WA), 58
Victorian Football League (VFL), 70
  clubs' feedback to Universal Football merger, 77
  establishment of independent commission, 41
  expansion plans for northern regions, 40–51
  'National Day' round 1952, 41, 43
  propaganda funding, 41
Victorian Rules, 56
  bias in sport history, 61–2, 69
  in colonial Adelaide, 60
  in colonial West Australia, 57, 58–9
  first inter-colonial game, 41
  See also Universal Rules
Victorian Rules Australasian Football Council, 70
Viduka, Mark, 157
V'landys, Peter, 3–4, 48, 124, 148
  attitude towards introducing a WA team, 44, 59
  on clubs taking financial responsibility, 149
  vision for rugby league, 171

W

'Wagga Effect,' 27–8, 43
Wagga Leagues Club, 46
Wagga Wagga City Council, 46
The Wallabies, 11, 109
Wanderers Club, 64
Waratah club v Carlton club (1977), 41
Waverley Park, 32
Webster, Andrew, 46
Wei Chuan Dragons, 12
Wellington Phoenix, 154, 170
Wentworth Park, 31
Werner, Greg, 28
West Australia
  development of colonial football, 56–9
  first football match, 56
  map of AFL and rugby interest by region, 44
  newspapers push for Victorian Rules, 57
  as Olympian athlete hotspot, 27
  second and third rugby seasons 1883/1884, 58
  sport participation rates, 26
  switches from rugby union to Victorian Rules, 58–9
The West Australian, 57, 58, 59
West Australian Coastal League, 78
West Australian Football Association (WAFA), 57, 58, 77
West Coast Eagles, 57, 88
Western Bulldogs, 154
Western Force, 103, 114
Western Suburbs Magpies, 32, 33, 118
Western Suburbs Soccer Club, 88
Western Suburbs v Newcastle soccer match (1978), 88
Westralian Worker, 69, 75
Wests Tigers, 21, 35, 118
Whateley, Gerard, 166

Whimpress, Bernard, 53
white flight in sport, 131–2, 135
Wilkie, Douglas, 92
Wills, Tom, 1, 31
Wilmot, Reginald, 74
Wimbledon, 13
Winning Edge strategy (2012), 7
W-League, 13, 147–8
Woolloongabba stadium, AFL Grand Final 2020, 48, 49
women's attendance at football matches, 26, 29, 113
women in sport
    media coverage of AFL, 16
    soccer success in US, 83
    Spanish rink hockey league, 12
    See also Matildas; W-League
Women's Big Bash Leagues (WBBL), 13
Women's World Cup 2023, 85, 171
A World in Conflict: The Battle for Rugby Supremacy (Parkes), 97
World Rugby, 97, 109
    global game development, 155
    introduction of safe tackling trials 2018, 138–9
World Rugby Corporation (WRC), 96
World Series Cricket 1977, 1, 169
World War I
    disruption to formation of Universal Rules, 70, 78
    popularity of rugby league during, 78
Worrall, Jack, 74

Y

York Football Club, 58

About the Author

Hunter Fujak is a Lecturer in Sports Management at Deakin University in Melbourne, Australia.

His PhD explored sport consumer behaviour, specifically in understanding consumption patterns within Australia's crowded sport marketplace. He has previously worked in sport consultancy as an audience and sponsorship analyst for Australasia's largest sporting leagues and events, including the Australian Open Tennis, Rugby World Cup and National Rugby League.

He has also previously been engaged in market research consultancy for some of Australia's leading brands, including Telstra, Sportsbet, Foxtel and Woolworths.

Hunter has published extensively across sport broadcasting, consumer behaviour and sport culture, and is a regular media contributor to topics related to the business of Australian football.

Really good football books from Fair Play Publishing

The Australian Youth Footballer Regulatory Guide by Peter Paleologos (Popcorn Press)

The Away Game by Matthew Hall

The Time of My Football Life by David Picken

Surfing for England Our Lost Socceroos by Jason Goldsmith

Encyclopedia of Matildas by Andrew Howe and Greg Werner

Encyclopedia of Socceroos by Andrew Howe

'If I Started to Cry, I Wouldn't Stop' by Matthew Hall

The A-Z of Socceroos - World Cup Edition 2018 by Andrew Howe (with Ray Gatt and Bonita Mersiades)

Playing for Australia The First Socceroos, Asia and the World Game by Trevor Thompson

The World Cup Chronicles 31 Days that Rocked Brazil by Jorge Knijnik

Chronicles of Soccer in Australia - The Foundation Years 1859 to 1949 by Peter Kunz

Support Your Local League, A South-East Asian Football Odyssey by Antony Sutton

The Aboriginal Soccer Tribe by John Maynard

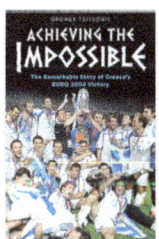
Achieving the Impossible - the Remarkable Story of How Greece Won EURO 2004 by George Tsitsonis

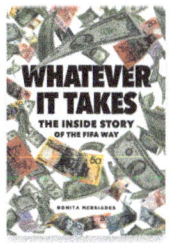
Whatever It Takes - The Inside Story of the FIFA Way by Bonita Mersiades (Powderhouse Press)

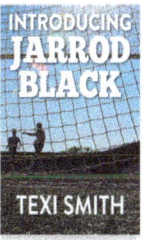
Introducing Jarrod Black by Texi Smith (Popcorn Press)

Jarrod Black Hospital Pass by Texi Smith (Popcorn Press)

Jarrod Black Guilty Party by Texi Smith (Popcorn Press)

www.fairplaypublishing.com.au/shop

www.fairplaypublishing.com.au

www.ingramcontent.com/pod-product-compliance
Lightning Source LLC
Chambersburg PA
CBHW040415100526
44588CB00022B/2831